The Universal Spirit

The Universal Spirit

Exploring Theosophical Questions

Douglas Keene

Foreword by Tim Boyd

tph

The Theosophical Publishing House
Wheaton, Illinois • Chennai, India

First Edition 2024

tph

The Theosophical Publishing House
P.O. Box 270
Wheaton, Illinois 60187-0270
www.theosophical.org

Cover and interior artwork by Alder Keene, www.alderkeene.com

All proceeds from the sale of this book will be donated to The Theosophical Society in America.

Library of Congress Cataloging-in-Publication Data

Names: Keene, Douglas, author.

Title: The universal spirit: exploring theosophical questions / Douglas Keene.

Description: First edition. | Wheaton, Illinois: Theosophical Publishing House, 2023. | Includes bibliographical references and index. | Summary:
"An exploration of the tenets of Theosophy, also known as the Ancient Wisdom Tradition or the Wisdom Religion. Topics include the cyclic nature of existence, beauty, good and evil, ethics and values, the nature of suffering, karma, and death"— Provided by publisher.

Identifiers: LCCN 2023027327 | ISBN 9780835609555 (paperback)

Subjects: LCSH: Theosophy.

Classification: LCC BP565 .K44 2023 | DDC 299/.934—dc23/eng/20230918

LC record available at https://lccn.loc.gov/2023027327

4 3 2 1 * 24 25 26 27 28 29 30

Printed in the United States of America

For all those who struggle

We must try to understand our own nature, and,
understanding that, we may see the path . . .
which leads to the realization of the Self.

—ANNIE BESANT

CONTENTS

PART THREE: PRACTICAL, LIVING THEOSOPHY

Illustrations

FOREWORD

At some point in our lives, we ask profound questions: Why am I here? What is the meaning of life? What happens after I die? How can I know what is true? Why do bad things happen to good people? Often these are questions that arise during our youth or as we near the end of this life, but for some they have an urgency that persists. Those who can't shake the questions generally turn to others for answers. But who can you ask about such things? The usual avenues of search lead toward scientific experts, philosophers, or religious figures—people who have, or who claim to have—a knowledge of such things. Because the deeper questions go beyond the reach of normal science and philosophy, many find themselves in the pews of churches or the ceremonies of temples searching for answers.

One advantage of the world's spiritual traditions is that their exploration of the questions and their methods to pursue them have been developed and tested over millennia. The results of generations of practitioners are passed on in the form of examples, advices, and scriptures. A disadvantage can be that with the passage of time these important matters tend to become formalized into rituals, beliefs, and dogmas that resist inquiry. Spiritual experience becomes institutionalized as religion, each with its own set of "Thou shalt nots." In effect, one is told what is true based only on what has been told before.

To be told what and how to believe serves a need for some. The comfort that comes from a sense of certainty protects from the sometimes disturbing need to grapple with questions. It is no exaggeration to say that millions of books have been written providing answers. Far fewer have focused on the exploration of the questions. Professors, pundits, and priests abound with answers and prescriptions for thought. The rarer individual is the friend—the spiritual friend who speaks *with* you, not at you; who shares their understanding, their journey, and their thought; who demands no compliance but invites you into a conversation about deep and difficult things.

The question may seem odd, but in matters of the inner life, where do we find conversation? Sermons and lectures are everywhere, but where is the person who can live the questions together with us? In today's world, conversation has been trivialized to some extent. For many it suggests a superficial social activity burdened with an etiquette and rules. But the root meaning of the word *converse* is "to live among" or "to keep company with." In Doug Keene's book, *The Universal Spirit: Exploring Theosophical Questions*, he takes this more unusual approach of inviting us to live among large thoughts and ideas. He takes the further step of applying this thought to issues we face in daily life.

All of us are shaped by our life experience. It gives us a perspective from which to see and interpret the world around us. A good deal of Doug Keene's perspective has been shaped by his profession as a doctor practicing medicine in mainstream America as well as in remote and underserved communities around the world. Witnessing the human spectrum from the glory of birth to the anguish of death and dying—equally, from the anguish of birth to the glory of death and dying, healing and decline in hospitals and huts—has a leavening effect.

One aspect of the Ageless Wisdom is that it is a system of thought embracing a cosmology, ethics, and description of the human potential, which, while consistent with science and contemporary understanding, exceeds them in many areas. For someone who feels drawn to it, an initial preparation is necessary. We develop a base of knowledge to familiarize ourselves with its spacious view of the human being and our place within the universe. But knowledge, even knowledge of Theosophy, is not enough. The deeper one goes, the deeper the recognition grows that real wisdom is something of a completely different order than knowledge.

As easy as it might be to content oneself with pursuing the ever-receding horizon of the limits of the Ageless Wisdom, at a certain point one realizes that some form of practice is required to step beyond mere fascination with knowledge. In closing his book, Doug directs our attention to three brief but powerful books—J. Krishnamurti's *At the Feet of the Master*, Mabel Collins's *Light on the Path*, and H. P. Blavatsky's *The Voice of the Silence*. Each one moves toward progressively deeper levels of experience. Although their focus is on the cultivation of the inner life, the distinctions between inner and outer, self and others, fade as understanding grows.

One of the strengths of Doug's book is his generous references from the many great people who have thought long and deeply on the wisdom Theosophy embodies. All of them found ways to exemplify it in their lives. There is a growing body of historical and academic studies of the Theosophical Society documenting its profound impact on global culture. With each day, the value of this wisdom tradition in extending the scope of human vision and moving the human family toward a recognition of Oneness becomes more apparent. In places around the globe, all fields of human endeavor—music, the arts, education, religion, science, even politics—are marked by the presence of great souls in whom teachings, service, and living are fused. The distinctions have disappeared. It is my hope that Doug Keene's book will be the catalyst that moves someone closer to such a life. Even in small ways, the realization of compassion, openness, freedom, and Oneness help all of us and our planet at a time of great need.

—Tim Boyd
International President of
The Theosophical Society
March 2023

Preface

Initially, I had no intention of authoring a book. It came about in a gradual, stepwise fashion. Five days after moving back to New Hampshire in late 2017, after a two-and-half-year medical excursion in the African country of Lesotho, I climbed on an airplane to attend the International Theosophical Society Convention in Adyar, India. In addition to the stimulating presentations prepared by the Society and the opportunity to meet old friends and new, the convention provided me with a useful retreat for reflection. I was at a crossroads. I was attempting to assimilate my experience professionally and theosophically and create a plan for moving forward. I was between jobs, although I did intend to apply for a position as medical director at a county nursing home. I wished to stay academically engaged; this would not be a full-time position and would give me the flexibility for other pursuits. Witnessing several theosophical talks, I struggled with whether I should (or could) speak on behalf of the Society. My natural reluctance at public speaking was balanced by a desire to contribute to the dissemination and interpretation of the Ageless Wisdom. Additionally, there were several topics about which I was curious and wished to further investigate.

At the time, I was a member of the board of directors for the American section. As I was going to be living in the United States again after a significant hiatus, I was motivated to visit lodges and study centers in my (Eastern) district. The next summer, during a Northeast Federation meeting at the Pumpkin Hollow Retreat Center, I offered to visit some of those locations. Frequently, the first question was, "Can you speak to our group?" Having by that time prepared some material, I offered to do so.

In 2017 and early 2018, I gave my first talk similar to the "Means, Motive, and Opportunity" material included here in chapter 4 approximately ten times. I presented it again at the Ojai Valley Lodge in January 2019 and at the National Headquarters at the Summer National Convention in July. During this time, other topics of interest arose, and I began researching and creating essays. In early 2019, another member of the TS (Theosophical Society) in New Hampshire and I started a small discussion group, meeting monthly. That sparked additional interest in pursuing more deeply the foundational tenets of Theosophy. The last three chapters of this book, comprising reflections of the three small theosophical classics—Jiddu Krishnamurti's *At the Feet of the Master*, Mabel Collins's *Light on the Path*, and H. P. Blavatsky's *The Voice of the Silence*—is derived from that work.

I had planned to do additional presentations when in March 2020 the coronavirus pandemic struck. Scheduled talks were canceled and virtually all travel ceased. It afforded me, however, more time to write. The essays/potential talks began to look more like book chapters. Further, I realized that no matter how often I gave a presentation, there might be many people who hadn't heard it but would wish to; I had received some requests to repeat the talks. Creating a book of the essays presents the topics in a more durable form for anyone who may have an interest in them.

In general, the chapters are directed toward a theosophically literate audience. For those who are new to these topics or wish to review them, chapter 1 provides an introduction to some of the major points addressed in the theosophical body of literature. In a sense, this entire book can be seen as introductory, although some of the chapters go more in depth regarding the thoughts and writings I have selected.

Because I wrote the chapters at different times and for different purposes, they may vary somewhat in tone, form, and depth of analysis. Chapter 12 is modified from an earlier exercise. There may occasionally be an overlap of topics or references. The denotation of the word *man* and its pronouns in the nineteenth and early twentieth centuries was intended to be gender neutral, evinced by its ubiquitous use by both male and female writers. This phrasing has not been modified in the quoted material, but it has been avoided in the current text.

I've included quotations from some of my favorite speakers and writers for the clarity and inspiration they offer. They also provide a sampling of theosophical expression. I believe it is critical to find the vibrancy and unity in our world that Theosophy offers.

All quotations of the Bhagavad Gita are from Juan Mascaró's excellent translation in *The Bhagavad Gita* (NY: Penguin Books, 1962). References to the Mahatma letters are from Vicente Hao Chin's *The Mahatma Letters: In Chronological Sequence* (Adyar, India: Theosophical Publishing House, 1998).

—Douglas Keene
Sullivan, NH
October 2020

Acknowledgments

Firstly, I would like to thank my wife, Risa, who has brought me great joy and happiness, as well as my three remarkable daughters, Alder, Kendra, and Woodra. I also wish to thank my editor, Sharron Dorr, for her countless hours of work and invaluable suggestions as she tried to educate me on proper exposition. And I wish to express my gratitude to Quest Books, especially business manager Pat Griebeler, and her assistants, for their help in the publication of this book. Many heartfelt thanks go to all the friends and mentors I've had, in and out of the Society, who have provided insight and inspiration. Finally, I want to share my profound appreciation to HPB and the early writers of Theosophy for bringing into manifestation their splendid expression of the Ageless Wisdom.

PART ONE

BASIC THEOSOPHICAL PRINCIPLES

1

A Brief Introduction to Theosophy

The whole order of nature evinces a progressive march toward a higher life.

—H. P. BLAVATSKY

"It was once said of the Christian Scriptures," wrote early Theosophist Annie Besant, "that they contained shallows in which a child could wade and depths in which a giant must swim." Theosophy is similar, she went on, "for some of its teachings are so simple and so practical that any person of average intelligence can understand and follow them, while others are so lofty, so profound, that the ablest strains his intellect to contain them and sinks exhausted in the effort."[1] Besant, who became the second president of the international Theosophical Society in 1907, was speaking over a century ago. And even now, when members of the Society are asked, "What *is* Theosophy, anyway?" they have difficulty responding with a short and simple explanation.

Indeed, many search for years trying to find the true nature of Theosophy. Theosophical thought and commentary spanning numerous topics and perspectives fill libraries (as just one example, approximately 28,000 books, periodicals, and video and audio recordings are housed at the US national headquarters in Wheaton, Illinois). The scope of Theosophy is broad, the depths layered, and the content inexhaustible. It has been called a religion, a philosophy, and a spiritual movement based on the Ancient Wisdom Tradition. None of these descriptions suffice to encompass the complexity of the subject, as students and swimming giants know.

The modern Theosophical Society was founded in 1875 in New York City by Helena Petrovna Blavatsky, Henry Steel Olcott, William Quan Judge, and a small number of other students. The term *Theosophy*, however, goes much further back in time, and its core concepts even further. *Theosophia*, a Greek term combining *theos* (god) and *sophia* (wisdom), is often defined as "divine wisdom" or "wisdom of the gods." It has been used in Greek and Latin writings and is contained in Gnosticism and Neoplatonism. Theosophical views have been endorsed by Rosicrucians and Freemasons as well as taught in ancient mystery schools and secret societies in Egypt, Chaldea, and other locations. Adding to potential confusion, many philosophical organizations today—including branches of the original society founded in New York, as well as non-associated groups in organizations such as Freemasonry, Anthroposophy, and New Age movements—use the term. In *The Key to Theosophy*, as the fictitious Enquirer asks, "What is the real meaning of the term?" the reply of Mme. Blavatsky herself is illuminating:

> "Divine Wisdom," (Theosophia) or Wisdom of the gods, as (theogonia), genealogy of the gods. The word *theos* means a god in Greek, one of the divine beings, certainly not "God" in the sense attached in our day to the term. Therefore, it is not "Wisdom of God," as

> translated by some, but *Divine Wisdom* such as that possessed by the gods. The term is many thousand years old.[2]

She noted that the term comes to us from the Alexandrian philosophers and "dates from the third century of our era and began with Ammonius Saccas and his disciples."[3]

Mme. Blavatsky (known to her students as HPB) once described *Theosophy* as "the shoreless ocean of universal truth, love, and wisdom, reflecting its radiance on the earth, while the Theosophical Society is only a visible bubble on that reflection."[4]

Charles W. Leadbeater, another foundational theosophical author, explains, "Many thousands have learned wisdom in that school, yet to the majority its teachings are still unknown, and they can give only the vaguest of replies to the query, 'What is Theosophy?'"[5]

Mme. Blavatsky published her magnum opus, *The Secret Doctrine*, in 1888. Its subtitle—*The Synthesis of Science, Religion, and Philosophy*—is perhaps a useful way to regard Theosophy as a whole.

Theosophy is a science in the sense that it can explain our natural world in many ways that have been mysterious to conventional science but are often later confirmed by discoveries such as Mme. Blavatsky's apparent foreknowledge of the wave/particle duality of light.[6] It goes much further than mere physical manifestation in describing many layers of "superphysical" existence on higher planes, each with a delicate balance of spirit and matter. Natural laws apply as well to these higher planes, but they are largely uninvestigated by today's scientists. People with clairvoyant ability have in some cases studied these realms. As Leadbeater describes this advantage,

> It asserts that man has no need to trust to blind faith, because he has within him latent powers which, when aroused, enable him to see and examine for himself, and it proceeds to prove its case by showing how those powers may be awakened. It is itself a result of the awakening

> of such powers by men, for the teachings which it puts before us are founded upon direct observations made in the past, and rendered possible only by such development.[7]

Theosophy is a religion in the sense that many of its tenets are incorporated in today's religious beliefs, particularly at the esoteric level. Mme. Blavatsky used the term *wisdom-religion* and describes it thus:

> It is from this WISDOM-RELIGION that all the various individual "Religions" (erroneously so called) have sprung, forming in their turn offshoots and branches, and also all the minor creeds, based upon and always originated through some personal experience in psychology. Every such religion, or religious offshoot, be it considered orthodox or heretical, wise or foolish, started originally as a clear and unadulterated stream from the Mother-Source. The fact that each became in time polluted with purely human speculations and even inventions, due to interested motives, does not prevent any from having been pure in its early beginnings.[8]

This quotation shows the jaundiced eye and sharp tongue HPB had for human distortion of divine teachings. The motto of the Theosophical Society is "There is no religion higher than truth." The philosophy of Theosophy, often termed *esoteric* (hidden) *philosophy*, refers to a body of knowledge about the cosmos, the Divine, and the human being that takes into account not only the visible aspect but more predominantly the invisible, metaphysical, and spiritual dimensions. HPB notes that "Esoteric philosophy, teaching an *objective* Idealism—though it regards the objective Universe and all in it as *Māyā*, temporary illusion—draws a practical distinction between collective illusion, *Mahāmāyā*, from the purely metaphysical standpoint, and the objective relations in it between various conscious *Egos* so long as this illusion lasts."[9]

This esoteric knowledge is protected to a degree in that it is understandable and accessible fully only to those who are dedicated to the search and who, through a series of initiations, can come to a perfected state of awareness and insight.

Much more could be said on each of these three aspects, but this is not the place to explore them further. Additional illumination of theosophical thought may be gained through the Theosophical Society organization.

The present mission statement crafted by the International Theosophical Society in 2018 reads as follows: "To serve humanity by cultivating an ever-deepening understanding and realization of the Ageless Wisdom, spiritual self-transformation, and the unity of all life." One may ask, then, "What is this Ageless Wisdom?" The answer might be given that it is Divine Wisdom, but this really gets us no further along in understanding. Yet, it appears self-evident that Divine Wisdom cannot be communicated in a few words (or even ten thousand). Borrowing from the Sanskrit words, *jnana* (knowledge) may be a beginning but cannot take us the entire route. *Bhaki* (devotion) is also necessary. *Karma* (service and action) is a sine qua non. Now it is becoming more obvious why *Theosophy* is difficult to define.

At the time of the founding, Three Objects were established that are core to the teachings of Theosophy. These have been essentially unchanged since that time and presently are listed as follows:

1. To form a nucleus of the Universal Brotherhood of Humanity, without distinction of race, creed, sex, caste, or color.
2. To encourage the study of comparative religion, philosophy, and science.
3. To investigate unexplained laws of nature and the powers latent in man.

Regarding the first object—to form a "brotherhood of humanity"—*brotherhood*, of course, was presented as a nongender term for the unity, compassion, and mutual service of the human race. It is predicated on the belief that all beings—in fact, all manifested (and unmanifested) matter—is interconnected and an aspect of a universal whole. This object is to form a "nucleus" of those who are aware of this unity and can model and share it with those who are not yet able to see. Despite the illusion, we are not separate beings, and any action to help or harm another, in truth, helps or harms us as well.

The second object—to encourage the study of comparative religion, philosophy, and science—is critical for having a deeper understanding of past and present approaches to our natural world and for being conversant in central belief structures; it also shows a respect and appreciation for contributions of other individuals and organizations, small and large. It is only by understanding our roots in these disciplines that we can hope to integrate the highest aspects into our own comprehension and have a yardstick against which we may judge new notions and ideas. Additionally, pursuing this object will provide unity among different traditions, emphasizing similarities over differences and perhaps finding that at their essence all pursuits have a harmonious relationship.

Finally, regarding the third object, which addresses the "unexplained laws of nature" and the "powers latent in man," there appear to be powers in the universe unknown to us and abilities in individuals that are difficult to explain. This confusion is in part due to our myopic views of nature, confined primarily to the physical plane, and even they are distorted through habituation and training. We hear stories daily about telepathy, precognition, clairvoyance, psychokinesis, and other paranormal phenomena. Descriptions abound of near-death experiences, and many books are written on the subject annually. Do we really know who and what we are? What are the depths of human existence and consciousness, and how can we attain them? These are profound questions that have engaged the human mind from time immemorial. We are encouraged to "investigate" and look for answers. In some sense, Theosophy helps point the way.

Theosophy teaches that the human being is not a single body but in fact seven, superimposed on each other at different vibrational frequencies. All manifestation, in fact, is of a septenary nature. These layers of being are often called seven "principles." They have different names and are sometimes categorized differently, but generally they are divided into the lower four (the lower quaternary), consisting of the physical body, vitality, the astral body (or etheric double), and the emotional body—all of which are mortal and sequentially perish—and the higher three (upper triad), which are immortal. This triad is comprised of the higher mind (Skt. *manas*), the intuition (Skt. *buddhi*), and the spirit (Skt. *atma*). The common conception that human beings are a body and have a soul is reversed: the theosophical belief is that human beings are a soul and have a body. Our physical form is simply a vehicle, a collection of attributes and characteristics, manifested in a specific time and place, that carry our eternal being. Therefore, death is merely a temporary transition to another form and eventually to another body. Bishop Leadbeater notes:

> What is called death is the laying aside of the vehicle belonging to this lowest world, but the soul or real man in a higher world is no more changed or affected by this than the physical man is changed or affected when he removes his overcoat. All this is a matter, not of speculation, but of observation and experiment.[10]

This line of thought leads to the linked concepts of reincarnation and karma. A human lifetime truly is just a day in the eternal life of the real self, the soul. Theosophical sages such as the Mahatmas, Blavatsky, Besant, and Leadbeater tell us that we have experienced numerous past lives, perhaps hundreds or even thousands, and will experience many more in the future, as is inherently necessary for spiritual evolution. We will likely inhabit all sorts of human forms, of different ethnicities, any gender, and various physical characteristics. We will be born into different societies and experience a myriad of circumstances. Therefore, any notion of being "superior" or "privileged" is quickly erased. It is through each lifetime that we learn, wittingly or unwittingly, how to live a noble and righteous life. We all will make many errors but over time learn from our mistakes, sometimes slowly. This is where karma has a great influence. The Sanskrit word *karma* means "action" or "deed." It is sometimes translated as the law of retribution and refers to the law of cause and effect. It is not punitive and does not give rewards in the sense of "bad" karma and "good" karma; rather, it is always a consequence of thought and behavior in order that we may open our eyes.

Annie Besant writes the following in her book *Esoteric Christianity*:

> As every object has two sides, one of which is behind, out of sight, when the other is in front, in sight, so every act has two sides, which cannot both be seen at once in the physical world. In other worlds, good and happiness, evil and sorrow, are seen as two sides of the same thing. This is what is called karma—a convenient and now widely used term, originally Sanskrit, expressing this connection or identity.[11]

Our life circumstances are created from karmic consequences, individual and collective, to optimize our opportunities for development. We may wish to rise to prominence and positions of importance, but these are not necessary to fulfill our duties, nurture our loved ones, advocate for social equity, and deepen our understanding of our larger world. Leonardo da Vinci is quoted as having said, "Wisdom is the daughter of experience," and Will Rogers once quipped, "Good judgment comes from experience, and a lot of that comes from bad judgment." Others have expressed similar sentiments. This notion at its heart is very theosophical. We have an opportunity to learn from our mistakes. How quickly we assimilate these lessons is up to us.

When there is discussion of the planetary chains, rounds, and races in Theosophy, some eyes gloss over. This can be a challenging topic due both to its complexity and to the vast sums of time involved. Just as a human physical life is only "one day" in our true existence, the history of our planet is also only one day in its existence. We are told that our present earth is one "globe" in a series of seven incarnations, descending from the spiritual planes into the physical and then back again to the spiritual. The middle globe of the sequence is our present earth and the most material, for it presides at the bottom of the loop schematically. Of course, these are not actually separate planets in separate places but merely the vibrational state and stage of development at a specific time. For each globe, seven "root races" occur. It must be clear that these are not races in the modern sense. Instead, they are epochal expressions of humanity. We are presently in our fifth root race on this planet, the full complement being seven. The descriptions of prior root races can be mystical; our previous root race (the fourth) is said to be Atlantean. Each root race has sub-races, again seven in number, and we are presently in the fifth, moving toward the sixth.

In addition, each cycle through seven globes constitutes one "round." The life wave that moves through the globes descends into matter and ascends back into spirit, as previously noted. Seven of these rounds, also descending into matter and re-ascending into spirit, constitute a "chain." Leadbeater writes:

> Each chain consists of seven globes, and both globes and chains observe the rule of descending into matter and then rising out of it again. In order to make this comprehensible let us take as an example the chain to which our Earth belongs. At the present time it is in its fourth or most material incarnation, and therefore three of its globes belong to the physical world, two to the astral world, and two to the lower part of the mental world. The wave of divine Life passes in succession from globe to globe of this chain, beginning with one of the highest, descending gradually to the lowest and then climbing again to the same level as that at which it began.[12]

Humanity is presently also at the fourth round of this chain. Therefore, when looking at the entire planetary scheme, we are just slightly past the midpoint, still nearly in the most material (and least spiritual) form. Our globe forms the nadir of the cycles, and our root race, being the fifth of seven, is just slightly past it. The aforementioned Atlantean civilization would be the direct midpoint.

Leadbeater goes on to say, "There are ten schemes of evolution at present existing in our solar system, but only seven of them are at the stage where they have planets in the physical world."[13] This means that the other planets in our solar system are not inert pieces of rock and ice. Rather, they are the lowest physical manifestation of a complex series of globes that support the evolution of life of a description that is difficult to fathom. And our solar system is only one of an infinite number in the universe, where similar schemes of evolution may be taking place.

Each night passes into day, winter is followed by summer, birth is followed by death. We see cycles and periodicity everywhere. Our planet, our solar system, and our universe are no different. Each phase of manifestation of the universe is cyclical, having an outbreathing and an inbreathing. In theosophical terms, the period of manifestation is known as a *manvantara*, and the period of non-manifestation (or rest) is known as *pralaya*. Mme. Blavatsky, in *The Secret Doctrine* under a section known as the Three Fundamental Propositions, writes, "The Eternity of the Universe *in toto* as a boundless plane; periodically 'the playground of numberless Universes incessantly manifesting and disappearing,' called 'the manifesting stars,' and the 'sparks of Eternity.' . . . 'The appearance and disappearance of Worlds is like a regular tidal ebb, flux and reflux.'" [14]

The expanse of time and space can be mind boggling. The time for a major cycle of manifestation (*maha-manvantara*) is said to be in the hundreds of trillions of years. Mme. Blavatsky has been criticized that her "system" is too complex and abstract to be accepted by the general public. It is curious that the same concerns have not been applied to quantum physics and viral immunology.

No discussion of Theosophy can be complete without reference to the Masters of Wisdom. As evolution progresses and humanity unfolds, some people reach the pinnacle of existence and become "perfected beings." Of these, some, through their own choice, remain to assist and elevate humanity. It is these beings who are referred to as the "Masters of Wisdom" or variously as the "Adepts," the "Arhats," or the "*Mahatmas*" (Skt. Great Souls). In her book on the Masters, Annie Besant writes, "The great religions bestow on this Perfect Man different names, but, whatever the name, the same idea is beneath it; He is Mithra, Osiris, Krishna, Buddha, Christ—but he ever symbolizes the Man made perfect. He does not belong to a single religion, a single nation, a single human family."[15] These Adepts who retained an interest in our fledgling earthly existence have been described as the "Great White Brotherhood." Again, although the phrase is potentially emotionally laden, it is not meant to have any implication regarding race or gender (*white* refers to light, *brotherhood* to all humanity), as the Masters are free of these attributes, except when they occasionally take physical bodies as vehicles. The Masters attempt to guide the evolution of our species, and two in particular have been responsible for the development of the Theosophical Society, as well as other religious initiatives in our history. Those two are known as Master Koot Hoomi and Master Morya. Mme. Blavatsky said that they live "beyond the Himalayas," although they do travel astrally and occasionally in physical form. Blavatsky was a disciple of the Master Morya and met him on several occasions. She writes that "a Mahatma is a personage, who, by special training and education, has evolved those higher faculties and has attained that spiritual knowledge, which ordinary humanity will acquire after passing through numberless series of reincarnations during the process of cosmic evolution, provided, of course, that they do not go, in the meanwhile, against the purposes of Nature."[16]

In the early days of the society, A. P. Sinnett, an Englishman living in India who was interested in theosophical ideas, asked Blavatsky about initiating correspondence with the Masters. She encouraged him to try, and over several years there was an exchange of written communication. These letters have survived and are known as the "Mahatma Letters." Initially a private exchange, decades later they were published, and the originals still exist at the British Library in London. The letters have been a rich resource of theosophical theory and instruction and are revered by many students of Theosophy. N. Sri Ram, a former president of the Theosophical Society, notes about the Masters that "all the Adepts of whom mention has been made have physical bodies, but many, we are told, do not have such bodies but remain in touch with the earth in their subtle bodies; they have not gone away from the world."[17] The work of the Masters is thought to be behind some of the deepest religious and philosophical writings that have been provided through others over the centuries. Koot Hoomi (known as Master KH) writes, "Then you will, of course, aim to show that this Theosophy is no new candidate for the world's attention, but only the restatement of principles which have been recognized from the very infancy of mankind."[18]

What, then, is the purpose of life from a theosophical perspective? This question has no single answer but varies by perspective and emphasis. We are beginning the return path to Divinity from our deepest excursion into materiality. This is a natural cycle of humankind and of consciousness. It is accomplished through character development, compassion, and service. Gaining knowledge through the doctrine of the eye and intuitional wisdom through the doctrine of the heart are both critical. By being aware of deeper states of existence through knowledge (study) and experience (meditation), we can develop spiritual wisdom. Annie Besant, writing about *yoga* (meaning "deep, spiritual union," not simply postures or asanas) says that there

> desire must cease; and the Self-determined will must take its place. The last object of desire in a person commencing the Path of Return is the desire to work with the Will of the Supreme; he harmonises his will with the Supreme Will, renounces all separate desires, and thus works to turn of the wheel of life as long as such turning is needed by the law of Life. Desire on the Path of Forthgoing becomes will on the Path of Return; the soul, in harmony with the Divine, works with the law.[19]

Charles Leadbeater, in discussing the purpose of life, describes the downward arc into materiality and the upward arc into spirituality this way: "In this stage the spirit, having learnt perfectly how to receive impression through matter and how to express itself through it, and having awakened its dormant powers, learns to use these powers rightly in the service of the Deity."[20]

Socrates is famous for saying, "The unexamined life is not worth living." Perhaps this is a succinct way of noting that introspection, self-observation, self-understanding, and striving to ascertain life's purpose are essential to the inner development of the soul during our terrestrial journey. Who we are and how we relate to ourselves, our fellow travelers, our environment, and our collective Divinity define our nature in the present. Our potential, however, goes much further. Legitimate spiritual teachers have attempted to point the way. We can take comfort in the fact that many have traveled this path before us, both ancient and modern. However, none of them will carry us over the threshold. We must each take our own steps and find our own way. Each path will vary in its challenges and accomplishments.

To be an adherent of Theosophy requires no belief in doctrine, save the unity of all humanity. Each is free to explore avenues and corners to which he or she may be attracted. There is no need to recite or even believe in any particular teaching. We are constantly being told not to accept a specific concept because it was spoken by someone with recognition or written in an acclaimed book. We are counseled to explore for ourselves, to search where we may, and then to make up our own minds. We need not delve into the writings of the Masters or even recognize their existence. If Mme. Blavatsky's writings are too recondite, many other authors are available. If we find the talk of globes, rounds, and chains overwhelming, we need not dwell on them.

Theosophy, like all traditions, has a history variegated with personalities and opinions. But it is something much more. It has an aliveness and an immediacy. It begins to lift the veil of life's secrets. It embraces the mystery of who we are and what we can accomplish. It vibrates deep inside us and emanates through our universe, seen and unseen. It is the love we share, the joy we touch, and the common link of all we experience. Each breath brings us closer to Divinity. Blavatsky told her students:

> There *is* a road, steep and thorny, beset with perils of every kind, but yet a road, and it leads to the very heart of the Universe: I can tell you

how to find those who will show you the secret gateway that opens inward only, and closes fast behind the neophyte for evermore. There is no danger that dauntless courage cannot conquer; there is no trial that spotless purity cannot pass through; there is no difficulty that strong intellect cannot surmount. For those who win onwards there is reward past all telling—the power to bless and save humanity; for those who fail, there are other lives in which success may come.[21]

2

The Divine Seed

The soul in sleep gives proof of its divine nature.

—CICERO

"Nurturing the Divine Seed" was the theme of the 144th International Conference of the Theosophical Society in Varanasi (2019–20). What does the concept of the divine seed mean to a theosophical audience? The divine seed can be defined in numerous ways, but generally it refers to the spiritual self within each evolving entity. In Theosophy, we speak of the *monad*, or the individual (permanent) aspect of human nature, the spirit or spiritual soul. The higher nature of the human being has puzzled our species ever since we developed the capacity for self-reflection. The existence of that nature can be known through inference, revelation, or direct experience. Many religions and spiritual traditions have been based on various methods for establishing connection and communication with the deeper aspects of our Self.

The most fundamental questions may be, Does this divine seed (or higher nature) exist? followed by, Where and how does it manifest? Multiple theosophical authors confirm that there is a higher nature in each human being, perhaps dormant and unrecognized, and yet present, destined to unfold in the evolution of what Blavatsky calls the "Cycle of Incarnation (or 'Necessity') in accordance with Cyclic and Karmic law."[1]

The symbology of the seed is spread throughout Eastern and Western literature. It captures the potential for growth and maturation that we see in the development of plants, especially in those with the cycle of flowering and fruit. The miracle of nature that we observe in the metamorphosis of acorn to oak reminds us of the dynamic and largely unseen forces at play all around us that manifest with the breath of life. The embryo becomes the babe, the babe the adult, and the adult acquires wisdom and purpose. The inherent genetic manifestation of a plant is predictable if all the essential elements are present, including fertile soil, nutrients, hydration, protection, and later the warmth and energy of the sun. Just as this process unfolds in our physical world, it seems possible, even probable, that an analogous unfoldment can occur in the less tangible planes of our existence. As HPB comments,

> The Lotus, or Padma, is, moreover, a very ancient and favorite simile for the Kosmos itself, and also for man. The popular reasons given are, firstly, the fact just mentioned, that the Lotus seed contains within itself a perfect miniature of the future plant, which typifies the fact that the spiritual prototypes of all things exist in the immaterial world before those things become materialized on Earth.[2]

The symbol of the lotus, although it varies in its application and implications, often refers to the inner, divine nature at the core of every human being. In theosophical terminology, this generally equates to the dual monad (*atma-buddhi*) or the triple monad (*atma-buddhi-manas*), terms that are frequently used interchangeably. In *The Key to Theosophy*, Mme. Blavatsky defines the monad this way: "Monad. It is the Unity, the ONE; but in occultism it often means the unified duad, Atma-Buddhi,—or that immortal part of man which incarnating in the lower kingdoms and gradually progressing through them to Man, finds thence way to the final goal—Nirvana."[3]

Dr. I. K. Taimni, in *Man, God, and the Universe*, shows that many different similes are used in Hinduism to explain the relationship between the individual pilgrim (Skt. *jivatma*) and divine unity (Skt. *paramatma*). Each has its strengths but also some weaknesses, and each must be taken in context as a teaching mechanism rather than as a literal equivalent.

Like all analogies, that of the divine seed, for instance, is not a perfect one. Below, Taimni addresses both its usefulness and its limitations:

> Perhaps the most suggestive simile used for the relation between the Logos and the Monad is that of a tree and its seed. The most striking resemblance between a seed and the Monad is the presence in both of the potentiality to grow gradually into the likeness of their parents from which they are derived. The seed grows into the likeness of the tree from which it has come when it is sown in the earth; and so does the Monad when it is sown in the soil of *Prakṛti* or matter. The former also needs the light of the physical sun for its growth, and so does the Monad need the internal pressure of the Divine Life to make it unfold all its Divine possibilities on the lower planes. This simile also like the previous ones is defective in some respects. For instance, a seed is derived from the tree into the likeness of which it grows, but the Monad is not derived from the Logos Who provides him only with a field for his unfoldment. He is derived from the *Śiva-Śakti Tattva*. Again, the seed like a spark does

> not maintain any constant and continuous relation with the tree from which it has come. It becomes independent of the tree.[4]

Other analogies exist to describe the monad and its relationship to the universal Atma. HPB has used that of the dewdrop in the ocean. Another common analogy is that of the divine spark related to the cosmic fire. This can be useful in the sense that a spark, although physically separate from the fire that generated it, can continue to burn and even ignite sparks in others and is not substantially different from the "parent," capable of expanding the small fragment into a roaring blaze. It also has the advantage of representing the burning passion in the fire of commitment that can be observed in individuals who sense that deep connection to an intrinsic sense of purpose. It frequently represents desire, whether selfless or otherwise. The monad can be represented by a spark, which C. W. Leadbeater explains more fully in his *Textbook of Theosophy*:

> Man is therefore in essence a Spark of the divine Fire, belonging to the monadic world. To that Spark, dwelling all the time in that world, we give the name "Monad." For the purposes of human evolution the Monad manifests itself in lower worlds. When it descends one stage and enters the spiritual world, it shows itself there as the triple Spirit having itself three aspects (just as in worlds infinitely higher the Deity has His three Aspects). Of those three one remains always in that world, and we call that the Spirit in man. The second aspect manifests itself in the intuitional world, and we speak of it as the intuition in man. The third shows itself in the higher mental world, and we call it the intelligence in man. These three aspects taken together constitute the ego which ensouls the fragment from the group-soul.[5]

The nature of the divine seed is elusive and challenges description. Many have attempted, both directly and indirectly, to describe the higher nature of humans. Prominent theosophists have written about it with its various divisions, nomenclature, and attributes. Perhaps the truest understanding comes through direct experience of these realms—mysterious, difficult to access, and yet the deepest part of our own nature. Once established within an individual, recognized or not, it is essentially immortal and lives eternally. As Pablo Sender explains in *Evolution of the Higher Consciousness*, only in the rare circumstance in which an individual becomes extremely corrupt and immoral is the bridge (Skt. *antahkarana*) between the higher and the lower selves broken for a time—or, more rarely, permanently.[6]

The divine seed exists regardless of our awareness or knowledge of it. It is as the sun, constantly radiating; only the illusion of it vanishing, through clouds or darkness, blocks our vision and experience of it. Therefore, the divine seed needs to be not controlled but contacted. The transformational impulse is in every human, no matter how deeply buried and neglected. The desire to truly "know oneself" is the pilgrimage that each of us will in time experience in our attempt to understand the nature of our deeper aspects in the universe in which we live. Different teachers recommend various methodologies and techniques, and each seeker must find his or her own path to the Divine. At the same time, devoting too much attention to advancing on the spiritual path is not pure of all selfishness and is thus self-defeating.

The divine seed exists in this world of manifestation only through the lower aspects of our nature and does not act directly in situations or circumstances. It is, therefore, not only the source of self-knowledge for us as individuals, but it can also be a fount of spiritual direction and education that may be useful to others, if we can channel ideas and motivations from a deeper consciousness (or conscious "nonconsciousness," as HPB described it) for altruistic service. Any acts of selflessness and service will have ripple effects within both ourselves and the planetary system. These vibrations coalesce and open new influences and pathways in the larger systems in which we live our lives.

What might be an incentive to investigate our own higher nature, by whatever name we may call it? Those of faith may wish to discover outer Divinity through an inner spark of connection to the unity of which we are all part. Those who are more analytical may wish to understand the deeper workings of mentation, consciousness, and beyond. Some are prompted by pain and loss, often nearly unendurable, to search for answers and understanding. Annie Besant notes that "people learn that selfishness can breed only sorrow and have no other offspring than misery. If they will not learn by love, they must learn by pain."[7] Whether this pain is brought on by selfishness, illusion, or sacrifice is not always clear, but it can be a powerful driver to generate self-observation and self-exploration.

Many search in vain for the inner self. Whether the motivation to do so at a particular time is devotion, curiosity, love, compassion, or inextricable pain, or whether it is simply the inherent desire to discover one's true nature, does not initially change the wish to look deeper inwardly. What are the parameters of consciousness, the milestones of meditation, the landmarks of self-introspection? Where do you find this deeper awareness, this immortal self? Mabel Collins uses a symbol of the song of life for the inner self and writes about it this way in *Light on the Path*:

> Listen to the song of life.
>
> Look for it and listen to it first in your own heart. At first you may say: "It is not there; when I search I find only discord." Look deeper. If again you are disappointed, pause and look deeper again. There is a natural melody, an obscure fount in every human heart. It may be hidden and utterly concealed and silenced—but it is there. At the very base of your nature you will find faith, hope, and love.[8]

Can we discover this melody for ourselves? Collins says to listen to it first "in your own heart." How can this be understood metaphorically? Is it a measure of our love and devotion? Is it compassion for others that we know and love? Is it the compassion for a stranger or even an opponent that is the true nature of our own deepest commitment? HPB notes in *The Secret Doctrine* that "there is one absolute Reality which antecedes all manifested, conditioned being. This Infinite and Eternal Cause—dimly formulated in the 'Unconscious' and 'Unknowable' of current European philosophy—is the rootless root of 'all that was, is, or ever shall be.'"[9] This unity is the basis of our connectedness to all objects in the universe, both seen and unseen, but especially with other sentient creatures. We are not only inextricably linked but also connected in the sense of unity, a single continuous entity, indivisible as water. Then HPB reminds us in *The Voice of the Silence*, "Thou shalt not separate thy being from Being, and the rest, but merge the Ocean in the drop, the drop within the Ocean."[10] It is a sense of unity, however imperfect, that can lift our insight and compassion, for none is outside our sense of self and our sphere of concern. How can we transcend the "us and them" mentality which leads to divisions—economic, social, religious, and political? If we can see others as encapsulating the higher nature or divine seed, just as we ourselves do, we may feel less separation and greater concern for their welfare.

How are we to know what feelings and actions will lead to a greater awareness? Through self-observation, we can learn which are selfless and pure and see who would benefit, particularly in the near term. To which things and actions are we particularly attached? What is the source of that attachment? Should we be paralyzed, afraid to act for fear of producing unwanted karma and selfishness? Actions are often based on mixed motives, some selfish and some selfless. We need to examine them objectively and purify the roots of action as much as possible.

Although knowledge of the divine seed can be intensely alluring for one who seeks understanding of the mysteries within ourselves and in the universe, devotion to the path of self-development can still reside in the lower self with strains of selfishness for achievement and recognition. Only with pure intention can one achieve progress. It may be difficult to filter the impure from the pure, as on the journey many of us have conflicting motives of thoughts and actions. Pablo Sender has pointed out that many who are on the spiritual path may not know it; moreover, they are not particularly concerned about whether they are or not and do not feel the need to identify where on that path they might be. Their focus will be on others who may be hungry for comfort and higher knowledge.[11]

Competition, pride, and power can all still exist in spiritual matters, and we must be alert to identify these qualities when they occur and take steps to counteract them. It is perhaps safer for the aspirant to forget his or her own path for the inner self and instead focus on those in various types of need. By being willing to sacrifice their time and energy to lift up those around them, they will, in time, unfold themselves. We can be confident that when the time is ripe for us to open to greater self-awareness, it will be accomplished naturally and without excessive effort, whether during an incarnation or between incarnations. We must always consider service and compassion paramount in our efforts to be useful in all that we do, even if it appears that our strengths and gifts are limited. We are born into circumstances and experience situations that are most conducive to our own internal development. Challenges may be difficult, particularly when they appear to be recurrent, through laws of karma, but we must welcome them as educational opportunities that we still need to experience. We need to "forget" ourselves in order to know the Divine. The Master Serapis states:

> My brother understands that once the germs are sown they must be left to themselves and Nature; any too impatient hand that will

> interfere with them daily, trying to help to their growth by pulling them upwards, and will not leave them quiet, is more than likely to bring them to wither, dry up and die forever.[12]

For this germination to occur, the seed needs the essential elements and then only quiet, warmth, and time. Some might say that then the Divinity of the seed itself unfolds in a prescribed way. A scientist may purport that the seed is just following genetically prescribed natural law—and certainly this is true as well, only using different terminology. The growth of a plant seed faces many hazards, just as does the development of the divine seed planted deep within the human constitution. Each of us may take solace in the fact that we are following a pattern, usually unseen. Rarely do we get to view the map of our own development, but in retrospect our journey may have more meaning. Insight may be achieved regarding questionable occurrences in our lifetime that led to some unexpected outcome in which we gained some strength or skill. Perhaps this knowledge will occur only after our present incarnation, but it is useful to realize that the pattern exists, even if the details are opaque. We do not need to see the journey's end to know that we are guided. Clearly, we have free choice and may take many detours along the way. Often, we repeat those lessons innumerable times until we truly incorporate them into the most fundamental aspects of our being, having fully learned a particular lesson.

To continue the metaphor, the divine seed grows into maturity when the plant flowers in its most radiant form. The inner Divinity extends, in the fullness of time, into the fruition of its potentiality. Mabel Collins, in her commentary in *Light on the Path* when discussing the Adept, provides the following description: "His life is not his own, but that of the forces which work behind him. He is the flower of humanity, the bloom which contains the divine seed. He is, in his own person, a treasure of the universal nature, which is guarded and made safe in order that the fruition shall be perfected."[13]

Annie Besant, in her London lectures of 1907, made a similar commentary. Again when describing the development of an Adept, she uses the universal concept of a seed in nature: "In Him that divine seed of Spirit has unfolded into flower and fruit. When you sow a seed in the soil of your garden, you sow it in the full belief that it will grow, that it will become a plant with leaf and flower and fruit."[14]

This process, both in the garden and in the human constitution, does not come easily or quickly, but it does have an inexorable process to it. It is not immune from external dangers, which can forestall or even destroy the burgeoning new unfolding and the expanding life within it, but the life wave continues even if rechanneled temporarily. There is a pattern that exists unseen before it can come into manifestation. Although we may be ignorant of those patterns, in time—through self-observation, increased awareness of our environment, and listening to our internal voice—it does become apparent that such patterns exist. We must find the ingredients to support the seeds, so that they can flourish and rise into actualization, bringing with them sensitivity, awareness, and intuition.

How, then, can we nurture the seed? What behaviors will elevate us? Many methods and trainings have been described. In Buddhism, the Noble Eightfold Path defines the steps toward purification. In Theosophy, we often see the triad of knowledge, devotion, and service. Annie Besant, in *The Spiritual Life*, notes that the first step is often stated as "cease to do evil." The second step is an active one: "to do right." She states "it is said that 'the Self is not found by knowledge nor by devotion, but by knowledge wedded to devotion.' These are the two wings that lift us up into the spiritual world."[15] There is a plethora of techniques, both religious and nonreligious, addressing avenues to higher consciousness and improved awareness.

HPB uses the concept of a seed for the fledgling Theosophical Society. In its early years, as today, it needed a good deal of nurturing in order for it to grow into its full potential to aid both individuals and humanity, the latter of which the Masters described as the "Great Orphan." We can recognize that a tremendous amount of progress is yet to be made as we look at global events. Human nature is not all that we wish it to be and that it someday can be. It is up to those who are able and willing, through their decisions and actions, to pursue kindness, compassion, and justice. HPB emphasizes the study of comparative religions with an unbiased mind in order to understand and respect other branches of the human community. Through appreciating another's sacred belief, not only do we know and possibly accept that individual more readily, but we can more clearly see the commonality of various religious traditions and how they can be expressions of similar origins. Mme. Blavatsky writes,

> Our Theosophical Society is the humble seed which, if watered and left to live, will finally produce the Tree of Knowledge of Good and Evil which is grafted on the Tree of Life Eternal. For it is only by studying the various great religions and philosophies of humanity, by comparing them dispassionately and with an unbiased mind, that men can hope to arrive at the truth.[16]

The divine seed is a useful analogy for the deepest essence of our own being as well as that of others. The seed may be small, but the concept is enormous, representative of our truest nature as we attempt to discover meaning in our lives and direction for our behavior. It connects us to the entire universe, manifest and unmanifest, animate and inanimate, near and far. Nothing can abolish it—not injury, not damage, not suffering, not even death. It may not be embedded in our awareness, due to being unrecognized or at times even rejected.

But it is there to be discovered and in time will require attention. It sits unnoticed and yet influences our lives, our circumstances, our preferences, our choices. Some will seek it out due to soaring inspiration, others due to agonizing despair. Some may wish to rely on it, others to ignore it. Some will follow the urgings of the lower vehicles—the mental, the astral, and the physical. But in due time the intuition, through transformational prodding and the search for understanding, will prevail, and each pilgrim will recognize the need for self-examination. The most famous maxim from the Oracle of Delphi was "Know Thyself." Aristotle expanded it slightly by saying, "Knowing yourself is the beginning of all wisdom." How to realize that goal is life's greatest mystery.

3

Beauty and Where We Can Find It

Everything has beauty, but not everyone sees it.

—Confucius

Beauty. What does it mean? We've heard the familiar expressions "Beauty is in the eye of the beholder" and "Beauty is only skin deep." But what is beauty, and how does it affect our daily lives? Is it quantifiable? Is it transferable? Is it predictable? Is it discoverable?

Beauty is a core human value such as goodness, truth, and justice that is inherent in all philosophies dating back at least to the ancient Greeks and likely eons prior to their writings. The Greek concept of aesthetics (derived from *aisthetikos*) is defined as a perception by the senses, related to appreciation or response to art, design, or beauty. Generally, the perception is experienced as pleasure or satisfaction. Beauty, like other core values, can be idealized, imitated, discussed, and attributed. But is there agreement on what attributes contribute to or define beauty, or is the consensus that it exists only "in the eye of the beholder"?

One of the core differences of opinions on beauty is whether it is subjective or objective. Experience suggests that it cannot be exclusively either but is a combination or blending of the two. Is it an internal or an external phenomenon? Can it exist separate from ourselves? Or, like turning sound waves into sound, does it require an internal perception that exists only within a sentient being? In the eighteenth century, the Scottish philosopher David Hume argued that beauty—whether it be visual, auditory, or of other senses that perceive it—could not be objective but was only subjective as interpreted by the experiencer: "Beauty is no quality in things themselves: It exists merely in the mind which contemplates them; and each mind perceives a different beauty. One person may even perceive deformity, where another is sensible of beauty; and every individual ought to acquiesce in his own sentiment, without pretending to regulate those of others."[1]

Nonetheless, beauty does seem to have an objective component, especially regarding the common beauty that may enter our environment: if one perceives a beautiful bloom or a dramatic sunset, we know that most others would also share an appreciation for it. This likelihood does not exclude the influences of individual preferences. One observer may be moved by the quiet tranquility of a mountain lake, and another may prefer an oceanfront scene for its calming sensibility. The eternity of the tides and the expanse of sea draw many to our shores. One person may enjoy hiking outdoors in inclement weather, and another would prefer the balmy comfort of a clear summer day. Are these differences explained merely through light, shape, and color?

Visual beauty depends first on the sense of vision. Colors are displayed in an array of given wavelengths, arranged in such a way that is pleasing to the eye. Subtle differences occur in hues, their relative placement and intensity, and the blending in such a way that is endearing to the observer. Color, of course, is a perception of electromagnetic waves of varying frequencies, and it is only the artist, divine or human, who can create the combination in an arrangement that will be elevating, satisfying, and even moving to the observer.

The classical conception of beauty rests heavily on the concept of proportion in painting and sculpture.

> The central idea of the Italian Renaissance is that of perfect proportion. In the human figure as in the edifice, this epoch strove to achieve the image of perfection at rest within itself. Every form developed to self-existent being, the whole freely coordinated: nothing but independently living parts. . . . In the system of a classic composition, the single parts, however firmly they may be rooted in the whole, maintain a certain independence. It is not the anarchy of primitive art: the part is conditioned by the whole, and yet does not cease to have its own life.[2]

Proportion, balance, harmony, and unity are central qualities that contribute to beauty in the representation of the human form as well as the natural world. But these qualities are not limited merely to the visual aspect of historic, tangible art. They are equally vital to creation in other mediums, be it in acoustics—classical or modern—or in opera, ballet, literature, film, sports, or any other such endeavor in the human experience. This reality does not suggest uniformity or blandness, for in any such medium contrast and even conflict may enhance the drama and elevation of experience to the point that we may describe it as "beautiful."

Individual persons are often described as beautiful. Physical beauty was certainly admired by the Greeks and the Romans as it has been in all other civilizations, including our present one. Although we may be able to recognize physical beauty, can we define it more clearly? Is it a certain placement of the eyes, the shape of the mouth, the line of the jaw?

Helen of Troy is known for having had the "face that launched a thousand ships."[3] She was the wife of King Menelaus of Sparta; but, because of her beauty, Paris, the prince of Troy, abducted her, with the result that Menelaus waged war. Due to her countenance and her effect on Paris, a series of events was initiated that precipitated historic consequences. No doubt, innumerable other choices and actions occur based on our appreciation of physical beauty.

We may find beauty in motion if it is strong, graceful, and fluid. A group of wild horses galloping across an open meadow may be beautiful to some. A game ending in a double play by one's favorite baseball team may be perceived as beautiful by others. Still others may thrill to the sublime ballet slides in *An American in Paris.* Human and animal movement in the right context can be extremely moving, be it staged or spontaneous. Beauty has a deep resonance, an inner satisfaction, a glowing quality that enhances our sense of being. John Denver wrote about the "serenity of a clear blue mountain lake" and the hiker in Colorado who would "be a poorer man if he never saw an eagle fly."[4] Beauty is both personal and shared. It touches us emotionally and often evokes sensations of wonder. It can trigger memories and aspirations deep inside our nature, sometimes surprisingly so, bypassing mental processing and assessment.

Beyond beauty in action, there are beautiful acts. These are generally gestures of kindness and selflessness. Any activity that involves service over benefit, sacrifice over acquisition, and assistance over greed contains an element of beauty due to its selfless nature. Such acts occur every day and are everywhere around us, frequently going unnoticed, unappreciated, and often apparently unrewarded. It is the mother who gives up her own comfort for that of her child, the teacher who spends long hours trying to instill curiosity and discipline in the teenager, and the police officer who risks her own life to ensure civil stability. In the nursing home, it is the nurses and aides who care for our vulnerable elderly, those who are often demented and need near-total care as their bodies and minds deteriorate in the final stages of life. There is beauty here, deep and clear, but rarely registered. It can be appreciated as the beauty of the soul that is manifested in caring for others.

Hopefully, such actions can be reciprocated in some fashion as we pass through our physical incarnations and perhaps beyond. But these actions are taken generally not in hopes of future reward but in an altruistic sense in which we recognize the needs of others and are able to apply ourselves toward them. Certainly, acts of heroism can be beautiful, but it is the ordinary, everyday, selfless acts that are just as radiant, just as glorious, just as exalting and inspiring as those that might be recorded. Each of us should be grateful and feel even elevated regarding such behaviors, as they contribute to the cohesiveness of our society as well as individual welfare.

In Buddhism, we read of the Four Noble Truths that address the truth of suffering, the truth of the cause of suffering, the truth of the end of suffering, and the truth of the path that leads to the end of suffering.[5] But is this concept pessimistic, and does it exclude beauty in our world? Suffering appears to be an inevitable part of our incarnated existence in contrast with the divine life. In the periodical *Tricycle*, Kurt Spellmeyer quotes the Adittapariyaya Sutta, where Buddha says, "Seeing thus, the well-instructed disciple of the noble ones grows disenchanted with the eye, disenchanted with forms, disenchanted with consciousness at the eye, disenchanted with contact at the eye. And whatever there is that arises in dependence on contact at the eye, experienced as pleasure, pain or neither-pleasure-nor-pain: With that, too, he grows disenchanted."[6] (And the Sutta itself adds: "Disenchanted, he becomes dispassionate. Through dispassion, he is fully released.")[7]

Spellmeyer acknowledges that in this release achieved by dispassion, the attachment to beauty would be sacrificed: "If disenchantment takes us to awakening, the case for beauty looks like quite a stretch. What kind of beauty can exist, after all, once we renounce 'contact at the eye'?"[8]

In Buddhist psychology, certain types of qualities such as kindness, generosity, and honesty are described as being beautiful (Pali *sobhana*). Was this the type of beauty for which Buddha had the most regard? In the Dhammapada, he said, "Mere talk or beauty of complexion does not make an envious, greedy, dishonest person become respectable. The one in whom all these are destroyed, torn out by the very root, who is free from hate and is wise, is called respectable."[9]

These contrasting quotations appear to emphasize the difference between physical (earthly) beauty and moral (divine) beauty. The former certainly has a role as a wonderful aspect of life, as long as undue attachment to physical beauty and unethical behavior to be in possession of it does not ensue. The rejection of the physical, the "disenchantment with form," may be more an admonition not to be attracted by "glittery objects" that may not have the depth and substance for which the spiritual seeker yearns. However, beyond personality, the *paramitas,* or six perfections of Buddhism (generosity, morality, patience, energy, meditation, and wisdom), do contain a beauty worth noting and pursuing for those wishing to deepen their connection to the spiritual planes and proceed on the path of uplifting consciousness.

How do we find beauty? Blavatsky reminds us in *The Voice of the Silence* that "before the soul can see, the harmony within must be attained, and fleshly eyes be rendered blind to all illusion."[10] This is the concept of discrimination, which is described in part 1 of *At the Feet of the Master* and many other spiritual writings. Other terms for *discrimination* can be used, such as *discernment* (see ch. 16 of this work). The Sanskrit term is *viveka*, and this quality allows us to distinguish that which is Real (everlasting) from that which is unreal (transient). Part of the allure of beauty is that it is transient in the experience. The relatively brief blooming of a flower is all the more precious because it lasts only a few weeks. The stunning majesty of a sunset occurs only with the right combination of conditions and lasts only minutes or even less. It is the ineffable and ephemeral attributes that elevate the sense of wonder even further. But the underlying quality of beauty, be it through visual, auditory, or other sensations, is enduring. It can be found by opening our awareness and appreciating the exquisite beauty in previously mundane objects and situations.

Mystical experience is often described as beautiful, usually beyond words. The sensations are difficult to communicate due to the lack of a common language that can capture such moments. Annie Besant, in *An Introduction to Yoga*, describes withdrawing consciousness into a sheath followed by a dim sensing of other vibrations:

> You feel as though surrounded by a dense mist, conscious that you are not alone but unable to see. Be still; be patient; wait. Let your consciousness be in the attitude of suspense. Presently the cloud will thin, and first in glimpses, then in its full beauty, the vision of a higher plane will dawn on your entranced sight.[11]

What she describes is an uncommon beauty for most of us who have difficulty accessing superconscious states. We access such states naturally when dreaming, and many do experience such dreams, including the quality of beauty, although much of it may be blunted or even lost as the memory of it is filtered by our lower mental state upon awakening to ordinary consciousness. What spaces do we travel in, and which are we able to recall, separate from the physical brain and body?

In *Beethoven and the Spiritual Path*, author David Tame suggests that Beethoven yearned to reach the Divine in his composing and to reflect to the earthbound public the celestial beauty of higher states of conscious awareness through his symphonies and sonatas. He suffered from the vicissitudes of life as most mortals do, but he never lost sight of the divine inspiration that drove him in striving to capture the transformational power and glory of the highest aspects of his nature and the communion with superphysical energies that allowed him to compose many of the world's most exquisite orchestrations. How this was accomplished must be left to speculation, but, two centuries later, his efforts remain among the most beautiful and sublime we have in the repertoire of classical music. His sentiments are reflected in this passage from his journal in 1815: "All things flowed clear and pure out of God. Though often darkly led to evil by passion, I returned, through penance and purification, to the pure fountain—to God—and to your art. In this I was never impelled by selfishness; may it always be so."[12]

As we are seeing, beauty comes in many forms and dimensions. Human qualities are often beautiful as they are displayed in thoughts and actions. Virtues such as generosity, compassion, and justice contain beauty as well. John Keats, in "Ode on a Grecian Urn," concludes the poem with the famous lines,

> When old age shall this generation waste,
> Thou shalt remain, in midst of other woe
> Than ours, a friend to man, to whom thou say'st,
> "Beauty is truth, truth beauty,—that is all
> Ye know on earth, and all Ye need to know."

Keats equates beauty with truth, which suggests that beauty is enduring, timeless, inexpressible, and inexhaustible. Philosophers debate whether true beauty needs to be everlasting, in which case its more temporal expressions would simply be a facet of the deeper nature of the quality. However, if beauty is truth, then can we say by extension that truth is subjective as well as objective? Traditionally, truth is considered to be based on factual information of mutual acceptance; therefore, it must have a strongly objective quality in order to be considered true. Yet Keats sees the more subjective quality of beauty and the objective quality of truth as being mirrors of each other.

Truth, beauty, and goodness are often discussed together. This theme runs through Christianity, Buddhism, and all major religious and philosophical traditions. It is often referred to as the Platonic Triad due to Plato's writings about the idealized human condition. The triad can be viewed as three points on a triangle, each interrelated to the others, inseparable and dependent, and each a reflection of the complementary two.

Some authors feel that the three qualities represent the ideal of science (truth), the arts (beauty), and morality (goodness). But they are more intertwined than that. Beauty infuses all aspects of life, and human activity would be barren without it. Would truth be truth without beauty? These are divine qualities, wherever they occur, and need to be recognized, nurtured, and developed. Beauty, in its broadest sense, relates to harmony, unity, and connectedness. It reflects the nature and purpose of the universe and our place within it. It appeals to the transformational impulse, manifest or latent, that is within all creatures on the path of evolution.

Essentially, every teacher of the Divine Wisdom will refer to higher levels of consciousness with superlatives including beauty, although further articulation may be wanting. Dr. Taimni notes that "the whole Truth in its perfection and transcendent beauty can be realized only within the innermost depth of one's consciousness when all the limitations and illusions of the mind have fallen away. We are then not looking at this Truth from a *particular* point of view. We have then become the Truth itself."[13] He goes on to explain that the superconscious Truth cannot be claimed by any specific religious movement, system of philosophical thought, or personality cult, for it belongs to universal humanity, open to those who wish to pursue the path and explore the deeper aspects of the inner self. Just as no one can claim to have a unique possession of knowledge or truth, no one individual or tradition can monopolize beauty. It exists freely in our universe, as do wind and sunlight. There are pursuits that may promote a specific methodology for connecting with higher regions of consciousness, and they may or may not be successful for some, but the higher consciousness itself is accessible to all who wish it, should the appropriate conditions be brought into existence. The revelatory beauty of higher consciousness surpasses any earthly definition according to those that have experienced it. As is true of many qualities, we can extrapolate from what we know from our earthly existence into the higher planes. However, like most extrapolations, the result will be an estimate at best; and our earthly words, often clumsy when used to express nonearthly qualities, will fall short of their intended meaning. Even if the word accurately describes a superphysical phenomenon, if we have not experienced that phenomenon or a similar one, then the use of the word does little to clarify the image that the speaker is attempting to communicate. Words are helpful in describing ordinary experiences, but they fail when trying to convey a mystical vision.

Many words can help point the way, though, with beauty being one of the major adjectives. To continue with Dr. Taimni's narrative, he writes that

> at best such a presentation can be an attempt to provide faint and blurred glimpses of this Truth in order that people may intuitively feel its beauty and grandeur within their heart, and begin to seek it there earnestly and purposefully. For the same reason no Teacher of

> the true Wisdom ever tries to put forward the claim that his teaching is new or exclusive. Even the Buddha said, "I have seen the ancient way, the old road that was taken by the former awakened beings, and that is the path I follow."[14]

Even though the opening to the universal defies description with language, it can be hinted at. Yet at the same time, mystery remains. Ravi Ravindra, in his book on the Bhagavad Gita, quotes Albert Einstein saying,

> The most beautiful and deepest experience a man can have is the sense of the mysterious. It is the underlying principle of religion as well as all serious endeavor in art and science. He who never had this experience seems to me, if not dead, then at least blind. To sense that behind anything that can be experienced there is a something that our mind cannot grasp and whose beauty and sublimity reaches us only indirectly and as a feeble reflection, this is religiousness. In this sense I am religious. To me it suffices to wonder at these secrets and to attempt humbly to grasp with my mind a mere image of the lofty structure of all that there is. The scientists' religious feeling takes the form of a rapturous amazement at the harmony of natural law, which reveals an intelligence of such superiority that, compared with it, all the systemic thinking and acting of human beings is an utterly insignificant reflection.[15]

Dr. Ravindra, when discussing the mystery of sacred knowledge that Krishna teaches the warrior prince Arjuna, states that "this mystery is accessible not by thinking but by direct perception."[16] One can make the same argument for beauty. In general, beauty is a quality of direct experience, even if at times that experience involves a thought process, such as the beauty in a puzzle, in a mathematical formula, or in principles of astronomical physics.

From a theosophical perspective, beauty is an inherent quality in all that we see, do, and experience. There may be degrees of beauty, particularly for each individual, as one's life path unfolds before him or her. There is an enhanced beauty to be recognized as we are able to open awareness and appreciate the harmony and bliss of our natural world as well as places unseen and unknown. H. P. Blavatsky, when discussing the spiritual path in *The Key to Theosophy*, notes that "from strength to strength, from the beauty and perfection of one plane to the greater beauty and perfection of another, with accessions of new glory, of fresh knowledge and power in each cycle, such is the destiny of every Ego, which thus becomes its own Saviour in each world and incarnation."[17]

Therefore, it is not an exaggeration to say that beauty is omnipresent. It is striking to the ear and eye. There is beauty in action and in stillness. There is beauty in thought and in tranquility. There is moral beauty, and there is the beauty of compassion. There is beauty in the animate and in the (so-called) inanimate. There is beauty in the world we know and still greater beauty in the worlds we may not know. It is inherent in the way we live and breathe. We do not need to seek beauty. We need only to open ourselves to it, appreciate it, savor it, and see the Divine in it. As divine beings ourselves, we can never separate from it, although we can become blind from time to time. Let us acknowledge it, treasure it, and participate in it. What greater gift is there than in sharing our inherent love for and reflection about all things beautiful?

4

Means, Motive, and Opportunity

The Keys to Change

Peculiar travel suggestions are dancing lessons from God.

—KURT VONNEGUT

We are all familiar with the well-known line of questioning that occurs in popular murder mysteries when a suspect is taken into custody. Did he/she have the means, motive, and opportunity to commit the crime? If one or more of these components are missing, the investigators need to reconsider their supposition about the accused's guilt and perhaps look elsewhere for the perpetrator. It occurred to me that these components are necessary not only to commit what constitutes a crime but also to make a shift in one's attention or activity. This can apply to fairly small changes such as interest in a new hobby, literature, or group of friends as well as to life-changing circumstances such as pursuing a new profession, living in a new culture, or adopting new spiritual beliefs. The components in question do not necessarily appear simultaneously and may come into focus only gradually, over a significant period of time. One element may be missing that makes the change impossible, at least for the present. One factor may appear and then stimulate a person consciously to pursue the other two. Or, it's quite possible to experience one component—say, motivation—and to forget about it for a significant period of time, only to have the component of opportunity present itself much later, possibly when the component of means is also conducive. Often this dynamic is not obvious in real time but becomes more apparent in retrospect. On several occasions in my life, I have had a desire to participate in a particular activity that was thwarted initially but eventually came to fruition. Whether the initial impetus was foreshadowing the activity by planting a seed in consciousness or whether it was an invitation that brought other conditions into manifestation is not clear, and the distinction may not be relevant. It does appear that when we have a wish, it is somehow addressed.

Many clinical models have been developed regarding behavioral change. They have been described somewhat differently by various authorities and in different applications. Frequently, behavioral change has been proposed as occurring in five stages: precontemplation, contemplation, preparation, action, and maintenance. My intention is not to focus on this now-classical approach but rather to examine what moves a person through the stages.

In the preface, I mentioned that in 2017 I had returned to the States following an extended medical excursion in Africa. After having worked for twenty-five years in a fairly traditional medical practice, I had accepted the position as a faculty member training native physicians in the small African country of Lesotho. Many have asked how I came to this decision. It was not initially my intention to make this change. I have had a long-held interest in global health and had made several trips to Haiti to do short-term volunteer medical work. Initially I had joined others who have a shared interest and eventually started leading teams of my own. We usually would spend a week to ten days working in pop-up clinics, typically held in a church or school.

Often working in this type of setting evokes a feeling of wanting to do more and create a deeper and more durable impact. I was drawn to the notion of furthering my education through a Masters of Public Health degree. In 2013, I had the opportunity to retire from my present position and, although I did not desire to retire from medicine, I did see it as an opportunity to change direction.

During that time of considering retirement, I began to feel restless. I wanted a different type of milieu. The thought of routine activities such as going to the local hardware store, taking community classes, or deciding on the most appealing restaurant on a Friday night felt trivial. The homogeneity of life in New Hampshire was uninspiring. I read medical journals with pictures of physicians working in refugee camps and felt envious. There seemed to be great excitement in both the academic and service components of medical work in the developing world, and I felt I just had to be involved in some way.

I did leave my practice and was able to find a program to obtain my master's degree in public health in less than a year. Because of my growing interest in international health, I decided to attend a conference of the World Organization of National Colleges, Academies, and Academic Associations of General Practitioners/Family Physicians (WONCA). It was there that I encountered a physician who was leading a program in Lesotho, an isolated country of approximately two million people completely within the borders of South Africa. The program's educational initiative is to train local physicians while encouraging them to choose careers in their own country. There is a high disease burden and a shortage of resources, both human and monetary. Further, the physician leading the program was a man with whom I had done my specialty residency thirty years earlier.

After completing my master's degree, I reached out to the Lesotho organization but did not hear back for many months. I was considering other opportunities when the Lesotho group, known as LeBoHA (Lesotho Boston Health Alliance), finally did contact me, saying they were looking for an additional faculty member. As I was considering my answer, I realized a path had been cleared for me to commit to such an opportunity. I had the financial means to afford a voluntary (or nearly so) position for two years. Professionally, I was able to shift to using my training and experience with the new population. Personally, my children were young adults and could manage on their own (of course, with electronic communication and support), and my wife was willing to engage in this experience with me. In short, means, motive, and opportunity had coalesced in such a way that I felt the door had opened and an invitation had been delivered. Perhaps with some mild trepidation, but with great enthusiasm, I accepted this new challenge.

Did this opportunity find me, or did I find it? Perhaps I drew it toward me in some unconscious way or created the circumstances in which it could occur. I think of it as a dance, a partnership, in which I create the desire and "the universe" responds.

Whether one considers it as an answer to a prayer, the implementation of karma, or the whispering of the cosmos, it appears that when intention is created an opportunity presents itself. This has happened at other times in my life as well, and I'm certain each of you has also experienced it. What is this connection that appears to open doors, and how do we choose when it is manifest? One decision, of course, leads to many others. Much has been written about saying yes to these opportunities, but we must first recognize and secondly commit, with confidence and courage, when they present themselves. These circumstances may provide useful experiences related to our own development, such as purification, service, or education, that may ultimately allow our personal unfoldment and expansion of our humanity. They do not need to be transformational spiritual experiences, however.

Many ask how they can be of service. Annie Besant noted that her contemporaries often asked her this question. They might have wished to go to India to serve the Masters there. She was adamant in her reply of *no*. Each of us, through individual karma, is placed in a life and conditions most conducive to developing the parts of our nature that are necessary at the time. Additionally, Besant was quite clear that we should do our own work that has been provided for us. It is better to do our own work well than that of another. For this reason, comparing one's experience with another is unhelpful. Individual karma is specific and cannot be adapted to another context. Our means, motive, and opportunity are not transferable. Although my work in Africa was important to me, I understand that such a venture is not realistic, or even appropriate, for many others. However, each life invites openings to explore.

Charles Leadbeater writes, in *The Masters and the Path*,

> We can do nothing on our side but steadily work at the improvement of our character, and endeavour in every possible way, by the study of Theosophical works, by self-development, and by the unselfishness of our devotion to the interests of others, to fit ourselves for the honour which we desire, having within our minds the utter certainty that as soon as we are ready the recognition will assuredly come.[1]

Means is the ability or method of obtaining a particular result. It includes the physical, financial, emotional, and/or logistical support necessary to allow a particular behavior or activity. Often, it is the limiting factor in making a decision pertaining to a change.

However, this limiting factor contains two components: One concerns *objective* limitations such as depleted finances or primary family obligations. The other concerns the *subjective* determination that the obstacles are "overwhelming," where in fact only a shift in vision and priorities is necessary to find the means to accomplish the goal. This sense of being overwhelmed often occurs at moments of crisis or moments of inspiration. Nelson Mandela famously said, "It is always thought impossible until it is done."

One's course of action may involve considerable risk. It has become fashionable to talk about "risk tolerance," which, of course, can impinge on many aspects of our sense of safety. At times, we choose a course of action simply because it "feels right" or "has to be done." A pianist was once asked, when participating in the grueling Van Cliburn competition, why he would put himself through such scrutiny and pressure with little chance of success. He answered simply. "I couldn't not do it." Whether such persistence is due to karma, destiny, or free choice seems to be less important and is only a matter of semantics.

Motivation is notoriously mercurial. Let's take a simple example. I have met many patients who say they cannot give up smoking. They have tried various methods, all of which have ultimately failed. They essentially resign themselves to continuing this unhealthy habit because they believe they lack the determination to quit. Then perhaps they have a catastrophic event, such as admission to the intensive care unit with pneumonia or a heart attack. They see the immediacy of their mortality and then have a greatly enhanced resolve as they understand the clear relationship between discontinuing smoking and continuing to live.

We all experience changes in motivation in smaller and perhaps less dramatic ways. Taking a Tai Chi class might not work in our schedule one year, but maybe it will in another. As we become more attracted to the concept of Tai Chi, we may make it a priority. Or, we may have a strong motivation to travel to Europe, but the opportunity is not available. Once the opportunity presents itself, the motivation may be gone. Yet again, we may wish to work for a certain company that we envision has views compatible with our own, but an opening is not available. In time, when we release this desire, perhaps an opening will be created in that or a similar company.

Often, motivation is realized in a considered, rational choice. Motivation can also be realized in an impulsive, emotional response. Our decisions in relationships are often a combination. Our attractions to people and ideas can certainly ebb and flow over time. At times, we are motivated in ways of which we are unaware. I believe each of us is propelled to certain actions by unconscious (or perhaps superconscious) motivations when we see only one course available to us. It seems clear that, if we do not "push" ourselves, life will "push" us into challenging situations.

One motive to change our life is to make it more spiritual. This may be something in which we wish to be actively involved, or there may be forces at work that we do not completely understand. In *The Spiritual Life*, Mrs. Besant writes about changing motives:

> I just now used the word "duty," for that is the first step. It does not matter what your work in the world may be if you begin to do it, not because it brings you a livelihood—though there is nothing to be ashamed of in that—but slowly, gradually, more and more you do it because it ought to be done, not because you want to gain something for yourself. Then you are taking the first step toward the spiritual life, you are changing your motive; all activities of your day will have a new object.[2]

In Mahatma letter 92, Master KH, while writing in defense of HPB, states that "*motive* is everything for us";[3] therefore, this may be the most powerful of the three components. Now, because we are familiar with the theosophical context, we can reflect on how this understanding might be relevant to our lives.

Inherent in our discussion so far, we've looked at how opportunities may present themselves for our consideration. The conflicting axioms of "Look before you leap" and "He who hesitates is lost" perhaps convey that no uniform rule will suffice. Only each of us alone can determine whether an opportunity should be taken in a given set of circumstances. Some opportunities are predictable and can be prepared for. If one wishes to enter a school of higher education, that person can take the necessary prerequisites and testing to determine if they are qualified. Other opportunities are completely unexpected. Perhaps a casual meeting of another person on a plane leads to a job opportunity. Perhaps a friend of a friend invites you on an excursion to a foreign country. Perhaps a supervisor is injured or leaves unexpectedly and you are promoted into a position entirely unanticipated. Whether these are chance encounters or predetermined occurrences can be debated. But they do occur with regular frequency, and we might wonder if they are somehow "opened" to us in superphysical spheres. Whether they lead to joy or pain cannot determine the necessity of welcoming the experiences that come to us. Each change in which we engage leads to further changes. We may be able to see, not the future, but only the present and perhaps a few next steps. Similar to driving in foggy weather, we need only to see the few feet ahead of us to progress; if we have the benefit of the road and a map, we can make the full trip. In life, most of us do not have the foresight of knowing the path ahead, but we can intuitively follow what we see as our dharma (our right way of living/duty), knowing that—perhaps trusting that—we will find the opportunities we need.

We know that matter is in constant motion, as are all parts of the universe. Our bodies, our needs, our sense of self are similarly moving. Some prepare for and seek change, and others have it thrust upon them. We are who we are today through a series of circumstances and choices. Through dawning awareness, we can consciously participate in our own development and unfoldment. These comments are not necessarily about seeking a spiritual path, although they may include it. They are more about recognizing that choices are a sharing between the rational and the irrational, between the seen and the unseen, between the expected and the unexpected. It is about the willingness to invite the door to open and then having the courage and determination to walk through it. In small and large ways, we can attract our own circumstances. Means, motive, and opportunity often don't come together as a package, at least initially. Perhaps the motive may need to germinate for many years. Or perhaps it may need to be long forgotten when the opportunity to act on it comes. Instead of a giant leap, we may choose an incremental step. But many steps create a pathway, and a pathway leads to something new. Whether that new thing can be useful to us and to our work depends on multiple factors, but it is likely to change us. Are we willing to find out?

5

Ethics in the Age of Greed

Finding One's Way in the Morass of Immorality

The first step in the evolution of ethics
is a sense of solidarity with other human beings.

—ALBERT SCHWEITZER

This is a time of great upheaval politically, socially, and economically, leading to dazzling displays of greed in many facets of our society. Self-interest is not new, of course, and financial interests have frequently pervaded politics (along with many laudable efforts by compassionate voices in opposition), but it feels more pivotal and dangerous today. We cannot help but reflect upon (and regret) that there is such a flagrant abuse of civility and lack of respect for the downtrodden in certain quarters. Nightly headlines seem to scream to us of excesses of power and greed.

What are we to think about the values in the world in which we live? Are we to find our way without admirable role models in all levels of our public and private leadership? How can we find our place in a system that appears stunningly corrupt? A selfish attitude has a ripple effect as it infuses into our society, changing us culturally and individually. Perhaps we are more likely to be influenced by such behavior and say to ourselves and others, "Everyone does it," or, "This is nothing compared to such and such situation." The corruption begins to erode our moral structure (or we let it do so). Where can we turn for moral direction? Are our ethics passé or even naïve? Let us investigate this dilemma and try to find the light in the darkness.

Ethics and *morals* are two words that relate to right and wrong and are often used interchangeably, although they have distinct meanings and therefore implications. *Ethics* is derived from the French (*éthique*) and the Greek (*ethos*), meaning "character." Its application leads to professional or legal guidelines to help direct behavior regarding the individual and collective actions of a particular unit. *Ethics* refers to rules generally provided by an external source as a code of conduct such as in a medical, legal, business, or religious setting. These ethical principles are recognized by a particular group or culture to help them define behaviors that are acceptable. The word *morals*, on the other hand, is derived from the Latin word *moralis*, which refers to individual principles regarding right and wrong and ultimately to an individual's choices and behavior that may or may not be congruent with the ethical standards (or lack thereof) in the larger group. Morality can transcend (or fall short of) cultural norms. We might follow an ethical pattern because society or some smaller group has determined that it is proper, while we will make a moral decision based on what we personally think is right or wrong. There may be differences in flexibility. Since ethical rules are based on certain cultural theories and practices—which certainly can change but usually not abruptly—they tend to be stable or evolving. Morals tend to be consistent with an individual person's worldview. These, too, can be flexible, depending on circumstances and experience, and can undergo dramatic changes at times.

Can we imagine situations in which moral choices and ethics are not aligned? Such situations may actually occur quite commonly. Suppose a defendant is on trial for murder and is assigned a public defender. That attorney may feel that murder is reprehensible. She may even be convinced that her client is guilty of the crime. However, due to her professional ethics she feels duty bound to give the defendant a fair trial and perhaps even to achieve an acquittal. In the medical profession, a doctor may believe in a patient's right to die and not feel that euthanasia is a crime (which it is in this country, but not in all countries). Disagreeing with the medical ethics that prohibit active euthanasia, this doctor may even attempt to break the law and administer a lethal injection. You might say that his morals transcend the ethical recommendations of his profession, while others may see his behavior as illegal and immoral.

Complicating matters is that ethical guidelines can vary from place to place and from time to time. Take, for example, the difference between ethically prescribed behavior in civilian life and in military conflict. While in civilian life murder is considered a most serious crime, many people who are loathe to harm and certainly to kill another are sanctioned to perform this activity in times of war. In this instance, some may still refuse and be labeled as conscientious objectors. Although combat is ethically permissible, they may see it as personally repugnant. The conflict between public and private ethics can create an agonizing struggle for the individual forced to make a choice.

Ethical theory can be broken down into several approaches. *Utilitarianism*, founded in modern guise by Jeremy Bentham

(1748–1832) and developed by John Stuart Mill (1806–1873), is the theory that the highest ethical purpose is to promote the greatest happiness of the greatest number of people. *Deontology*, advanced by Immanuel Kant (1724–1804), is the theory that people should base ethical decisions on their prescribed obligations and duties instead of on the consequences of an action. *Communitarianism* is based on the values of the community in which the actor is immersed. *Casuistry* entails deciding dilemmas by looking at precedent and previous decisions in similar cases; this method is prominent in our legal system as well as in ecclesiastical settings. *Character ethics*, sometimes called the "virtuous man theory," posits a virtuous person or entity with ideal ethics and then supposes what decision that person might make. The common response of What Would Jesus Do (WWJD) falls into this category. These and other ethical theories are listed below.

There are several sets of ethical principles in which the numbers can vary slightly but generally include at least four. Autonomy, beneficence, nonmaleficence, and justice comprise one such set, derived by the ethicists Tom Beauchamp and James Childress.[1] Other principles such as truthfulness, dignity, respect, fidelity, integrity, competence, and respect for rights are sometimes included, but these are essentially inherent in the first four. Each of these can be discussed in considerable detail, which we will not pursue now.

What about the role of law? We have libraries full of laws. Are these not adequate to direct ethics (and morals)? There are several problems with relying only on established legal statutes. First is that the law may be silent on important issues. Also, the law may change from time to time and differ from place to place. The law may allow unethical practices, as many behaviors that are legal are nonetheless unethical. Additionally, many laws may be inconsistent and conflicting.

Traditional Ethical Theories

THEORY	BASICS	MAIN FEATURES
Utilitarianism	Consequence-based theory	Greatest good/happiness for the greatest number of people
Kantianism	Obligation-based theory	Intention, duty or obligation to do the right thing
Liberal individualism	Rights-based theory	Positive and negative individual rights with obligations and responsibilities
Communitarianism	Community-based theory	Communal values, needs, and rights are paramount
Ethics of care	Relationship-based accounts	Interpersonal relations, care, and compassion emphasized
Casuistry	Case-based reasoning	Practical decisions based on real- life case studies
Character ethics	Virtue-based theory	Personality and character (key traits and virtues) taken into account

Figure 1. Traditional major ethical theories in the current medical literature. Critical to note is that theories vary according to emphasis of values; none apply to all situations. Reproduced from Robert Mash, *Handbook of Family Medicine* (Cape Town: Oxford University Press, Southern Africa Ltd., 2017), 410.

What about intuition as a guide to ethics? We might feel that we know right from wrong in a given situation, but this view is also certainly problematic. Intuition is subjective and often differs substantially among individuals. Further, it is reflexive and not based on systematic considerations. It does not allow for the review of practice and ethical theory. One can easily conflict with existing ethical guidelines in whatever sphere one is operating. Reference to intuition can be difficult to justify in the absence of a supporting foundation.

When dealing with ethical or moral decisions, as mentioned, justice is a core principle that we must take into consideration. *Justice* can be interpreted as equality, equity, and fairness. *Equality* is defined as a state in which the quality, quantity, measure, and value are equal or balanced. *Equity* implies fairness but is more in accordance with one's specific needs than is just blind equality. *Fairness* is a concept closely related to justice, but it can vary depending on one's perspective.

An example, sometimes used in ethical circles, is one in which a small business celebrates its success by purchasing a cake. That cake can be cut in equal-sized portions, but how can it be divided most fairly? Perhaps one might believe in an equal size for each member present. Yet one thoughtful member might advocate including five extra pieces in the equal measure for the five employees who cannot be present that day because they need to continue working. Perhaps the president of the company feels that due to her elevated rank she is entitled to a larger portion. One of the salesmen might mention that he has been the most successful in sales for the quarter and therefore should have a larger slice. Another employee might note that, due to circumstances of employment, he has been unable to be present for the last two celebrations and therefore is owed a debt of cake accordingly. Another chimes in that equal portions of cake for people who are very different in size is really not fair at all; the pieces should be proportional to the person's weight. Another notes that many people don't even care for cake, and so they should sacrifice for the ones who most savor it. One woman says she desperately needs a larger piece of cake because she has not eaten for the last day.

Each of these arguments sees the fairness of dividing the cake from a different perspective. This somewhat amusing example can be very serious in a time and place of limited resources. Suppose we live in a land of restricted food and medical availability. Discussions regarding fairness that revolve around presence versus absence, rank, value, need, past injustice, and desire are very relevant, and at times it is difficult to find the balance. Rules of allocation might be seen as unfair by some. Can such distribution be done in an objectively just manner?

Beyond personal ethics are the ethics of communities and governments. Through our state and national governments, do we collectively perform ethically? Can these political entities represent a diverse population fairly? Do international organizations such as the World Trade Organization, the International Monetary Fund, and the World Bank follow ethical principles? And what are the constraints on such organizations, internal and external?

Many look to religion to provide a system of ethics that can guide our own morality. Such religions provide commentaries on right living and behavior that go back to the early days of each core tradition. Buddhism, for example, provides what is known as the five precepts, which are a distillation of Buddhist ethical theory. The following list is from the Buddhist Centre Online:

1. Not killing or causing harm to other living beings. This is the fundamental ethical principle for Buddhism, and all the other precepts are elaborations of this. The precept implies acting nonviolently wherever possible, and many Buddhists are vegetarian for this reason. The positive counterpart of this precept is love.
2. Not taking the not-given. Stealing is an obvious way in which one can harm others. One can also take advantage of people, exploit them, or manipulate them. All these can be seen as ways of taking the not-given. The positive counterpart of this precept is generosity.
3. Avoiding sexual misconduct. Over the centuries different Buddhist schools have interpreted this precept in many ways,

but essentially it means not causing harm to oneself or others in the area of sexual activity. It includes avoiding breaking commitments in the area of sexual relations, and avoiding encouraging others to do the same. The positive counterpart of this precept is contentment.

4. Avoiding false speech. Speech is the crucial element in our relations with others, and yet language is a slippery medium, and we often deceive ourselves or others without even realizing that this is what we are doing. Truthfulness, the positive counterpart of this precept, is therefore essential in an ethical life. But truthfulness is not enough, and in another list of precepts (the ten precepts or the ten *kusala* dharmas) no fewer than four speech precepts are mentioned, the others enjoining that our speech should be kindly, helpful, and harmonious.
5. Abstaining from drink and drugs that cloud the mind. The positive counterpart of this precept is mindfulness, or awareness. Mindfulness is a fundamental quality to be developed on the Buddha's path, and experience shows that taking intoxicating drink or drugs tends to run directly counter to this.[2]

All other ethical decisions must be derivative of these principles in the Buddhist tradition. Of course, the central messages of these precepts are also common in many, if not most, other religious traditions, both Eastern and Western. In essence, each one promotes selfless behavior and admonishes against the selfish aspects of our nature. We should not cause harm to others (or ourselves) through thought, speech, or actions. We must remain humble and not use any situation to our advantage, especially without the knowledge and consent of those with whom we are interacting.

In Hinduism, from which Buddhism evolved, there are also five major themes, known as the *Panchavrata*. The following excerpt from the Rigveda sums them up: "Violence, womanizing, drinking liquor, gambling, stealing, falsehood or lying, and association with those who commit these sins; one who commits any of these sins is a sinner."[3]

Although the Rigveda text is ancient, the translation appears more modern. Not surprisingly, given the close relationship of Hinduism and Buddhism, the essential concepts are quite similar. A core treatise of Hinduism is the Bhagavad Gita, and many commentaries have been written on the ethics expressed in this sublime work. Some authors list nine commandments expounded in the Gita.[4]

One critical commandment is that of *ahimsa* (Skt.), often understood to mean respect for all living things and the avoidance of violence toward others.[5] This means abstention from inflicting not only physical harm but psychological harm as well. It includes not only harmful actions but also harmful speech and thoughts. But does this commandment imply passivity in all situations? In *The Wisdom of Patanjali's Yoga Sutras*, Ravi Ravindra discusses ahimsa and its opposite, *himsa*:

> In the Bhagavad Gita, himsa is the violation of right order; it does not necessarily mean physical fighting or harming. . . . External action alone does not determine whether there is himsa or not; intention, motive and the relationship between the parties involved are also relevant. Externally an action may appear violent, but it may arise because of love and compassion. . . . Krishna urges Arjuna to fight while he maintains that the characteristics of a wise person are 'ahimsa, truth, absence of anger, non-identification, peace, loyalty, compassion for all, lack of greed, gentleness, modesty, reliability.'[6]

This reasoning suggests that there may be a role for strength and even force in certain situations, depending on the motivation involved—such as that of a defensive nature based in love and compassion. The issue comprises one of the central conflicts of the Bhagavad Gita, as Arjuna does not wish to commit violence against his opponents, many of whom are his relatives, teachers, and friends. Ethical decisions about the uses of action, particularly when they are violent, can be complicated. Although war is reprehensible, is it always unethical? Would we use violence to defend that which we hold most sacred? (This question is explored further in ch. 6.)

Patanjali's *Yoga Sutras* is a revered text that offers us a guide to right living. This is done through the yamas and niyamas, a series of ethical rules within Hinduism and yoga. As stated by Kripalu, a major yoga center,

> The yamas and niyamas are yoga's ethical guidelines laid out in the first two limbs of Patanjali's eightfold path. They're like a map written to guide you on your life's journey. Simply put, the yamas are things not to do, or restraints, while the niyamas are things to do, or observances. Together, they form a moral code of conduct.[7]

The five yamas are, in Sanskrit, *ahimsa* (nonharming), *satya* (benevolent truthfulness), *asteya* (nonstealing), *brahmacharya* (unity, nonexcess, celibacy, containment) and *aparigraha* (simplicity, generosity, nonpossessiveness, nongrasping). Some of these terms have different interpretations emphasizing different nuances of the core meaning. We will not delve into each one here, but it might be helpful to look more closely at *aparigraha* as an example. Ravi Ravindra notes:

> Non-possession or non-grasping (*aparigraha*) is recommended as a practice by Patanjali. It is as relevant to psychological possessions as to physical or material ones. The force of possession is primarily psychological and we can be addicted to an accumulation of goods, of power, of knowledge, or of thrilling experiences. That is why there is the repeated suggestion by the sages, such as Krishnamurti, that in order to be free, one needs to die to the habit of accumulation. Dying to oneself is to die to this accumulator, which is more psychological than physical.[8]

The five niyamas are *saucha* (clarity, purity), *santosha* (contentment, cheerfulness), *tapas* (discipline, sacrifice, training your senses), *svadhyaya* (self-study, self-exploration, one-pointedness), and *ishvara pranidhana* (surrender, service to something bigger, ability for Self-realization). These can be explored further with any in-depth text on yoga.

How does Theosophy view ethics? H. P. Blavatsky comments on this in *Key to Theosophy* as follows:

> ENQUIRER. But are not the ethics of Theosophy identical with those taught by Buddha?
>
> THEOSOPHIST. Certainly, because these ethics are the soul of the Wisdom-Religion, and were once the common property of the initiates of all nations. But Buddha was the first to embody these lofty ethics in his public teachings, and to make them the foundation and the very essence of his public system. It is herein that lies the immense difference between exoteric Buddhism and every other religion. For while in other religions ritualism and dogma hold the first and most important place, in Buddhism it is the ethics which have always been the most insisted upon. This accounts for the resemblance, amounting almost to identity, between the ethics of Theosophy and those of the religion of Buddha.[9]

Hence, we see that the ethics of Theosophy are reflected in Buddhism and other major traditions, although there is a difference of emphasis in different schools of Buddhism as well as between exoteric and esoteric Buddhism. When establishing ethical standards, we can look to religious and spiritual texts for guidance, but they may not directly apply to our own particular circumstances. Another method for gaining insight into a quandary involving ethical choices is to look deeply into our own being. In common parlance this may be expressed as "soul-searching," but there is a fountain of wisdom deep inside us that may be accessed in certain times and situations. It is generally thought to be in the higher bodies of the septenary nature of the human and can be expressed as the triple monad or the atma-buddhi-manas. The connection between the higher triad and the lower quaternary, often conceptually referred to in Hindu as *antahkarana* (referring to the totality of mind), in Theosophy relates to purity extending from the upper mind to the lower mind. This understanding can be expressed schematically as shown below:

Principles of Human Consciousness

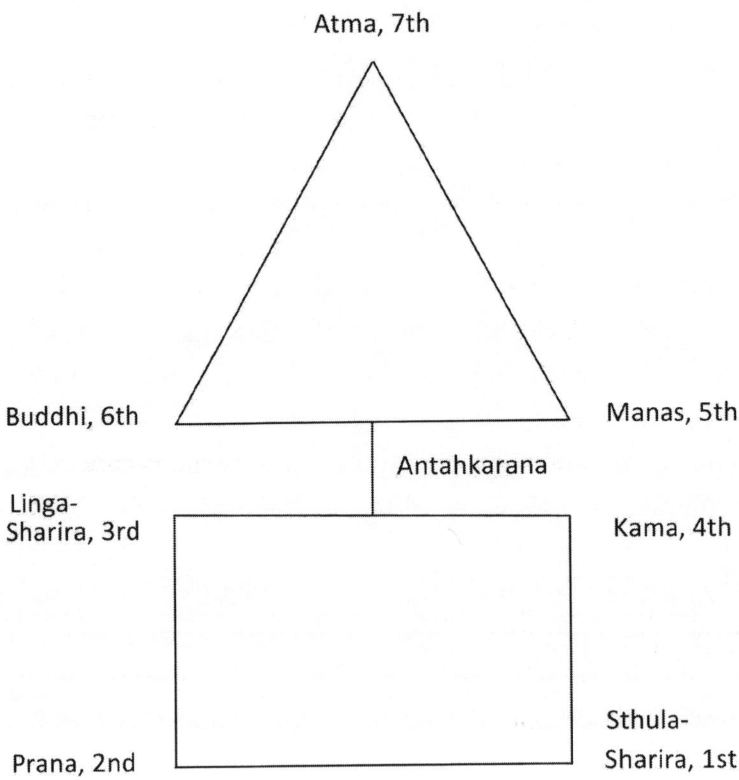

Figure 2. Principles of Human Consciousness. Illustration derived from H. P. Blavatsky, *The Key to Theosophy*, section 6. Also see letter 72 in Vicente Hao Chin, *The Mahatma Letters to A. P. Sinnet: In Chronological Sequence* (Adyar, India: Theosophical Publishing House, 1998).

As Pablo Sender points out in his book *Evolution of the Higher Consciousness*, this bridge can serve as a connection to our deeper nature where we can access inner wisdom. He notes that the antahkarana is not only the source of "all good and noble aspirations" expressing through the lower nature but also the bridge for transferring any valuable personal experience to the higher ego.[10] It can be an inexhaustible fountain of inspiration and insight; however, the reverse is also true. Be it ignored and neglected, it will atrophy and the connection will be lost, at least temporarily. The connection must be nurtured and sustained. Pablo goes on to write, "When a person systematically ignores the voice of his conscience, the field of choice gradually diminishes and the process of thinking becomes more and more instinctive and mechanical. In extreme cases, where a person is completely selfish and blinded by the influence of matter, there can be a severing between the higher and the lower."[11]

Having discussed these principles, how do we put them into practice? As HPB observed, "Modern ethics are beautiful to read about and hear discussed; but what are words unless converted into actions?" [12]

Why is ethical behavior sometimes challenging? If we wish to be moral and ethical individuals, should we not always choose the higher road? There are many reasons that ethics can become muddied and confusing.

Firstly, there can be a conflict between self-interest and selfless behavior. If we act selflessly, we may be harmed either physically, financially, reputationally, or in some other manner. It is often difficult to overcome this instinct of self-preservation and self-promotion.

Secondly, there may be a conflict among favorites in the general population. Suppose we had a son participating in a sporting activity, and there were some way to give him an advantage that others might not have readily available. Would we like to see our loved ones succeed over others? What if there were a way to help our daughter get into a prestigious college? Might there be a situation where ethics are bent to one's advantage?

Thirdly, there can be significant resistance to taking the more ethical path. It might require more time, work, soliciting the input of others, and surrendering control in a particular setting. It may seem much easier and expeditious to take a direct path that would not be as clearly ethical. Suppose, for instance, we wish to make a decision in our marriage without consulting our partner. Certainly, it may be more efficient to make a decision ourselves, but if it affects both parties, to do so would not truly be the most ethical path forward.

Another reason that ethics can become confusing might have to do with the conflict between recognition and anonymity. We may work for a good cause but have mixed motives. We want to be recognized for the good works we see ourselves doing, and that motive may distort the choices we make.

Lastly, there might be a conflict between ethical principles themselves. One example is autonomy versus beneficence: we allow people to make their own decisions when they are competent to do so, even if it appears that their choices are harmful to themselves—such as a medical patient who chooses to live alone at significant risk or an alcohol-dependent person who insists on going to public drinking places. Whether and when to intercede can be complicated and depends on the specific conditions involved, without a clear path that is superior from an ethical viewpoint.

So, even for the well-intentioned, life can be fraught with ethical dilemmas, and there must be a sustained effort to overcome the conflicts we face. Perhaps recalling the words of Mabel Collins may give us some perspective: "Regard most earnestly your own heart. For through your own heart comes the one light which can illuminate life and make it clear to your eyes."[13]

Blavatsky summarizes the practical nature of theosophical actions in this passage:

> Finally: if you ask me how we understand Theosophical duty practically and in view of Karma, I may answer you that our duty is to drink without a murmur to the last drop, whatever contents the cup of life may have in store for us, to pluck the roses of life only for the fragrance they may shed on *others*, and to be ourselves content but with the thorns, if that fragrance cannot be enjoyed without depriving someone else of it.[14]

In closing, we return to the words of Ravi Ravindra: "In the right development of a human being, development of conscience needs to precede the development of consciousness."[15] The implication appears to be that the conscience (i.e., the inner voice of ethical behavior) is essential to achieve consciousness, which we must interpret as "higher" consciousness, as it is clear that everyday, mundane, waking consciousness occurs in many individuals without ethical awareness. Ethical behavior, in addition to its own merits, can have a purifying effect on the individual and will be necessary for the pilgrim who seeks deeper understanding. Each step toward purification also makes ethical behavior more achievable and more necessary.

6

Violence in Reformation

Method or Metaphor?

I object to violence because when it appears to do good, the good is only temporary; the evil it does is permanent.

—MAHATMA GANDHI

Humans are a violent species. To be convinced of this statement takes only a cursory look at our history and the current world situation. The examples are ubiquitous; yet why are we driven to violence? We kill in the pursuit of food as do many animals. We can be violent in defending our territory and possessions, again not uncommon among less-developed species. But humans have taken it further, using violence for social and political ends. An aggressive monarch will move to expand his or her empire. Explorers will wish to dominate new lands. An oppressed people will rebel when possible.

Can violence ever be justified? This question occurred to me in the recent past when I was reading three historical accounts in close succession, each containing violent interactions associated with social upheavals. The first was Ron Chernow's *Alexander Hamilton*, recounting the early days of our nation and describing the seeds of revolution:

> Back in Manhattan, the young captain found a city engaged in a spree of wanton violence against Tory sympathizers. Many Loyalists were subjected to a harrowing ritual known as "riding the rail," in which they were carried through the streets sitting astride a sharp rail borne by two tall, strong men. The prisoners' names were proclaimed at each street corner as spectators lustily cheered their humiliation. One bystander reported, "We had some grand Tory rides in the city this week. . . . Several of them were handled very roughly, being carried through the streets on rails, their clothes torn off their backs and their bodies pretty well mingled with the dust. . . . There is hardly a Tory face to be seen this morning.[1]

Next, I read Nelson Mandela's autobiography, *Long Walk to Freedom*. It is a detailed personal and political history of the struggle against apartheid in South Africa. That nonviolent tactics were initially employed was due mostly to operational considerations and not to the repugnance of violence. Nonhuman targets were pursued but, in time, the rebellion targeted human oppressors, less for vengeance than for strategic impact. In his statement at the opening of his trial in 1964, Mandela said,

> I must deal immediately and at some length with the question of violence. Some of the things so far told the court are true and some are untrue. I do not, however, deny that I planned sabotage. I did not plan it in a spirit of recklessness nor because I have any love of

> violence. I planned it as a result of a calm and sober assessment of the political situation that had arisen after many years of tyranny, exploitation, and oppression of my people by whites.[2]

The third work I read was *Playing with Fire: The 1968 Election and the Transformation of American Politics* by Lawrence O'Donnell. In it, he traces the turbulent politics of the 1960s, the rise of Richard Nixon to the presidency, the Vietnam War protests, and the contentious 1968 Democratic Convention. Although the war protesters were mostly peaceful, social disobedience was rampant and confrontations were frequent.

> On April 22, [Mark] Rudd published an open letter to the Columbia administration. In it, he flatly rejected university president Grayson Kirk's call for obedience. Taking a page from the pants-down Yippie approach to revolution, he got threatening while trying to be comedic.
>
> "We will destroy at times," Rudd said, "even violently, in order to end your power and your system." And Rudd ended his letter to "Uncle Grayson" with this: "Up against the wall . . . this is a stickup."[3]

So, when can violence be justified, if ever, and even found useful for the "greater good"? We might feel the instinct to be violent when we feel threatened as individuals or regarding that which we hold sacred. When I was working in Haiti, on one occasion we were hosted by a young missionary family consisting of a husband and wife and two small children. The husband's father had done similar work in years past. The day our team was leaving we got word that the two children had been kidnapped. Dressed as police, the perpetrators had stopped the mother's car after school pickup, thrown the mother from the car, and driven off with the two children still seat belted in the back. The police and other law enforcement were summoned, including the American FBI. The horror of this crime was palpable and weighed heavily on all of us for a week. It was likely a ploy for ransom, but such atrocities often end poorly. Fortunately, in this case the children were safely returned. The kidnappers were killed. Was violence in the rescue of the children justified? These are difficult questions that frequently don't have a satisfying answer. What are we willing to do to defend ourselves, our family, our property, and even "our way of life"?

We might suggest turning to religious traditions on the use of violence. The Buddha noted that "hatred does not cease by hatred, but only by love. This is the eternal rule."[4] Jesus Christ is quoted in Matthew as saying, "But I tell you not to resist an evil person. But whoever slaps you on your right cheek, turn the other to him also."[5] Spiritual literature is filled with similar expression of forbearance, tolerance, compassion, and love in the face of animosity and aggression. But religious movements themselves have often been violent and bloody. We need only to consider the Crusades, the Thirty Years War, the Protestant–Catholic conflict in Ireland, the Israeli-Palestinian conflict, the 9/11 terror attacks, the Bosnian War, the Hindu–Muslim partition of India, and the Shia–Sunni conflicts in the Middle East, for a few examples.

Many social reformers follow the principles of nonviolent resistance, which is the attempt to achieve social change without violent actions and methods. Nonviolent tactics include protests, economic or political noncooperation, civil disobedience, and other peaceful strategies. Civil disobedience is usually defined as an act that violates the law, is performed intentionally, and for which a perpetrator anticipates punitive measures. The risk with any nonviolent but illegal activity is that it could turn violent when authorities are threatened.

Satyagrahi, a Sanskrit word developed by Mahatma Gandhi, is translated as "insistence" or "holding firmly to" and was used widely in the Indian independence movement. This movement represented a series of activities with the ultimate aim of ending the British rule in India. Gandhi was famous for many such efforts, including the Salt March and the Quit India Movement. He gained international recognition for his nonviolent efforts at social reform and contributed greatly to the ultimate freeing of India in 1947. Martin Luther King was deeply influenced by Gandhi while studying at Crozer Theological Seminary, and Gandhi's works informed many aspects of the civil rights movement of the 1950s and '60s.

Henry David Thoreau wrote a volume called *Civil Disobedience* and was often considered a reformer. Many others have advocated social resistance through nonviolent strategies. Some researchers (Chenoweth, for example) feel that nonviolent resistance is ultimately more successful in effecting change than violent campaigns.

Although the principle of nonviolence is reflected in the sixth commandment of the Judeo-Christian theology and inherent in most religious traditions, the concept of ahimsa is a spiritual doctrine shared by Hinduism, Buddhism, and Jainism. It is often translated as harmlessness and more broadly as respect for all living things and avoidance of violence toward others. In Sanskrit, it literally means "noninjury." It implies abstinence from creating any harm to any creature not only by action but also by words and thoughts. Ravi Ravindra notes that this interpretation

> is not wrong, but it is a partial meaning; and partiality is itself a form of *himsā*, the opposite of ahimsā. *Ahimsā* means "nonviolation," "nonmanipulation," and "noninterference." This [meaning] certainly includes nonviolence but is subtler and more comprehensive. Ahimsā is the very first one in the list of constraints (*yamas*) in the *Yoga Sutras* (2.30); later, it says, "In the presence of one who is established in ahimsā, there is cessation of hostility." (Yoga Sutras 2.35)[6]

The lack of violence or harm in thought, word, and deed is not exactly the same as taking a path of passivity. Perhaps the paradigmatic example of this conflict is portrayed in the classic Hindu treatise of the Bhagavad Gita. In the opening scene, the battle lines of a great war have been drawn and Arjuna, the great warrior, sits upon his chariot in full battle dress and takes up his bow. Yet he pauses with indecision. He tells Krishna, his charioteer, to drive his chariot between the two armies. He states this is so "that I may see those who have come here eager and ready to fight, in their desire to do the will of the evil son of Dhrita-rashtra" (BG 1:23). Arjuna experiences strongly ambivalent feelings regarding his role in this drama:

> Then Arjuna saw in both armies fathers, grandfathers, sons, grandsons; fathers of wives, uncles, masters; brothers, companions and friends. When Arjuna thus saw his kinsmen face to face in both lines of battle, he was overcome by grief and despair and thus he spoke with a sinking heart.
>
> Arjuna: "When I see all my kinsmen, Krishna, who have come here on this field of battle, Life goes from my limbs and they sink, and my mouth is sear and dry; a trembling overcomes my body, and my hair shudders in horror; My great bow Gandiva falls from my hands, and the skin over my flesh is burning; I am no longer able to stand, because my mind is whirling and wandering. And I see forebodings of evil, Krishna. I cannot foresee any glory if I kill my own kinsmen in the sacrifice of battle." (BG 1:26–31)

The dialogue that ensues between Arjuna and Krishna (the Divine) constitute this seminal work. It ranges among many metaphysical topics and, in the end, Krishna advocates action. Although there is action in inaction and inaction in action, we cannot be passive. In the eighteenth discourse, Krishna responds, in part,

> Krishna: "The works of a Brahmin are peace; self-harmony, austerity and purity; loving-forgiveness and righteousness; vision and wisdom and faith. These are the works of Kshatriya: a heroic mind, inner fire, constancy, resourcefulness, courage in battle, generosity and noble leadership. Trade, agriculture and the rearing of cattle is the work of a Vaisya. And the work of the Sudra is service. They all attain perfection when they find joy in their work. Hear how a man attains perfection and finds joy in his work. A man attains perfection when his work is worship of God, from whom all things come and who is in all. Greater is thine own work, even if this be humble, than the work of another, even if this be great. When a man does the work God gives him, no sin can touch this man. And a man should not abandon his work, even if he cannot achieve it in full perfection; because in all work there may be imperfection, even as in all fire there is smoke." (BG 18:42–48)

Inaction is not an option for Arjuna or for any of us. We must fulfill our nature, whether it be of the brahman, the warrior, the merchant, or the worker. These actions might occasionally be seen as violent but should come from an intention of loving-kindness and guidance. When seeking justice, perhaps a more assertive intervention may at times be warranted. In order to oppose cruelty, strength is required. To challenge aggression, a defensive posture is often necessary. To love our children, at times limits must be imposed and lessons taught.

Continuing with Dr. Ravindra's commentary,

> It is necessary to distinguish between the use of violence and the use of force. It is not possible to be violent without using force, but it is possible to use force without being violent. No action can be undertaken and nothing can be accomplished without energy, power,

and force. Having energy gives one power; a misplaced application of energy is violence.[7]

Can Theosophy add additional understanding to this consideration? How and when can force, possibly even violent force, be acceptable? Annie Besant notes that violence in and of itself is not evil but merely part of the ever-changing and evolving universe. However, violence directed toward an individual being with the intent to harm *can* be described as evil in some circumstances. It can also be strengthening if applied appropriately. Perhaps looking at the three objects of the Theosophical Society can be helpful, the first of which is "to form a nucleus of the universal brotherhood of humanity, without distinction of race, creed, sex, caste, or color."[8] This concept of unity is based on the oneness of the universe and the essential connectedness of all living beings.

If we see the manifested universe as a single entity, an ever-interconnected dependence among all its parts, then any injury we do to another we are in fact doing to ourselves. We cannot gain advantage by destroying other lives, for they are reflective of our own. However, there may be personal and social situations in which an abuse of power needs to be curtailed, offenses need to be challenged, and injustices need to be righted. These efforts at reformation, whether on a small or large scale, are often fueled by feelings of anger and revenge. Although motivating, hatred during social disruption is not necessary and often not useful. The same actions might be taken from a source of love, devotion, and intense desire for social order and justice. We need not disdain the oppressors or evildoers but rather approach the conflict with compassion, understanding, and ultimately forgiveness.

One example might be the Truth and Reconciliation Commission that was formed in South Africa after the end of apartheid with the goal of restorative justice. Amnesty was given to the perpetrators from civil and criminal prosecution if they provided testimony. Both sides were invited to give statements of their experiences, and many were given in public hearings. It was generally felt to be successful in the transition to a full and free democracy in South Africa. Although no human institution or political change is flawless, and this commission had its critics, its work was seen as a crucial step toward healing a diverse nation by contributing to the breaking of the cycle of violence.

There is widespread pain and suffering in the world in which we live. Oppression and injustice abound. We need not accept as inevitable all that we see. Reformers will intervene and try to form a more perfect society. We should employ nonviolent techniques such as the persuasion of public opinion, lawful protests, and even civil disobedience at times. Risk of escalation is frequently present. We must examine our motives and purify our intentions to the deepest extent possible. We must recognize the humanity of all participants and reach for fairness for all stakeholders. Violence should be shunned when possible. Ultimately, though, ahimsa is not the act itself, but, to quote Ravindra again, the "intention, motive, and the relationship between the parties."[9] As Master KH has stated in the Mahatma letters, "*Motive* is everything for us."[10]

7

Freedom Is Just Another Word for . . . What, Exactly?

Only from the heart can you touch the sky.

—RUMI

Freedom is a word that is frequently used in a multitude of contexts throughout history and particularly today. In the 1950s and '60s, it was not uncommon to hear someone assert their individuality by stating, "It's a free country!" We would hear on the nightly news which countries were free and which were not (many of the latter being behind the "Iron Curtain" of oppression). The US president was often considered the leader of the "free world."

Within the political context, there was individual freedom, often seen as being personally free to choose one's own values, vocation, relationships, and lifestyle. There was a rebellion throughout the 1960s (as perhaps there is in all generations) as children rejected their parents' worldviews and attempted to establish their own. This cultural shift was spurred by liberated sexual mores, music, environmental sensitivity, alternative religious and social gurus, and a sense of rebirth and deepening of substance. One of the more popular ballads of the time was "Me and Bobby McGee," written by Kris Kristofferson and initially popularized by Janis Joplin. It contains the line,

> Freedom's just another word for nothin' left to lose;
> And nothin' ain't worth nothin' but it's free.[1]

What is the sense of freedom being implied here? It seems the author intends to convey the sense of disappointment at the loss of his lover; he is now free of commitment and obligation, but in a very hollow sense—a pyrrhic accomplishment. The wonderful elation that we associate with the relaxation or removal of restraints is paradoxically absent in this refrain.

But what is true freedom, particularly in a spiritual sense? Is it freedom from responsibility? Is it freedom of choice?

On January 6, 1941, President Franklin D. Roosevelt gave a well-known speech as the United States was debating whether to enter the war in Europe. Officially, it was the State of the Union speech, but it was informally known as the "Four Freedoms" speech. It was about the national security of the United States and the threat of the Axis powers to global stability. Roosevelt articulated the four freedoms—freedom of speech, freedom of worship, freedom from want, and freedom from fear—to be some of the core benefits to be derived in a democracy.[2] These freedoms are not only ideals; the first two are also protected by the First Amendment of the Constitution. As a consequence of his third freedom, the freedom from want, Roosevelt endorsed a broader human right to economic security, which led to a wider concept of human rights codified as the Universal

Declaration of Human Rights, a document adopted by the United Nations in 1948. Although the nature and responsibility of human rights is fertile ground for a fascinating discussion, it leads to a more political and social arena regarding freedom and expectations.

Freedom is multidimensional. Each aspect can be differentiated and addressed separately. The four freedoms cited above are societal. Other freedoms include the physical freedom from disease and restraint and the social freedom in being able to move about geographically—freedom from confinement. There is also freedom from family responsibility and freedom from our own nature. Each of us has wants and desires that we may or may not feel fully free to express. But do we have unlimited personal freedom to perform any actions that we might wish? Do we have absolute freedom of choice? Can we ever be free of consequences (some would say karma)?

The following quotation is attributed to the Buddha: "No one outside ourselves can rule us inwardly. When we know this, we become free."[3] Here, being free is understood as not being attached to any person outside the self, commonly referred to as the "other." The suggestion is that each individual can (or should) control his or her own choices in order to be free. In this translation, Buddha's word *rule* refers to control of any type, whether physical, emotional, social, or political. How often we feel we are subject to the thoughts and actions of others, whether it be our parents, spouses, bosses, or the myriad of other people with whom we daily come in contact! Yet Buddha asserts that no one should be able to control us internally. So, while others may have dominion over our behavior in certain settings, we must realize that they cannot "rule us inwardly." While messages we receive throughout our life may shape our self-esteem and influence our opinion of ourselves, they do not necessarily reflect our true value, talent, and worth. Eleanor Roosevelt is famously credited as having said, "No one can make you feel inferior without your consent."[4]

But even in an ideal sense, does being free from all external influences (especially the negative) define the essence of freedom? Do we also need to find a way to be free from our past, from our nature, from ourselves?

The concept of spiritual freedom is often equated with the Sanskrit term *mumuksutva*. Dating back thousands of years in Hinduism and other traditions, this concept is described as "an intense longing or burning desire for liberation, freedom and self-realization."[5] The source goes on to say that mumuksutva "is a particularly important concept in advaita vedanta and jnana yoga, which both see it as an essential requirement for finding *moksha*, or liberation. They believe that a practitioner is not ready to hear the truths of the sacred scriptures until they have mumukshutva."[6] (See ch. 15 for further discussion.) The quest here is for liberation from physical existence itself and the ties that bind us to the lower planes, sometimes referred to as *skandhas* in Buddhism. This intensity of desire for liberation must be central, even absolute, beyond life itself, if one is successfully to make progress along the path of ascension, according to this tradition. There are many interpretations of how this quality may be expressed in the manifested world. Seeking spiritual liberation does not need to require a rejection of our place in civilization, although the quest to find the Divine often entails forgetting ourselves.

In the seventh discourse of the Bhagavad Gita, Krishna says to Arjuna, "For those who take refuge in me and strive to be free from age and death, they know Brahman, they know Atman, and they know what Karma is" (BG 7:29). Here, Krishna indicates that to survive mortality (aging and death) one must know Krishna (the Divine) as well as one's Higher Self (the monad in theosophical terminology) and by so doing achieve freedom. This freedom is that of self-knowledge, enlightenment, and immortality. Is it an ultimate form of freedom? If so, how is it to be achieved?

Arjuna is certainly confused. In BG 8:1, he states in response, "Who is Brahman? Who is Atman? And what is Karma, Spirit Supreme? What is the kingdom of the earth? And what is the kingdom of Light?" Krishna attempts to teach Arjuna (and us). Because these dilemmas are universal and delve into the very nature of humanity's deepest questions, this seven-hundred-verse scripture has become extremely popular and revered in the Hindu tradition as well as the greater world. Ravi Ravindra states:

> Since the Bhagavad Gita represents a summary of the Upanishadic teachings, it is also called the Upanishad of the Upanishads. It is sometimes said that the Upanishads are the cow and Krishna, the cowherd, milks the cow in the presence of Arjuna, the calf, and the milk is the Bhagavad Gita! The Gita is also called a *mokshashāstra*, or scripture of liberation, since it deals with the science of the Absolute and teaches the way to freedom without measure.[7]

Here the way to freedom is consistent with spiritual elevation and ultimately enlightenment. Is this the type of freedom that most seek? It is quite different in concept from what we might think of as political or social freedom; we define ourselves through our physical, emotional, and mental bodies, and the concept of surpassing them is somewhat foreign to us culturally. In addition, spiritual freedom appears to be quite a distant goal, since most of us are constrained (mired) in the lower worlds through desire and attachment. Even if we wish to supersede our daily lives, we have little inkling of how to do so safely and effectively.

However, the impulse to look beyond ourselves and the known universe is inherent in our very nature, and we become restless without it. We feel somehow incomplete, as if something important were absent. This impulse may manifest in an unsolicited curiosity, a wanderlust, a midlife crisis, disturbing dreams, and dozens of other ways. We may feel confined and uninspired in our lives, despite external successes and apparent tranquility. It is unlikely that we will find equipoise and peace of a sustained quality without addressing our deeper spiritual needs and questions.

We really cannot talk about freedom without addressing the topic of free will. Free will is defined as "the power of acting without the constraint or necessity or fate; the ability to act at one's own discretion."[8] Debates regarding the presence and nature of free will have engaged philosophers (and the rest of us) for millennia. The concept does, in fact, have some significant theoretical and practical challenges. The debate can be couched as the alternatives between libertarian free will—whereby we act as an agent of thought and choose between a number of alternative actions based on beliefs, desires, and temperament—and hard determinism, which is the belief that every action and reaction exists in a world of cause and effect. Just as a baseball is hit with a certain velocity, direction, and energy that will predetermine its arc, human decisions can (in the mind of some) be reduced to a series of causes, known and unknown, that ultimately lead to a predetermined "choice."[9]

The latter argument is based in part on the theory that the mind is closely related to the physical instrument we know as the brain and is perhaps dependent on or even a byproduct of it. However, this concept of the mind is not universally accepted. Certainly, the expression of the mind through an individual requires adequate functioning of the brain, but this condition does not disqualify the existence of a separate mind. A broken radio disturbs or obstructs the beautiful melody but does nothing to interfere with the broadcast of that melody. That the mind functions at some level of awareness without the brain is suggested by many examples such as dreams, near-death experiences, and spiritual revelations.

The second challenge to free will is karma. In Hinduism and Buddhism, *karma* is defined as "the sum of the person's actions in this and previous states of existence, viewed as deciding their fate in future existences."[10] This notion, however, is significantly oversimplified. Many essays and even books are written attempting to describe and communicate the essence of karma, including those by Annie Besant and Mabel Collins.[11] Karma, sometimes described as the Great Law, is a teacher and influencer. We can understand and cooperate with karma in our efforts to tread a spiritual path. While karma cannot be ignored, like gravity, it can be used to our benefit, correcting us when we need instruction and lifting us when we know its purpose. In her small treatise on karma, Mrs. Besant writes:

> That we live in a realm of law, that we are surrounded by laws that we cannot break, this is a truism. Yet when the fact is recognized in a real and vital way, and when it is seen to be a fact in the mental and moral world as much as in the physical, a certain sense of helplessness is apt to overpower us, as though we felt ourselves in the grip of some mighty power, that, seizing us, whirls us away whither it will. The very reverse of this is in reality the case, for the mighty power, when it is understood, will obediently carry us whither *we* will; all forces in Nature can be used in proportion as they are understood—[as the Master says,] "Nature is conquered by obedience"—and her resistless energies are at our bidding as soon as we, by knowledge, work with them and not against them. We can choose out of her boundless stores the forces that serve our purpose in momentum, in direction, and so on, and their very invariability becomes the guarantee of our success.[12]

In this sense, karma does not imply fatalism, at least when we have developed to the point that we can harness its energies through congruence of purpose and desire. When we are able to align our motives with those that are divine, karma will be our benefactor. This understanding is indicative not of servitude in the usual sense that we associate with lack of freedom but of an opportunity to fulfill our highest purpose. Geoffrey Hodson notes, "To some minds the existence of the Law of Karma and of a Plan for the evolution of life and form suggests determinism and even fatalism. Yet Theosophy teaches positively that man is above all things free. The Great Plan, therefore, must be flexibly fixed!"[13] After describing the multiple forces in the universe as the "pieces in the great chess problem of life," he summarizes the idea this way:

> One may think of the Masters as working amidst these forces, combining the good to intensify beneficial effects, directing the good against the evil to modify adversities, yet all the time most respectful of each individual's divine nature and right to freedom of action. Thus there is a certain Egoic freedom in the great weaving process which the operation of the Law of Karma resembles and in which humanity constitutes the material, each individual contributing his share of the pattern, his colours, kind of thread, and so on.[14]

Again, in reflecting on this passage, we can see that karma is a force not to be feared but to be recognized. It does have ramifications, reflecting the cause and effect inherent in our universe. Yet it does not eliminate freedom but in fact enhances it. Free choice remains viable. But free choice, like free speech and free activity, does not indicate freedom from consequences. We may choose to neglect these consequences, but we cannot escape them. In time, we will learn that we need to try not to avoid them but only to learn from them. As we are fallible human beings, the journey is never smooth, but we can ease the discordance as we discover our deeper essence.

In order to accomplish freedom (or anything), we must enlist the powers of the will. This is the motivating force that we need to harness in order to proceed in any endeavor. Will alone, however, is not adequate and must be tempered by wisdom and lifted by love in order to find its way. I. K. Taimni makes the following comment regarding will and freedom:

> This peculiar characteristic of pure will, i.e. the absence of any predetermined and fixed method of achieving the objective, should be kept in mind, for it is this flexibility upon which depends its efficacy and the certainty of finally gaining the end. It is this freedom to adopt one means or another or adjusting means to ends, giving up a particular course of action when necessary so that the accomplishment of the end is ensured, it is this relentless flexibility which ensures that the end will be accomplished sooner or later, by one means or another. The will concentrates its effort and attention on the *end* and leaves the question of *means* open. It is thus merely a state of consciousness capable of bringing to bear a tremendous concentration of purpose on any aim which has been deliberately chosen and pursuing that aim until it is accomplished.[15]

Here, Dr. Taimni is using the word *freedom* to indicate the ability to remain flexible and change directions when circumstances dictate that it becomes necessary. The power of the will can be applied freely in such a way that it can be most useful with the insight of wisdom. Without the mental clarity of wisdom and the freedom to adjust and amend our application of effort, will becomes no more than a blunt instrument, impulsive and capricious without focus or strategy.

We value our freedom of thought, both politically and spiritually, but this does not suggest we have a freedom of belief that justifies any behavior. While errant beliefs may be harmless, if they do not insult or injure others, they may be unhelpful to our own spiritual journey. Dr. Taimni states, "When we are dealing with these things pertaining to the inner realities of existence, let us be very careful and not misuse our freedom of thought to interpret things as we like, and in our foolishness and egotism tread the path of error."[16]

With freedoms come responsibilities, and one of those responsibilities is to strive for wisdom and understanding. It is not enough to claim freedom of thought without applying those beliefs in ways to nurture and sustain the elements of the ideal. We must seek wisdom if we are to be effective agents and collaborators in our own development and that of the external world. We may (and surely will) fail at times, but we must find the lesson hidden in the failure, if one is to be found. As HPB has noted, no failure is complete.[17] The outcome may be undesirable, but we are changed by the effort, as are frequently those around us. Every failure becomes a step toward success if we can reap the benefit of our actions connected to the outcome. Freedom from failure is not true freedom at all but merely a cocoon of protection that is stifling to the inner nature. Risk is inherent in action (and life) and we frequently need to suffer the adverse consequences of that risk taking in order to help mold ourselves in new and better ways. We are ever changing, and with that changing there are choices—those of which we are aware and those of which we are not—to be made. This is the responsibility of every human. As HPB states in *The Secret Doctrine*, "The pivotal doctrine of the Esoteric philosophy admits no privileges or special gifts in man, save those won by his own Ego through personal effort and merit throughout a long series of metempsychoses and reincarnations."[18] We do indeed have freedom in a spiritual sense, even if we are more constrained in our social or political situation. We have freedom of thought and belief. In *The Voice of the Silence,* Madame Blavatsky notes in passage 169, "The way to final freedom is within thy Self."[19] The pathway is through self-knowledge, but this can in no way be selfish. To experience this inner knowledge, we must know the inner self. To find the depths of meaning in the universe, we must find it in ourselves. In *Light on the Path*, Mabel

Collins writes, "Desire only that which is within you. Desire only that which is beyond you. Desire only that which is unattainable."[20] (These ideas are discussed further in ch. 16). Suffice it to say that to discover our truest nature we must observe ourselves and learn that we are more than what we might appear and feel ourselves to be. We are an unknown chasm of being of which we can only scratch the surface. To learn the deepest truths, we must unmask the real nature of ourselves, layer by layer, for this is the greatest mystery to behold. It is our destiny to find our way, however slow and erratic our efforts might be. One day we will awaken to all our inner nature can bestow and have the freedom to use our considerable abilities to elevate our consciousness.

What freedoms do we have, and how do they manifest? We saw in an earlier chapter that when we are behaving in a selfish way any potential activity or effort is seen in the context of how it may help us personally. What will I gain if I participate? we may say to ourselves. If I take this employment position, will the balance of favorables and unfavorables be to my benefit? If I join this organization, what will be my reward? If I enter into this relationship, will it be to my advantage? In time, and with maturity, our eyes may open to see a need to be fulfilled. Someone should provide that service, we may think. This thought may evolve further into the notion that we are ideally situated to provide assistance in a time of want and need. Eventually, we may wish happily and without reservation to help those who are disadvantaged. The joy of service is discovered in a selfless way in which benefit of personal gain is not considered. We desire only to serve those who cry out, no matter what the reason or cost to us personally. There is a strong admonition that we must seek and find those who are in need. By serving others we are also serving the Masters and our higher selves.

But how does this action relate to freedom? We continue to be free to choose our values and where we wish to put our energies.

Sometimes we seem to be directed by external forces, but within any situation, no matter how restrictive, we retain some element of choice. Geoffrey Hodson writes that "this [influence of the Great Plan] throws a new light upon the much-vaunted freedom of man, for actually the more highly evolved man is, the less is his freedom."[21] This statement, standing alone, may be intimidating to some. The more we evolve, the less freedom we have seems to be an unnecessary restraint and limitation. We may feel it as a cage to impede our options in our world. However, Hodson continues with a further thought that "yet advanced man is conscious of no restraint, for his only aspirations are those in accord with the divine mind and the divine will."[22]

So, we can see that, as we evolve toward purity and understanding, and as we become more altruistic in our actions, we have *less* freedom (primarily in the sense of variations to be in disharmony); but we are not in any way aware of limitations as it is our wish and prayer to be of service to our fellow beings. The wish and prayer then become a *choice* to be of service. The service is in harmony with the wishes of the Masters (if they can be determined), with our own dharma (work or destiny), and with the evolutionary forces of the Universal.

How, then, can we summarize the concept of freedom? It is not necessary to address all its meanings here, but as we look at spiritual freedom, we can interpret it in different ways: The first is freedom from our lower natures, often referred to as *liberation*, which sometimes extends to freedom from the necessity of incarnating entirely. This is an ultimate wish, perhaps, but not particularly practical in the here and now and not for everyone. The second meaning is paradoxical in the sense that the more we work selflessly, the less freedom we in fact have, not by physical or psychological bonds, but by choice. It seems counterintuitive to say that we choose less freedom, but that is often the case. We can rejoice in our efforts if they are selfless. There is no need or desire to choose differently. Earlier in this consideration, I cited Annie Besant quoting the Master as saying, "Nature is conquered by obedience." This concept could be extended variously as "Nature is conquered by harmony," or "Nature is conquered by service," or even "Nature is conquered by love." As a Master has noted, "None of us live for ourselves, we all live for humanity."[23]

This is the freedom not to be free. It is a freedom to obey. Just as a domestic employee may choose to remain in a loving household, we may elect to serve our fellows within our capacity, however small it may seem to us. None of us (with some possible exceptions) can do this perfectly in the fullness of our potential. We can take solace in the fact that we are evolving with each lifetime. And each step we take on our spiritual journey leads to the next. Each experience will open another door. Each selfless act will have a ripple effect, spreading to others and perhaps back to ourselves, allowing greater wisdom and ability to contribute in significant ways in the future. We are longing to find a home. It is here waiting for us.

8

Transitions

Birth, Death, and Life's In-Betweens

For life and death are one, even as
the river and the sea are one.

—KAHLIL GIBRAN

We live in the manifested, physical world. Some would say that the physical self and the physical universe are all that exist. Others would argue that, at the least, human beings exist variously on physical, psychological, and spiritual fields. Theosophy teaches that there are seven interpenetrating fields for both humanity and the universe, known and unknown. These are often described as "principles" in the theosophical literature. Annie Besant describes them thus:

> Man, according to the Theosophical teaching, is a sevenfold being, or, in the usual phrase, has a septenary constitution. Putting it in another way, man's nature has seven aspects, may be studied from

> seven different points of view, is composed of seven principles. The clearest and best way of all in which to think of man is to regard him as one, the Spirit or true Self; this belongs to the highest region of the universe, and is universal, the same for all; it is a ray of God, a spark from the divine fire.[1]

The cycle of life brings us through these different principles, including the lowest, or physical, by a process that we see as beginning with birth and culminating in death, an irreversible occurrence at least for the physical body. These transitions have often been seen as magical and mystical, containing sublime elements that can only be described as divine. While births are often wondrous events (especially for those giving birth and those connected to the generation of new life), deaths are seen, depending on the circumstances, as tragedies or blessings. Of course, it is difficult to know if there is pleasure or pain, gratification or dissatisfaction, for the infant being born or for the decedent after passing out of physical life.

As a practicing physician for forty years (and a member of the Theosophical Society for the same length of time), I have witnessed many of each of these two powerful transitions and wish to reflect on some thoughts regarding them. I witnessed the births of my three children (fortunately a more common occurrence these days) and performed approximately two hundred deliveries professionally. The birthing process, associated with the first breaths of life, never fails to impress by the ineffable quality of initiating a new journey, unknowable and likely full of adventure. Each neonate will grow and develop according to some celestial plan. Each will have challenges and choices as they unfold into some sense of self and relationship with family, community, and the universe at large. How each incarnating soul comes into a specific physical body has been written about at some length in various spiritual traditions. Whether the circumstances are chosen or random, and whether there is even any life existing preconception, is a subject of debate and belief that I do not intend to address here.

Historically, life has been short and harsh for the majority. Over the last several millennia, infant mortality has been close to 25 percent, and nearly half of the children have died before their sixteenth birthday. In the last two centuries, these numbers have dropped dramatically. Global infant mortality has declined by a factor of 10, and in the most advanced countries by a factor of 170. Pregnancy itself is not a benign state. Global maternal mortality is 0.21 percent, but in several countries it remains above 1 percent. Intrauterine fetal death (stillbirth) occurs in approximately 1.84 percent of pregnancies. Fetal death is often due to pregnancy and labor complications (approximately one-in-three preterm labor, multiple fetuses, and premature placental separation), poor function of the placenta (one in four), birth defects (one in ten), infection (one in ten), umbilical cord complications, blood pressure disorder in the mother (preeclampsia) and non-pregnancy related maternal medical disorders such as diabetes. Substance abuse during pregnancy contributes significantly to the risk of fetal death.[2] Almost half of stillbirths occur during labor. Infant mortality (death within one year of birth) was 2.9 percent globally in 2018 (or 4 million), down from 6.5 percent in 1990 (or 8.7 million).[3] A rough estimate is that half of infant mortality occurs in the first month of life, a quarter in the first week, and an eighth within the first day. The causes of neonatal death are, of course, manifold; the three most common globally are infection, prematurity, and birth asphyxia. This depends enormously on the setting in which the pregnancy and delivery occur.

So, for many, this glorious journey of life begins with great difficulty and threat. Many suffer birth-related trauma, severe illness, and lack of access to basic medical care. We may be puzzled by why some are so afflicted. Are these challenges random, societal, purely economic, or karmic? (More about discrepancies in birth circumstances later.) Many of us, especially if we are in good health physically and socially, feel that life is a blessing, but is it truly so universally? Why are some lives so burdened at the outset and set against unspeakable hardship? It is difficult to see why children who suffer birth-related trauma, illness, and lack of access to medical care are in any way culpable for their circumstances and nearly so their parents and larger families as well. What is the purpose of the life that lasts only a few hours or a few days, both for the child and for the family?

My first exposure to the tenets of reincarnation, karma, and celestial beings (beyond God and angels as presented in Christianity) was during an Eastern philosophy course in which I enrolled in college. The professor told an intriguing story about how a group of these elevated beings, as a prank, had stolen a cow. As punishment, they were sent into the physical world to suffer incarnated life. Seven were allowed to be released within the first year, but the ringleader was sentenced to a full life in the manifested world.

It turned out that this was from the opening of the Mahabharata, the great Indian epic that contains the Bhagavad Gita. A brief synopsis is that the divine being, Mahabhisha, took birth as Santanu, the noble son. He met and fell in love with a lovely maiden who was none other than the goddess Ganga. She consented to marriage with the condition that he would never interfere with her actions. Annie Besant continues the story in her book *Mahabharata*. Note that the storyteller she mentions would be Ugrasrava, the epic's narrator, and the word *rshi* in the story refers to a Hindu sage or inspired poet:

> Presently a child was born, and the queen took the child and threw it into the river, saying: "This is for thy good." The same thing happened with the second child, and with the third and fourth, up to the seventh. And the poor king grew very troubled and unhappy.

> He "could not approve of such conduct," says the storyteller. But he said not a word, lest his wife should leave him. But when the eighth child was born, and his wife, as before, was about to throw it smilingly into the river, the king, with a sorrowful countenance, and desirous of saving it from destruction, addressed her and said: "Slay it not!" . . . Then she explained to him that the eight Vasus, celestial beings, had, a long time before, stolen away from a great rshi the cow of plenty, Nandini; one of [the Vasus], named Dyau, being the actual thief. The rshi was very displeased, and declared that the Vasus should be born upon earth, as a result of their sin. They begged his pardon very humbly, so the rshi said that they should be set free again from human life within a year of their births, with the exception of Dyau, who, "for his sinful act, shall have to dwell on earth for a long time."[4]

This story struck me deeply at the time, not so much because it was feasible (which it may be) but because it was such a reversal of the usual way in which I, and largely those around me, have viewed life as a precious commodity and not as a punishment or incarceration. As my interface with Eastern thought expanded, I began to question further—or at least temper my opinion of—the Christian view of a single life leading to everlasting bliss or damnation. The Buddhist teaching of the Four Noble Truths and the Eightfold Path contributes to the concept that incarnate life is a restriction of our full potential and that our common view of life, bookmarked by birth and death, is not a full explanation of our deepest nature and our ultimate destiny. I began to explore alternative explanations for what we judge to be "reality," reading Carlos Castaneda's books on Yaqui shamanism, taking classes in mysticism and related topics, and sitting for past-life readings. Then I was given a copy of Besant's *The Outer Court*. This led me to investigate the Theosophical Society, and, after attending meetings of the local branch, I became a member. As I developed more familiarity with theosophical principles, my sense of marvel at the birth process grew.

The transition to death, the morbid sister of sleep, is equally fraught with obstacles, perhaps more so. Like birth, this process encompasses a spectrum of experiences from slipping away peacefully in one's sleep to an agonizing death deprived of all humanity. Fear of death is common and follows the fear of the unknown. For many, it is not so much physical death that is frightening but the process of dying. Socrates stated, "To fear death, gentlemen, is no other than to think oneself wise when one is not, to think one knows what one does not know. No one knows whether death may not be the greatest of all blessings for a man, yet men fear it as if they knew that it is the greatest of evils."[5]

Much is written in metaphysical and spiritual literature regarding postmortem states and purposes, but my task today is to reflect on the events of dropping the physical body, particularly among the aged. Death, of course, can be violent or nonviolent; painful or nonpainful; sudden or prolonged; with loved ones, with strangers, or alone. In my years of attending patients in the hospital and nursing home, I've seen many persons pass out of their physical vehicle. End-of-life discussions, decisions, and management can be complex. The hospice movement in recent decades has been enormously helpful, but it is a formalization and expansion of activities that have been carried out for millennia. Comforting the terminally ill is optimized by acquiring certain skills, but in essence it is a channeling of our most basic human qualities: to care, to touch, to talk, and to be present.

Certain patterns emerge. As a person approaches the last weeks and days of life, "hallucinations" are common, frequently of people in the room. While illness and medications can often cause visual and auditory phenomenon, they seem more common for end-of-life circumstances. Further, such "visitors" are frequently family members who usually have passed before. They are nearly always comforting and only very rarely distressing. This phenomenon may be in preparation for entering the next world. Sometimes, much less commonly, there is a terminal restlessness. The medical term is *akathisia*, and it can be severe. Patients become extremely agitated, sleepless, and at times even frantic. Although there is a reluctance to use medication as chemical restraints, sometimes it is necessary both for the safety of the individual and for those surrounding him or her. Often it requires multiple modalities of management, and, even then, it can be quite challenging medically. What neurocognitive changes are happening at the physiologic level is not clear. Finally, there is often a lucid interval within a couple of days of the person's death, particularly if there are family members present. It provides a chance to have a final discussion and express final wishes and love. It is an opportunity to reminisce regarding shared life experiences and affections. Family members usually find it extremely gratifying to have this opportunity to say goodbye.

Some know that they will be dying soon, some are aware they are actively dying, and some are apparently unaware that the end of life is happening. This latter state may be due to diseases that affect cognitive function, including dementia, sepsis, and other conditions such as hepatic encephalopathy (mental changes secondary to liver failure). It may also be due to denial, a very powerful psychological defense mechanism that is often employed to maintain a sense of self and preservation of the psyche. Our expectations of longevity vary from one individual to the next and in different stages of life. Frequently, I've heard, "If I can just make it to eighty, I will have lived a good, long life." But at eighty and beyond, depending on our situation, we may wish for more time. In fact, those who are hale and hearty may well wish to live far beyond the natural lifespan and perhaps forever. Many industries cater to this thinking with antiaging products, cosmetic surgery, longevity "secrets," and so on.

Another factor is intolerance of disability. Once people are no longer able to travel, work, talk intelligently, or eat, many feel that the end has come. "When I can no longer do X, just shoot me" is the common refrain. However, once we are at the door, we might feel differently. And, certainly, loving family members may not want to see their relative die just because his or her functioning has become more limited.

Future decisions are by their very nature hypothetical, and although we can express our preferences, decisions toward the end of life should be based on specifics whenever possible. Healthcare proxies have been very useful in this regard. I recently cared for a ninety-nine-year-old woman (she would correctly emphasize that she was ninety-nine and five months) who wished to live to be at least one hundred and preferably to 102, the age that her mother had passed. She was fully intact cognitively but unfortunately quite ill. The disease process did progress, and she did not survive the month. Many treatment options, including hospitalization, were considered, but they were unlikely to have been of any benefit to her. In the end, she was aware of her approaching death and accepting of it.

Although variation is great, end-of-life physiological changes often follow common pathways. Desire for food and liquids wanes, confusion increases, drowsiness and obtundation progress. Frequently there is chest congestion due to increased secretions and difficulty clearing them. Respiration cycles from rapid and shallow to slow and deep (called the "Cheyne-Stokes" pattern), and fever is not uncommon, even in the absence of infection. Even when patients are not responsive, there is evidence that hearing is preserved, and they may be more aware of their environment than we realize. Many near-death experiences suggest that, beyond the physical, there is an astral or spiritual awareness of developments in the room and often in adjacent rooms in the building. Frequently, patients report a floating sensation and having a perspective from above the bed where their body lies.

As patients cease to take in food and nutrition, they become dehydrated. This leads to compromised circulation and kidney failure and, eventually, death. The body preserves fluid to the extent it is able, and, remarkably, some patients can survive for two weeks or longer with no intake. Narcotics, such as morphine and hydromorphone (Dilaudid), are useful not only to control pain but also to improve respiration and decrease end-of-life anxiety and restlessness. Lorazepam (Ativan) is useful for agitation and anxiety. Anti-secretory medications can decrease saliva and mucous. In general, the armamentarium used in hospice and other medical settings can be quite effective in aiding the process of physical death and transition. Compassionate attention and presence by healthcare personnel, trained hospice workers, family, clergy, and other support persons appear to be of enormous benefit. How helpful this is to the individual to smooth the passing and facilitate arrival in the next world is difficult to know. What is clear is that there are significant benefits to those who remain.

The Center for Disease Control reports that 26 percent of adults have a disability today.[6] The US Department of Health and Human Services estimates that the likelihood that adults who survive to age sixty-five will need long-term services and support (LTSS) is 70 percent and those who will require some paid care during their lifetime is 48 percent. Twenty-four percent of this cohort will receive more than two years of paid LTSS, and 15 percent will receive more than two years of nursing home care.[7] The average length of stay in a nursing home is 13.7 months, of course with wide variation.[8]

As we age, we lose the ability to care for ourselves independently, and we need to rely on others. Activities of Daily Living (ADL) are basic self-care activities that are measured by caregivers to assess, in part, an individual's needs. These include eating, dressing, bathing, transferring (usually from bed to chair and the reverse), and toileting, although sometimes others are included. Instrumental Activities of Daily Living (IADL) are somewhat more complex tasks that include managing finances, handling transportation, shopping, preparing meals, using the telephone, managing medication, and doing laundry, housework, and basic home maintenance. The second set of skills is useful for living independently and managing life. Once IADLs and, more fundamentally, ADLs are compromised, the individual needs supportive care and often supervision. Many medical conditions, and sometimes just the aging process itself, lead to this situation.

As we enter a condition of general physical decline, often accompanied by neurocognitive deterioration, we must look for resources to meet our needs, either by ourselves or with assistance. Frequently, individuals can stay alone until an "event" occurs that precipitates contact with the police, the healthcare community, or some other responsible organization. Emergency rooms are very familiar with seeing patients who are found "acting strangely," wandering, exhibiting atypical behaviors, and generally not demonstrating an ability to care for themselves. We as a society struggle with finding and funding appropriate care for such people and with acting in their best interest. In optimal situations, a caring family member with a Durable Power of Attorney for Health Care designation can be activated. Frequently, legal guardianship must be sought. If the individual is not competent to act on his or her own behalf, the administration of care can be compromised.

As dementia and other neurocognitive disorders progress, the person's external world shrinks, gradually or suddenly, until that individual relies entirely on outside care for all ADLs. Immobility progresses to the point that a mechanical lift is necessary. They frequently become nonverbal—with only an occasional random word or groan—and need to be fed. Because of the excellent care many receive, this state of being can go on for several months or even years.

What is happening to the individual's consciousness as the physical body contracts in its abilities and the mental awareness appears absent? Are these residents in a condition of "suspended animation," unconscious at any higher level beyond the most basic instinct and need? Or are they having full lives of some description in another dimension, perhaps on the astral and mental planes? As all life is experience, we can suppose there is some purpose to these compromised states. Whether we are learning and evolving during the end of life, or simply waiting for the final breath so that we can pass into the higher realms, has not been established. It would, however, be reasonable to assume that, even in this constricted physical body, there is some value to life, some useful purpose we are serving, unknown perhaps at this stage. How we treat disabled and vulnerable individuals is a measure of our humanity and society, even if the benefits are at times obscure.

Some may conjecture that the physical tribulations preceding death are a form of punishment. Disabilities toward the end of life (as is true for disabilities in general) may be seen as retribution for some past, and perhaps unconscious, transgression. This view can be connected to a superficial and inaccurate understanding of karma. The law of cause and effect is educational but not specifically punitive. It is more complex than this, and therefore it is impossible to see or understand all the circumstances that may contribute to such a condition. Each life is precious, no matter the form. We are naïve to think we can understand the consequences of another's experience (we struggle enough to understand our own), and we risk misinterpretation and even arrogance if we care to comment on the causes of others' suffering. The only viable approach to such individuals is compassion. Through our human care and concern, we must attempt to ease the struggle for our brothers and sisters, particularly those who have difficulty advocating for themselves. We must demonstrate our humanity and sensitivity for those who rely on us as a society and as individuals to care for them. No matter how robust we may feel in our prime, our future is not known in this life or in lives to come. Disability may visit us tomorrow or not until some far, future date. We must not shy away from our responsibilities, even if they are at times distasteful. We must imagine ourselves in a similar situation, even if we have the good fortune not to be there now.

We may feel repelled by such a condition as being minimally responsive in a nursing-home bed. Life appears entirely unappealing, at least superficially, and we may judge that the inevitable death should be pursued. We may be appalled and repulsed and more than a little fearful. What can be the merits of such a life? It is easy to wish to put someone out of their misery, if indeed that's what it is. However, I would propose that the value of the ill person's life is unknown and perhaps—as it appears absent a sense of evolution, higher consciousness, and a spiritual path—we are comparing that existence to our own and finding it intolerable. Such patients generally do not appear to be in distress, though. Presumably, their own inner nature (or their divine agent) can cause cessation of life when the time is appropriate. Many patients simply draw their last breath, even when recent examination and laboratory tests have been fairly normal.

Are any of us in a position to say who lives and dies? There are times when aggressive medical intervention, such as hospitalization or ventilator support, is not warranted due to its significant discomfort and limited benefit. Most of us would wish to die in a familiar environment, cared for by people we know and having loved ones available rather than in the sterile, noisy, disorienting environment of an ICU. Hospitalizations near the end of life are common even for nursing-home residents. The average number of in-hospital deaths for these nursing home residents is approximately 23 percent, but with wide variations. Aggressive care at the end of life is not always consistent with an individual's preferences, if they can be determined. The reasons for these transfers are complex but include lack of available resources, liability, family wishes, and other contributing factors. On-site medical providers and a comprehensive, advanced-care planning program can lower the rate of hospitalization.[9]

Many practitioners feel hospitalization should be the exception for end-stage disease, "letting nature take its course" while managing day-to-day exacerbations in the home (which may be a nursing center). Optimally, this is a shared decision-making process involving the patient, family, and staff.

The physical body is our instrument for experiencing life in the manifested world. It is how we see, hear, and touch our surroundings. But individual life can be frail, and we are vulnerable in so many ways. As Shakespeare's Prince Hamlet says in his famous soliloquy:

> To die—to sleep,
> No more; and by a sleep to say we end
> The heartache and the thousand natural shocks
> That flesh is heir to. 'Tis a consummation
> Devoutly to be wished. To die, to sleep . . .
>
> (*Hamlet*, 3.1.60–64)

To be born, live, decline, and die entails enormous challenges. The physical body, while allowing the variety of experience we seek, can also be a barrier to those experiences and in fact can generate such trials and tribulations themselves. We need to nurture and care for our own bodies as well as for those who can't (or occasionally won't) care for themselves. We need to provide comfort without judgment, compassion without preconditions, and companionship without condescension.

The term *disability* has come into common use recently. If we expand the notion to those who suffer (realizing that the correlation is not one-to-one: many with disabilities would not claim to suffer, and a sufferer may not claim disability), we can readily see that all spiritual traditions have addressed this topic. How can we lighten the load of our fellow traveler as we tumble through this mortal world? Perhaps it is best to allow Mme. Blavatsky the last word:

> Theosophy has to inculcate ethics; it has to purify the soul, if it would relieve the physical body, whose ailments, save cases of accidents, are all hereditary. It is not by studying Occultism for selfish ends, for the gratification of one's personal ambition, pride, or vanity, that one can ever reach the true goal: that of helping suffering mankind.[10]

PART TWO

DIVINE FORCES OF LIGHT AND DARKNESS

9

Spiritual Darkness

Hope is being able to see that there is
light, despite all of the darkness.

—DESMOND TUTU

We live in a world of contrasts, polarity, and differentiation. The opposites of light and darkness characteristic of physical phenomena are also used metaphorically when applied to the spiritual path. As we seek the brightness of illumination of wisdom, we also encounter the disillusionment of darkness. Darkness can apply to ignorance, evil, confusion, pain, depression, and a myriad of other conditions that are generally felt to convey a negative connotation. Occasionally, darkness can imply a potentiality, a cloak, a mystery, such as conveyed by the term *divine darkness*. It can apply to the unknowable and undiscoverable.

The expression "Only in the darkness can you see the stars" is attributed to Dr. Martin Luther King, Jr.[1] There can be a comfort to darkness that allows involution and withdrawal from the outer world. But it also can be frightening, and our senses can betray us. We imagine unseen threats that may fall upon us. In the *Collected Writings*, Blavatsky explains, "Ever-Darkness means, I suppose, the ever-unknowable mystery, behind the veil—in fact, Parabrahm. Even the Logos can see only Mulaprakriti, it cannot see that which is beyond the veil. It is that which is the Ever-unknowable Darkness."[2]

There are developmental phases that occur in the evolution in humans, nations, planets, and other unfolding entities. These phases are often marked by initiations in occult terminology. There are minor and major cycles in the ebb and flow of opening the higher vibrational aspects. Geoffrey Hodson, in his 1953 article, "Steps on the Pathway to Divine Manhood," writes,

> In Christianity, for example, the five major steps on the Path are portrayed by means of allegories, supposedly descriptive of experiences through which Jesus passed, namely, Nativity, Baptism, Transfiguration, Crucifixion and Ascension. Every human being repeatedly passes through these self-same experiences before the "Way of Holiness" is entered upon. . . . Gethsemane, the dark night of the Soul, is frequently experienced by both individuals and nations, as also is betrayal and unjust condemnation. These tribulations can culminate in a sense of veritable crucifixion, when the quintessence of loneliness is known, as also are agonies of heartache and even bodily pain.[3]

The phrase *spiritual darkness* often relates to an individual either seeking or treading the spiritual path. In Christian literature as well as in other spiritual traditions, it is seen as separation from God or the Divine. It is widely described as inherent in any spiritual quest and frequently referred to as the "dark night of the soul" after a poem and commentary by the sixteenth-century Catholic priest St. John of the Cross, although he did not ascribe any title to the poem. His two books of commentary are *The Ascent of Mount Carmel* and *The*

Dark Night. The term *dark night of the soul* usually refers to a crisis of faith or belief and the questioning of one's most intrinsic core values, although the poem itself is more uplifting. Its eight stanzas are excerpted here:

> Once in a dark of night,
> Inflamed with love and yearning, I arose
> (O coming of delight!)
> And went, as no one knows,
> When all my house lay long in deep repose . . .
>
> And in the luck of night
> In secret places where no other spied
> I went without my sight
> Without a light to guide
> Except the heart that lit me from inside. . . .
>
> I stayed there to forget.
> There on my lover, face to face I lay.
> All ended, and I let
> My cares all fall away
> Forgotten in the lilies on that day.[4]

In *The Spiritual Life*, in a chapter about spiritual darkness, Annie Besant writes:

> Few of the perils that beset the path of the serious aspirant are more depressing, more fatal in their effects, than what is called spiritual darkness—the gloom that descends on the heart and brain, wrapping one's whole nature in its somber folds, blotting out memories of past peace, hopes of future progress. As a dense fog pervades a great city, stealing into every corner, effacing every familiar landmark, dimming even the brilliant lights, until, to bewildered wayfarers, nothing seems

> left except themselves and the foul, stifling vapor that enfolds them—so is it when the fog of spiritual darkness comes down on aspirants or disciples. All their landmarks disappear, and the way vanishes in the gloom; their familiar lights lose luster, and human beings are mere shadows that now and again push up out of the night and disappear into the night again. Aspirants are alone and lost; a sense of terrible isolation shuts them in, and no one shares their solitude. The faces that smiled on them have vanished; the voices that cheered them are silent: the love that caressed them has grown chill. Their "lovers and friends are put away" from them, and no words of comfort reach across the deadly stillness.[5]

Besant's descriptive language certainly conveys the sense of desperate isolation and loneliness often attributed to this state of being. It feels impossible to find one's bearings, to know which way to turn. What can cause such an apparent travesty and loss? We can't say specifically, for on every individual path, both the summits and the valleys depend on the individual's particular history, karma, constitution, journey, and other factors.

A crisis of faith, however, can fall into four main categories. The first is disillusionment with the Divine due to a tragic incident in one's life. The loss of a beloved family member or friend can trigger a rejection of a sense of any inherent worth or purpose. There is a sense of betrayal and disenchantment. Many lose trust in life's "normality," viewing it instead as a precarious adventure with random outcomes. Anger is prevalent, and later despondency and ennui may occur. There is an overwhelming feeling of being abandoned and alone.

The second category of spiritual doubt has to do with distraction. The practitioner may jump from one spiritual tradition to another to another, unable to find any real depth and meaning in the process. It is normal for a seeker to explore and experiment widely, trying to find teachings that resonate, but it is also quite common to be caught in the trappings of the ceremonies and not be able to delve into the experience of communion, particularly if it does not come quickly. Many "shiny objects" may distract and ultimately create the sense of hopelessness.

The third category of spiritual doubt concerns those who stumble and fall on their quest. One may indulge in pursuing emotional or physical sensations and therefore feel removed from the influence of the Divine. This is less a crisis of faith than it is a feeling of disconnection secondary to failure and a distancing from the Ineffable due to human frailty or moral impurity. We may feel that the spiritual path is insurmountable or at least that we are unworthy of it and that our faults and frailties prevent us from progressing and partaking in Divinity.

In the last category, the precipitant cause may be spontaneous and unknown. Belief, dedication, and commitment may dissolve for no discernible reason, at least to the present mind. This can add to the confusion and disorientation that accompanies this condition. We become adrift with no foothold in reality and no handle on the sacred. We are suspended in time and place without motive or direction and lament our loss and loneliness.

Gopi Krishna, in his well-known book *Kundalini*, describes his unintentional arousal of this primordial and divine energy and how he was torn between two worlds:

> Little did I realize that from that day onwards I was never to be my old normal self again, that I had unwittingly and without preparation or even adequate knowledge of it roused to activity the most wonderful and stern power in man, that I had stepped unknowingly upon the key to the most guarded secret of the ancients, and that thenceforth for a long time I had to live suspended by a thread, swinging between life on the one hand and death on the other, between sanity and insanity, between light and darkness, between heaven and earth.[6]

Unseen powers raged within him, indescribable and unknown, causing him to question his very sanity. He had no reference point, no safe harbor, no guide or mentor to help him navigate these surges of an invisible energy.

Water is frequently a metaphor for the spiritual journey. We leave solid ground as we sojourn to unknown worlds to reside on the "distant shore." The analogy could be that of being stuck in a fast-flowing river in grave danger, prevented from being swept away only by clinging to a branch (symbolically representing the familiar reality). We are told we must let go with confidence, that the universal forces will care for us, as frightening as that may seem. It is a sense of surrender and release of all we know, the giving up of one world before achieving the next, that can create the devastating loneliness that all the spiritual traditions describe.

Depression is a separate but related condition. Clinical depression is generally characterized by a persistently depressed mood or loss of interest in activities. The *Diagnostic and Statistical Manual V* (DSM-V) criteria for major depressive disorder require a minimum of five of nine symptoms and either depressed mood or loss of interest or pleasure. The symptoms must cause clinically significant distress or impairment in social, occupational, or other areas of functioning that cannot be explained by some other neurocognitive condition. The National Institute of Mental Health estimates that, in 2020, there were 21 million adults in the United States who suffered at least one major depressive episode, or approximately 8.4 percent of the US population eighteen and older. Depression is more prevalent in women than in men.[7] While pervasive feelings of hopelessness, worthlessness, sadness, and loneliness may be prolonged—even chronic—this condition of depression seems separate from spiritual darkness, although there is likely some overlap. Some attempts have been made to define the difference between the two. The classical vegetative symptoms of depression are frequently absent in episodes that are more manifestly a spiritual crisis.

Kevin Culligan, a psychologist and the former chair of the Institute of Carmelite Studies, also distinguishes between the dark night and clinical depression in the book, *Carmelite Prayer*:

> In the dark night of spirit, there is painful awareness of one's own incompleteness and imperfection in relation to God; however, one seldom utters morbid statements of abnormal guilt, self-loathing, worthlessness, and suicidal ideation that accompany serious depressive episodes. Thoughts of death do indeed occur in the dark night of the spirit, such as "death alone will free me from the pain of what I now see in myself," or "I long to die and be finished with life in this world so that I can be with God," but there is not the obsession with suicide or the intention to destroy oneself that is typical of depression. As a rule, the dark nights of sense and spirit do not, in themselves, involve eating and sleeping disturbances, weight fluctuations, and other physical symptoms (such as headaches, digestive disorders, and chronic pain).[8]

There has been some research into spiritually integrated treatment of depression; but it is relatively limited, and there are significant barriers to performing randomized controlled trials. John Peteet, of the Department of Psychosocial Oncology and Palliative Care at the Dana-Farber Cancer Institute and Brigham and Women's Hospital, Boston, writes in a 2012 article:

> Many studies have found an inverse correlation between religious/spiritual involvement and depression. Yet several obstacles impede spiritually integrated treatment of depressed individuals. These include specialization and fragmentation of care, inexperience of clinicians and spiritual care providers, ideological bias, boundary and

> ethical concerns, and the lack of an accepted conceptual framework for integrated treatment. Here I suggest a framework for approaching these obstacles, constructed from a unified view of human experience (having emotional, existential, and spiritual dimensions); spirituality seen as a response to existential concerns (in domains such as identity, hope, meaning/purpose, morality, and autonomy in relation to authority, which are frequently distorted and amplified in depression); a rationale for locating spiritually oriented approaches within a clinician's assessment, formulation, and treatment plan; and recognition of the challenges and potential pitfalls of integrated treatment.[9]

In the Bhagavad Gita, the warrior Arjuna is essentially in a spiritual crisis that one could describe as spiritual darkness. In the opening of the Third Discourse, Arjuna questions Krishna: "If thy thought is that vision is greater than action, why dost thou enjoin upon me the terrible action of war? My mind is in confusion because in thy words I find contradictions. Tell me in truth therefore by what path may I attain the Supreme" (BG 3:1–2).

As we can see here, and through the rest of the epic poem, Arjuna struggles to find faith that will lead him from the indecision that paralyzed him at the onset of the battle to confident understanding in subsequent action. How do we choose in conflicting circumstances without knowing the right path for ourselves? What guidepost can we find, what Northern Star can we adhere to that will not lead us astray or ultimately betray us? How can we restore faith in the Ultimate and therefore know that our decisions can be illuminated? We are lost in a sea of troubles and seek for an anchor of stability and shelter from the storm. Like Arjuna, without embedded faith, we are subject to the vicissitudes of nature and sway with the wind. Then we lose our place in the world and our sense of self, unable to orient our consciousness and to find a home.

When one is consumed by spiritual darkness (much as in depression), there appears to be no escape, no remedy, no option to quell the demons. Our hopelessness feels omnipresent and eternal. There is a pervasive sense of loss and of being lost. Our very identity disintegrates and dissolves. However, the condition is not static. To the individual it may feel eternal, but to an outside observer there is movement through it. We may fail and fall back to a state of lower consciousness, or we may transform to the higher. William Meader, in his talk "The Dark Night of the Soul," discusses this darkness as a prelude to new light.[10] It is a space of great potential, pregnant with new possibilities. And Joseph Campbell, the noted mythologist, has written, "The dark night of the soul comes just before revelation. When everything is lost, and all seems darkness, then comes the new life and all that is needed."[11]

This is the paradox of spiritual transformation. A "dark night" is a universal exploration, often on more than one occasion. However, it can lead to insight, profound understanding, and connection with the higher aspects of ourselves and the cosmos. But in order to reach the Divine we must surrender something. We must be willing to sacrifice all that we know and are. We must let go of the security of the familiar in order to experience the rapture of the exalted. We cannot coexist with our life in both worlds. We have to create a space for the new self to unfold. In seeking a grand excursion, we cannot be successful if we bring all the baggage that we have accumulated in our daily lives. We must let it fall away. It has a useful place and time, but it can only hinder us in our explorations inward. It can be only a fetter if we wish to soar.

As Annie Besant advises us,

> Limited as we are at present, every conception of God we form is limited, inadequate, even grotesque in its imperfection. Well may we try in gentlest reverence to improve and purify conceptions lower

> and cruder than our own, recognizing that ours must be equally low and crude in the sight of those beyond us, however inspiring they may be to us at our less developed stage. Let us worship the highest we can dream in our purest moments, and strive to live the beauty we adore. Worship and life reveal God above us, because they awaken the powers of God within us. We become that which we worship and love. When the two become one in Nirvana the quest is over, the spark has become the Flame.[12]

She writes about the spark that is inherent in each of us. This light may burn low, but it cannot be extinguished. We may be confident that however lost we may become, the divine spark remains and will guide us—perhaps imperceptibly at times—but nonetheless it takes us through necessary experiences for our own development. We may reject our own Divinity or feel that it has abandoned us, but this cannot occur.

We are never truly alone, despite feelings to the contrary. Our inner nature accompanies us, often in silence. Further, we are connected through our higher selves to the divine beings and consciousness of the universe.

We may be blind to this truth, particularly as darkness descends. But just as darkness in our physical world simply obscures but does not erase, the same principle holds true in the more subtle vehicles and planes of our environment. In a state of spiritual darkness, it is we who fail to see ourselves and our world; it is not as if that world is annihilated. If we lose our bearings, abandon our compass, eliminate our vision, life can be oppressive and pointless. We grieve the loss of the familiar. We lament the loss of a mentor. We struggle with a superficial existence. We search for meaning.

How can we find that divine spark? How can we find the ember and fan it to a warming blaze? Where is the fire of passion? How can we locate the path that leads onward? This is the subject of much spiritual investigation and writing. In *Light on the Path*, Mabel Collins tells us both to "seek the way by retreating within" and also to "seek the way by advancing boldly without."[13] Are these simply contradictory or paradoxical for our understanding? In *The Wizard of Oz*, the good witch Glinda tells Dorothy that she's always had the power to go back home. Like Dorothy, we all have the ability to find the answers in ourselves if we know where to look. This process is beyond the scope of these reflections, except to note that the spiritual darkness experience is real but the imagined isolation and abandonment are not. We retain the capacity for self-illumination, whatever the circumstance. Part of the ability for introspection is the belief that those elements reside within us. We will not search our inner nature absent the belief that there is something there to find.

To return to Geoffrey Hodson's quotation from his article "Steps on the Pathway" (see p. 110 above), the next sentence continues:

> Wonderful recoveries, ascensions from darkness, can lead to great happiness, whilst death itself, which comes to all, marks the ascension of the Inner Self from the limitations of earthly life. It is, perhaps, well for us all that we should recognize these universal human experiences for what they really are; for they are both results of the operation of the law of cause and effect and preparations for the time when, as steps upon the Path, they will be lived out in full, even as they are portrayed in the Gospel stories of the life of Our Lord.[14]

We see from this quotation that the darkness we experience is not only temporary but transitory. It is in a sense a test to ascertain our readiness to proceed along a spiritual path, despite the sensation of immobility while in the moment. While in the throes of the "dark night," we may feel the impulse to surrender, and surrender we must—surrender all that we have known in our earthly life, surrender our pleasure and pain, surrender even our sense of identity, if we are to reach that further shore. Faith alone can sustain us. Faith alone can accompany us in our despair. Faith alone can deliver us to our new world.

How can we prepare for such an experience? The answer varies by individual, but understanding and expecting the experience may ease its impact. To be able to maintain a thread of conviction and compassion, embedded not only in waking consciousness but in the deeper aspects of our being, may provide momentum to move through such a condition. We must know ourselves as completely as possible.

How will we know what choices are best for us? This is part of life's mystery that we must decipher. Some experiences come to us, and others we must seek out. Each is provided to us, however, for our benefit; and whether we find it pleasant or painful is less vital, for we are students, continuing to learn. N. Sri Ram, a former president of the Theosophical Society, writes regarding the art of living:

> It is for us to discover that point which is the goal, the summation of our aspirations, as well as the origin of our present being, and when we have discovered that point, that will be a theme that is all-sufficing, which all life can develop into an ever-enlarging symphony, knit together by an infallible logic.[15]

Each stage of our evolution is necessary and cannot be avoided. Through our experience and choices, this evolution may unfold in different time sequences, but the end result is inevitable: the flowering of humanity. The steps are challenging but need not be feared. Each hardship is educational; each elevation is inspirational. We know that we are more than what we seem. We know the path before us, hidden and mysterious, must contain wonders beyond any we can even fathom. We are not insignificant, despite our own perspective. As Joseph Campbell notes, we are the hero of our own story.[16] Our destiny is tremendous. Our nature is without limit. We will awaken to it. Even the "dark night" cannot defeat us.

As Master Morya says, "Happy is he who crosses the great gulf between *himself* and *us*—unscarred with doubt and free from the pollution of suspicion."[17]

10

The Absolute

Can We Know Anything about It?

The music of the soul can be heard by the universe.

—LAO TZU

The *Absolute* is a term that has its source in Latin as *absolutus*, meaning "not qualified or diminished in any way," "to set free and complete," and "detached," "pure." It is primarily a term used in philosophy or religion and frequently relates to that which is without attributes. The *New World Encyclopedia* notes that "something that is absolute, in itself, is not immediately or directly accessible by human perception, experience, and comprehension."[1] It can be described only in terms of negative qualifications, e.g., the rootless root or the causeless cause. Theologians such as Thomas Aquinas and philosophers such as Immanuel Kant discussed the epistemological challenges in accessing any knowledge that might be obtained through human observation or reasoning. Plato termed the Absolute as "the good," which he argued was an ethical principle that would be self-sustaining and presupposed by any human thought or activity.

Parallels are drawn in Christian theology between the Absolute or divine Unity and the concept of God, eternal and life sustaining. The concept of the Absolute, as it is free of attributes, exists beyond time and space. This idea, for some, involves imagery of what exists in our universe beyond the known and measurable matter that scientists describe and what existed before (and is separate from) our present universe. Cosmologists generally accept the big bang theory—that our universe was created suddenly out of nothingness 13.8 billion years ago. They came to this conclusion by examining an expanding universe and calculating backward the suspected origin in time and place. Although the big bang theory appears to be congruent with much of the evidence, the data supporting the theory is not uniform, and the how (and why) of the birth of the universe is not satisfactorily addressed. In recent years, a growing number of cosmologists have suggested the universe is one in an infinite series that is cyclic, more consistent with the beliefs of the Babylonians and Egyptians (and theosophists). This conception, which describes an endless cycle of expansion and contraction, has come to be known as the big bounce theory.

Are questions about such theories answerable, and do they help us with the concept of the Absolute? Scientific evidence may be compelling, but it is not infallible. Consider that once scientists believed that the sun revolved around the earth and, more recently, that the atom was indivisible. Other historical examples of the limited perspective of science at any given time are plentiful. Further, there is a presumption that all matter is acting passively in the universe without divine intelligence or active manipulation of any kind. Reverse calculation of the age of the universe through present-day observed expansion may be reliable, but unseen alterations may also have occurred.

In Theosophy, the Absolute is the Un-nameable in origin and contains all that exists in the past, present, and future. It is an infinite Unity, unknowable and indescribable. HPB writes, "Karma is an absolute and eternal law in the world of manifestation; and as there can only be one Absolute, as one Eternal, ever-present Cause, believers in Karma cannot be regarded as atheists or materialists, still less as fatalists, for Karma is one with the Unknowable, of which it is an aspect, in its effects in the phenomenal world."[2] In the proem of *The Secret Doctrine*, HPB lists a number of points in summary to give a clearer idea regarding the hierarchy of the universe. She states firstly: "The ABSOLUTE, the *Parabrahman* of the Vedāntins or the one Reality, SAT, which is, as Hegel says, both Absolute Being and Non-Being."[3] Manifestation is both derived from and contained within this Unity. Also, in *The Secret Doctrine*, as HPB is discussing the pilgrimage of the monad she concludes that "at the threshold of Paranirvāna, it reassumes its primeval Essence and becomes the Absolute once more."[4]

Spiritual writers have long struggled to describe the primary essence of the universe, the divine source of all being and manifestation. But do we possess the necessary capacity, both intellectually and linguistically, to know where and how to begin? The Absolute by definition is beyond attributes; therefore, anything we may ascribe to it would be not only inaccurate but contradictory. Is it presumptuous to suppose that the human mind can in any way be aware of that which is often referred to as the Absolute, the understanding of which humankind has desired for so long?

The Absolute is often referred to as the "Endless Darkness" or "Universal Silence." Is this because of the unknowable nature of such a condition, or because we associate darkness and silence with stability and eternity? We look at space and see primarily darkness except for a few twinkling stars. But is space in fact dark, or is it full of energy and even physical light that is not reflected? Annie

Besant notes that placing an object in space—even one that does not generate its own light but merely reflects it—makes that object become visible. This phenomenon would not be possible were the light-wave particles not already present. Should this unexpected presence of light shift the concept of the Absolute as the "Endless Darkness"?

Alternatively, "black holes" are curious objects in space that initially were invisible to scientists because no light or radiation can escape their gravitational field due to their massive density. It is only by indirect measurement that these astronomical bodies can be studied through gravitational distortion and other methodologies. Perhaps the Absolute is similar in terms of having potential attributes that we cannot see or hear because we lack the capacity for doing so.

In physics, we learn that energy can be kinetic or potential, with kinetic activity being visible and potential energy being undiminished, unseen but still present. For instance, we are not equipped to see ultraviolet light visually, but scientists have created instruments that can actually measure it, so we have a collective understanding that it truly exists. We cannot hear the sound of a dog whistle, but we can accept it as beyond our audible range. The absence of evidence to our senses either directly or indirectly through devices does not preclude the existence or possible attributes of that entity.

It appears that if any knowledge or comprehension is possible, it could occur in three possible ways (or some combination thereof): the first is direct spiritual experience; the second, scientific measurement and inference; and the third, logic regarding natural law. Each of these ways is fraught with imprecision and bias, if indeed workable at all, so caveats abound.

Many spiritual traditions have different deities of universality that are, if not the Absolute, portrayed as a source of all manifestation. Some may have attributes, at least in the lower aspects, that accept description. In the Bhagavad Gita (10:3), Krishna describes the protean aspects of his all-inclusive nature: "He who knows I am beginningless, unborn, the Lord of all the worlds, this mortal is free from delusion, and from all evils he is free." And, "I am the One source of all: the evolution of all comes from me. The wise think this and they worship me in adoration of love" (BG 10:8). Krishna goes on to depict the many aspects of his nature, saying, "Listen and I shall reveal to thee some manifestations of my divine glory. Only the greatest, Arjuna, for there is no end to my infinite greatness" (BG 10:19).

HPB, in *The Key to Theosophy*, writes, "For *Atman* or the 'Higher Self' is really Brahma, the ABSOLUTE, and indistinguishable from it. In hours of *Samadhi*, the higher spiritual consciousness of the Initiate is entirely absorbed in the ONE essence, which is Atman, and therefore, being one with the whole, there can be nothing objective for it."[5] Here she is equating the highest aspect of an individual with the universal Atman; indivisible, absolute, eternal. In its purest sense, however, it is free of all the attributes that can be ascribed to it. The term *Absolute* can be used in different descriptions with different connotations, but presently we are discussing the universal Absolute.

The *Absolute*, the *Eternal*, the *Everlasting*, the *Divine Unity*, the *All Powerful*—all are names sometimes used to indicate a supreme and unknowable entity. There is extensive revelation, commentary, and discussion on this subject in all religions and cultural traditions that are generally widely available today. Let us now examine some of the communication from the Masters, HPB, and other enlightened theosophists regarding the concept.

The Masters gave the following responses to A. P. Sinnett's questions that were recorded in Sinnett's Cosmological Notes in 1882. The numbers in parentheses show the position in the recorded list of questions and answers:

(17) APS: On the Hypothetical Absolute and Infinite Final Cause.

Masters: The absolute and infinite is composed of the conditioned and the finite. Causes are conditioned in their modes of existence and attributes, and as individual aggregates—unconditioned and eternal in their sum or as a collective aggregation.

(18) APS: If the Absolute is a blind law, how can it give birth to intelligence?

Masters: But passive latent intelligence, or the principle diffused throughout the universe which in its pure immateriality is non-intelligence and non-consciousness, and which as soon as it becomes imprisoned in matter is transformed into both—can.

(19) APS: The Absolute if intelligent, must be omnipotent, omniscient, and all-good?

Masters: Please give your reasons why!

[APS] In the East the Absolute, itself non-conscious, is linked to intelligence by emanations, supposed to be conditioned.[6]

In the well-known and controversial Mahatma letter 88, Master KH, when providing notes regarding A. O. Hume's writing of a "Preliminary Chapter on God," responds in part, "Parabrahm is not a God, but absolute immutable law. . . . The word 'God' was invented to designate the unknown cause of those effects which man has either admired or dreaded without understanding them."[7] In letter 69, Master KH, answering questions from Sinnett, writes, "the 'greater darkness' into which the perfected 'Siddha' is finally merged thereby, is that *Absolute Darkness* which is *Absolute Light*. The Real Knowledge here spoken of is not a mental but a spiritual state, implying full union between the Knower and the Known."[8]

Charles Leadbeater, in his *Textbook of Theosophy*, has a chapter entitled "From the Absolute to Man" where he comments:

> Of the Absolute, the Infinite, the All-embracing, we can at our present stage know nothing, except that It is; we can say nothing that is not a limitation, and therefore inaccurate. In It are innumerable universes; in each universe countless solar systems. Each solar system is the expression of a mighty Being, whom we call the Logos, the Word of God, the Solar Deity. He is to it all that men mean by God. He permeates it; there is nothing in it which is not He; it is the manifestation of Him in such matter as we can see. Yet He exists above it and outside it, living a stupendous life of His own among His Peers. As is said in an Eastern Scripture, "Having permeated this whole universe with one fragment of Myself I remain."[9]

Leadbeater goes on to explain that, although we cannot have direct evidence of the Highest One, we may be able to ascertain indirect knowledge through the works that surround us and that we see every day:

> Of that higher life of His we can know nothing. But of the fragment of His life which energises His system we may know something in the lower levels of its manifestation. We may not see Him, but we may see His power at work. No one who is clairvoyant can be atheistic; the evidence is too tremendous.[10]

Annie Besant describes the *Unity* as the *Logos* or the *mighty Life Breath*, among other terms. In the final chapter of *The Spiritual Life*, entitled "The Future That Awaits Us," she writes:

> Think for a moment, as far as thought is possible, of that high region of the beginning of the universe. From the great Logos from whom the universe proceeded, there issues a Breath which comes forth and returns but once in a manvantara. This is the mighty Life-Breath in which all systems, all worlds, all individuals live, breathe, and exist.

> Let there be in your mind for a moment a picture of that vast cycle of evolution—evolution as yet unaccomplished, evolution existing in the thought of the Logos but not in the facts of manifestation.[11]

Then when describing Nirvana, the highest known level of existence, she says:

> Then before the awakening soul unfolds a yet mightier world which dwarfs all that went before. One more range is still within the limits of their vision—within the reach, not of human thought, but to some extent of human apprehension. Nirvana binds up all these glories of humanity. Its possibilities are seen and realized, and are no longer mere lovely dreams. They include life beyond all fancy of living, activity in wisdom and power and love beyond any wild imaginings, mighty hierarchies of spiritual Intelligences, each seeming vaster and more wonderful than the one before.[12]

Dr. Taimni devotes two chapters to the Absolute in *Man, God, and the Universe*. He writes with clarity, simplicity, and readability when discussing metaphysical topics, in a way that is most appealing, saying that while contemplation of the Absolute is "beyond intellectual comprehension," it is yet still the most "profound concept in the whole realm of philosophy."[13] That this contemplation may not be "noble" in the usual sense of intellectual comprehension and discussion does not render it "impossible or undesirable."[14] Many classic religious texts offer indirect and peripheral suggestions even though language fails regarding direct description of such an *entity*—if we can even use that term—for something that is beyond the limits and attributes of our ken. The Absolute is profound in that it is at the core of the existence of humankind and the universe, and yet it is mysterious and enigmatic to thinkers and explorers alike. Most religious traditions, both

East and West, speak of an unknowable Divinity, the ineffable Substance (materially or nonmaterially) that underlies not only the structure of the universe but its purpose. Dr. Taimni states that this is a "Reality which is not only beyond the range of the intellect but beyond the range of Buddhi and Atmā and even beyond the range of the experiences of those high Adepts who can dive even deeper into the recesses of their own consciousness."[15] If knowledge of the Absolute is beyond even perfected beings, what hope can we ourselves have for meaningful insights and communication regarding its nature and how it may impact us individually and as a species?

Dr. Taimni offers an intriguing analogy: He presents the image of white light passing through a prism, dispersing the wavelengths and creating a spectrum of colored light as the energy passes out of the prism and onto a screen. There is no difference between the white light and the color spectrum energetically; the difference is only in the light's distribution. Indeed, if desired, the color spectrum could be passed through the prism in the opposite direction to reestablish the beam of white light.

Hypothetically, Dr. Taimni notes, someone living on the side of the prism where the colored light is could not imagine or describe in any fashion the *white* light, which again is simply a different configuration that exists on the other side of the prism. The reverse is true as well; someone living on the side of the white light would have no basis for understanding the alternative experience of colored light. For the person living in the colored world, comprehension of the white light is impossible; and if colors cease to exist, such a state must be imagined as darkness. Reminiscent of Plato's analogy of the shadows in the cave, Dr. Taimni writes, "We must leave the world of shadows if we are to know the realities which cast these shadows. We must leave the world of the mind if we are to know Consciousness in its purity, and, lastly, we must leave the world of relativity if we are to know the Absolute, if this is at all possible."[16] He discusses in some detail a quantitatively oriented image of the Absolute, noting that

> zero and infinity appear to be polar opposites. If we go on increasing the quantity of anything we approach the limit of infinity but never seem to reach it. If we go on decreasing the quantity, we approach the limit of zero but again never seem to reach it. Between these extreme and unattainable limits are contained all possible magnitudes of the thing we can imagine. . . . The point and boundless space are the two polar vestures of the Absolute, and Cosmic Rhythm, as we shall see later, is an eternal oscillation of consciousness between them. The properties of the zero and infinity are analogous to those of the point and space.[17]

Also interesting is Taimni's discussion of *Srsti* (Skt. manifestation, manvantara) and *pralaya* (Skt. dissolution, rest) in which he offers a model of a pendulum that swings between these two extremes. As the pendulum swings from manifestation to non-manifestation, matter transitions from infinity to an individual point and disappears, although in the analogy the pendulum continues to swing into pralaya, the unseen. This is a viable alternative image to the Life Breath that is sometimes associated with the Absolute.[18] He continues to delve into these concepts, and others regarding this topic, in greater detail.

Do we even *need* to know the Absolute? If we can see and feel and know even an infinitesimal portion of the Absolute that is our physical, emotional, and mental world and universe, can we not infer the majesty and glory of its origin? Does it not engender faith that there must be a Source for all we experience externally and internally each day, from the simplest daisy to the most magnificent nebula? From filial love to divine inspiration?

By attributing that manifestation to a greater divine Being, Intelligence, or Power, we are recognizing a cohesion and purpose in the universe of our experience and, by extension, in ourselves. To hold a conviction that there are greater creative forces in the universe whose nature and purpose we cannot fathom gives inspiration and solace to our meager and sometimes apparently random lives. Whether we hold this conviction due to constructs that are emotional or intellectual in nature is less important. Occasionally, divine forces can be known by direct spiritual contact with the higher planes. We can live vibrantly and compassionately each hour knowing we are within the sea of a "Perfect Whole" beyond description.

The source and essence of the universe is simultaneously life's greatest mystery, challenge, and inspiration. Is it possible, however tangentially, to learn or intuit any meaningful concepts in this regard? Is it possible to experience it, even in a faint and reflective way? Is the Absolute separate from the world we experience, or is it the divine Unity, of which we see evidence every day? Is it only that place, like infinity, that is beyond human conception and imagination, that can never be contained within mere description or imagery? Perhaps like the sun itself, its effects are for all to see, but its source, true nature, and origin are not to be known, at least for the present. Yet, there is some comfort even in knowing (or sensing) that the Absolute can or does exist, albeit we cannot begin intellectually to comprehend any qualifications that could be attributed to it. Perhaps we feel small and inadequate in a vast universe with unspeakably expansive dimensions of time and space and equally opaquely elevated levels of consciousness, but maybe there is some reassurance here as well: that we are all part of that One Life and purpose and that someday we will attain the heights of spirituality.

As Mabel Collins reminds us, "The principle which gives life dwells in us, and without us, is undying and eternally beneficent, is not heard or seen or smelt, but is perceived by the man who desires perception."[19]

11

The Question of Evil

No evil can happen to a good man, either in life or death.

—SOCRATES

The concept of evil has challenged humankind since the development of rational and reflective thought. But what exactly is evil, and how do we integrate it into our theosophical understanding of the workings of universal mechanisms in the development of higher consciousness? Most articles and presentations that speak of evil begin by stating that evil in our world is obvious—but is it? Often bad things happen, but to label something "bad" requires a subjective interpretation. One can acknowledge that pain and suffering are real and epidemic, but are they thereby "evil"? As we make our way in the world, we see widespread ignorance and inexperience in others (and perhaps some in ourselves), but are these characteristics commensurate with this concept? Does evil need to include malicious intent? Does it need to exclude ignorance, immaturity, and weakness? What are the "dark forces" in our universe? Is there a primal battle between good and evil, between God and Satan, as many believe? It may be helpful to see what enlightened theosophical authors have written on this topic in order to have a clearer concept as to the origins and nature of what is commonly referred to as *evil.*

In this case it is particularly important to start with a definition that is commonly accepted. *Merriam-Websters Dictionary* defines *evil* as "morally reprehensible" and "arising from actual or imputed bad character or conduct." Additional definitions pertain to "causing harm" or being "marked by misfortune." Some synonyms are *sinful, wicked, pernicious, unlucky, offensive, bad, dark, black, immoral, iniquitous, nefarious, rotten, unethical, unlawful, unrighteous, unsavory, vicious, vile, villainous, wicked,* and *wrong.* Like most synonyms, these give nuanced shades of meaning. Do they capture the concept of evil in the theosophical sense (if this is possible) that we are interested in today?

Philosophical and religious students often engage in the classic epistemological argument regarding whether there is evidence for or against the existence of God. The question is often presented this way: If God exists and if God is omniscient, omnipotent, and omnibenevolent (sometimes called an OOO Being), then is it contradictory to say that evil also exists? Some claim that the evidence of evil contradicts the existence of an OOO deity. The matter can be divided into the *deductive* problem of evil and the *evidential* problem of evil.

A deductive, logical sequence of thought can be pursued (if human logic can even be applied to inquiry about the Divine) wherein if God is all-powerful and all-beneficent, then He/She/It could and would eliminate evil. Therefore, and as the Australian philosopher J. L. Mackie (1917–1981) proposed, from a deductive standpoint evil and an OOO Being cannot coexist.[1]

Others claim that evil and an omnipotent God may coexist if that evil is for some grander (in this case, divine) purpose, which would eliminate this particular contradiction. But if evil exists for some ultimately good purpose, can it truly be characterized as *evil*, or is it just a delayed good?

Finally, the *evidential* model for approaching the question is that if we can identify *unjustified* evil (which a good and all-powerful God would not allow, we suppose), we can therefore disprove the existence of such a Deity, as argued by American philosopher William Rowe (1931–2015).[2] We will consider this argument further a bit later.

Let's start by looking at some quotes regarding evil from Gautama Buddha:

> Conquer anger by love, evil by good; conquer the miser with liberality, and the liar with truth.[3]
>
> What is evil? Killing is evil, lying is evil, slandering is evil, abuse is evil, gossip is evil, envy is evil, hatred is evil, to cling to false doctrine is evil; all these things are evil. And what is the root of evil? Desire is the root of evil, illusion is the root of evil.[4]
>
> Ceasing to do evil, Cultivating the good, Purifying the heart: This is the teaching of the Buddhas.[5]

We can see from these statements that Buddha is speaking of evil in the sense of harmful or bad, the opposite of righteous and good. This is certainly one interpretation of evil, but does it connote the malignant motive that some see associated with evil behavior, or does it simply imply selfishness and lack of awareness?

In *The Use of Evil*, Annie Besant speaks to this question. Her treatise addresses the origin, relativity, use, and ending of evil. She notes that "no universe can come into manifestation at all, that no manifestation can occur, that no multiplicity can become, that no diversity can appear, unless there be limitation."[6] She goes on to link limitation with the concept of duality by this line of reasoning: once duality is introduced into any system, it creates a polarity whereby pairs of opposites must necessarily manifest; and once duality occurs, imperfection is introduced and every object is therefore imperfect and limited. Hence emerges evil: "The perfect is unlimited; the limited, imperfect. . . . Now when that is realised, you have your origin of imperfection, of what is called evil. Thus imperfection is co-eternal with the universe."[7]

Besant notes that evil, like good, cannot exist in isolation or in a neutral body; it can exist only in relationship. If a ball is vibrating violently, it alone cannot be interpreted as evil; but if it comes into contact with a sentient object and causes pain or destruction, this occurrence introduces a subjective and negative quality that may be defined as evil. Further, she says the common assumption that *good* means "all that is working in harmony with the Great Law" and *evil* means "all that is working against it" can still be problematic in the specifics.[8] Selfishness and desire for material wealth, power, and fame may be an inherent part of our development during the initial stages of the spirit descending into matter, but now these characteristics "are evil as retarding the process of integration, as checking the inward-flowing tide of life toward the pole of Spirit."[9]

So, now we have actions that may or may not be evil depending on their context, motive, and circumstance. Which acts may contain evil may be difficult to judge, given our limited subjective and objective perceptions. Politics provides a clear example. One set of activities can appear noble to like-minded individuals but evil to those in opposition. Annie Besant goes on to discuss how apparently destructive forces—be they geological upheavals, predator–prey interactions, or even human war (as demonstrated in the Bhagavad Gita)—cannot be thought of only in terms of evil; they must also be thought of in terms of conflicting forces that reflect the "source of all life, the great One, the Lord . . . known sometimes as the Destroyer and sometimes as the Regenerator."[10] She explains that apparent evil may be useful in developing virtuous qualities within an individual or community. When there is a choice to resist darkness and support the causes of light, then we may expand our virtues in a setting conducive to their development. This is similar to the process of developing a muscle through isotonic or isometric exercises wherein the resistant weight is necessary for the growth and strengthening of the target tissue.

If good can thus be enhanced by resisting evil, then does evil meet the definition of being morally reprehensible, since its absence may be detrimental to the progress of forces aligned with universal harmony? Many historical examples exist in which a dangerous or malignant situation brings out the best in humanity, such as the Abolitionist movement in America and the Allied resistance to Naziism in World War II. Ms. Besant describes the phenomenon on a personal, spiritual level:

> Thus you are developing those qualities of Truth which, without opposition, you could never have evolved and which, in proportion to the energies evolved by your efforts against falsehood, will purify your nature from falsity, and render true the life which you are developing. So also with every other virtue. Courage is developed in the presence, not in the absence, of an object which you fear. If there were no objects which gave rise to the sensation of fear, then courage could never be evolved.[11]

Are these dark forces ultimately divine, regardless of whether they are for our own advancement or detrimental to it? In the Bhagavad Gita (10:23), Krishna says to Arjuna: "Among the terrible powers I am the god of destruction; and among monsters Vittesa, the lord of wealth. Of radiant spirits I am fire; and among high mountains the mountain of the gods."

Also, recall the famous passage where Krishna says, "I am the beginning and the middle and the end of all that is. Of all knowledge I am the knowledge of the Soul. Of the many paths of reason I am the one that leads to Truth" (BG 10:32). And again, "I am the cleverness in the gambler's dice. I am the beauty of all things beautiful. I am victory and the struggle for victory. I am the goodness of those who are good" (BG 10:36). Krishna's message to Arjuna is that all elements dwell in him. "But of what help is it to thee to know this diversity? Know that with one single fraction of my Being I pervade and support the Universe, and know that I AM" (BG 10:42). These words suggest that evil, too, is contained in Divinity. If this is true, evil may be an obstacle, but can it be outside of spirituality? Can it be held (and therefore controlled) by Krishna, the Divine?

The Masters address this question directly, most specifically in the Mahatma letters in the notes for letter 88. Master KH, when writing to Hume, first discusses the Masters' perspective on a personal God; then he goes on to express:

> *Our ideas on Evil.* Evil has no existence *per se* and is but the absence of good and exists but for him who is made its victim. It proceeds from two causes, and no more than good is it an independent cause in nature. Nature is destitute of goodness or malice; she follows only immutable laws when she either gives light and joy, or sends suffering [and] death, and destroys what she has created. Nature has an antidote for every poison and her laws a reward for every suffering. The butterfly devoured by a bird becomes that bird, and the little bird killed by an animal goes into a higher form. It is the blind law of necessity and the eternal fitness of things, and hence cannot be called Evil in Nature. The real evil proceeds from human intelligence and its origin rests entirely with reasoning man who dissociates himself from Nature. Humanity, then, alone is the true source of evil.[12]

Master KH attributes one third of the problem of evil to the selfishness of human nature. Later in the letter he points out that the chief cause of two thirds of the evils that pursue humanity "is religion under whatever form and in whatsoever nation."[13]

In *The Secret Doctrine*, HPB writes about the evil spirit, saying,

> Woe to those who live without suffering. Stagnation and death is the future of all that vegetates without a change. And how can there be any change for the better without proportionate suffering during the preceding stage? Is it not those only who have learnt the deceptive value of earthly hopes and the illusive allurements of external nature who are destined to solve the great problems of life, pain, and death?[14]

Here she is declaring that suffering is necessary for change. This is certainly a common concept and is reminiscent of Newton's first law of motion (i.e., that an object will remain at rest or in uniform motion in a straight line unless acted upon by an external force). But is it true that suffering is in fact evil, particularly when it leads to a greater good? Also, there may be other methods of change, such as education, inspiration, selfless sacrifice, and illumination. So, does the process of expansion and growth truly necessitate the existence of evil?

Joy Mills, in her commentary on the Mahatma letters, discusses the background and interpretations of many of the Masters' remarks. She has a number of comments regarding the Masters' view of evil and its resolution, including following the "chain of causation" that leads to the Four Noble Truths, reflecting basic Buddhist philosophy.[15] She notes that the problem of evil is addressed in many myths, from virtually every culture, as an oppositional force to good and harmony in the manifested world. Whether evil is seen as ignorance, desire, selfishness, or a malevolent supernatural force varies, depending on source and circumstance.

In *The Secret Doctrine*, Blavatsky addresses the subject of the evil spirit, taking aim, as usual, against the proponents of traditional theology, claiming that "one of their most sinful achievements in this direction was the transformation of the divine *alter ego* into the grotesque Satan of their theology."[16] She goes on to say:

> As the whole philosophy of the problem of evil hangs upon the correct comprehension of the constitution of the *inner* being of nature and man, of the divine within the animal, and hence also the correctness of the whole system as given in these pages, with regard to the crown piece of evolution—MAN—we cannot take sufficient precautions against theological subterfuges.[17]

She challenges the Church on the existence of a personal God as well as on the existence of demons and traces the roots of the Christian devil to the pagan demons of Egypt, India, and Chaldea.

Master Morya also addresses the "Chohans of Darkness" in Mahatma letter 30. As quoted by HPB, he says that "we do not find it either necessary or profitable to lose our time waging war on the unprogressed *Planetaries* who delight in personating gods and sometimes well-known characters who have lived on earth."[18] He notes that the "Dhyan Chohans . . . preside at every *Manvantara*" while the "Dark Chohans preside at the *Pralayas*."[19] Do these dark forces represent malevolence toward the safety and progress of the evolving humanity or simply inertia to provide a counterbalance as the pilgrimage to higher consciousness unfolds?

In *Theosophy: A Modern Expression of the Wisdom of the Ages*, Dr. Robert Ellwood has a chapter on "Theosophical Interpretations of Evil." After outlining traditional manifestations of evil, such as early death, material destruction, and physical and psychological harm that we inflict on each other, he discusses the possible causes of these manifestations from the theosophical point of view. He categorizes these causes in terms of the binary nature of reality, evolution, and karma, among others. There are "black magicians" who are on the left-hand path and also Dark Chohans, or "imperfect Gods." In his closing comments, he writes:

> Theosophy offers weapons to fight evil and fend off despair. We can contain the power of evil by understanding its purpose in karma and evolution; its initiatory role; its necessity to the universe of manifestation; its sometimes origins in black magic which can be combatted; its roots in spiritual illusions and cosmic entities above which we can rise.[20]

In *The Masters and the Path*, Charles Leadbeater has a section on "The Dark Powers," in which he describes such powers in this way:

> There is an obscure law in Nature which produces this rather curious result, that whenever there is a great outrush of higher and grander forces, there is also a corresponding efflux of undesirable energy. It may seem strange, but it undoubtedly is so; it has been put sometimes that when the Great Ones, working on the side of evolution, permit themselves to give an unusual benediction, in some curious kind of balance or fairness, they must allow a similar outflow of force on the other side. We have heard much of Darker Powers, of black magicians, of Brothers of the Shadow. These men are following an absolutely different line from ours, a line which brings them into collision with the Masters of the Wisdom, with the Hierarchy which directs the world and the solar system. Naturally that opposition acts not only upon those great Adepts, but upon us, their humble followers.[21]

It is not clear exactly who these dark powers are and what their place in the universe is. Are they similar to the demons and Satan of the Judeo-Christian tradition? Perhaps they are metaphors for our lower natures, oftentimes harsh and cruel. Do they exert sway in the manifested universe, in the destiny of human and superhuman advancement? Do they represent the battle between the gods, as ancient myths depict? Or are they more symbolic of the struggle within the human heart?

In a video on a Theosophical YouTube channel, Pablo Sender gives a thoughtful discussion of the history of evil in the world and in our consciousness.[22] At the end of his talk, he notes that evil is ignorance, for if we understood the true nature of our evil actions, we would choose differently. The existence of evil (perhaps better labeled by another term) adds uncertainty to our world. It often makes life seem irrational, hopeless, even impossible. Every life encounters suffering and loss that can lead to anxiety and fear. These eventualities can be crippling for many (consider suicide, depression, PTSD, and related disorders) and often create lifelong limitations and disabilities. And yet uncertainty in life in many ways contributes to life's appeal, in the sense that success does not come without risk, nor love without sacrifice.

"Evil" appears to be a part of the universe with which we must cope, however we understand its causes and effects. Is it due to malevolent gods or moral turpitude and self-indulgence? Is it a counterweight for us to gain purity and strength or the self-correction of selfish action through karma? It may be some or all, depending on circumstances. Perhaps we can find ways to oppose it, diminish it, or transform it and not succumb to it. We must attempt to challenge ignorance and purify ourselves whenever possible.

12

Theism in Theosophy

Searching for the Ineffable

Love is the joy of the good, the wonder of the wise, the amazement of the gods.

—PLATO

The search for God and the Divine appears to be intrinsic to the human condition. From the first stirrings of the human heart, we yearn to know where we came from and what the purpose of life is. The ancient religious traditions—dating from the Vedas and the Torah and expressed through the wisdom of Krishna, Buddha, Christ, and many others—speak to this yearning. The traditions based on the philosophy of Socrates and the scientific inquiry of Aristotle also attempt to explain the world in which we live.

God is a concept that is both widespread and very individual. God is usually conceived of as a supernatural being with qualities of omnipotence and omniscience and is also seen as the creator of the universe and of humankind. But the concept of God is not static and not uniform. Different cultures (and at different times) have described God quite differently. Even in the Judeo-Christian tradition, attributes ascribed to God have changed throughout the course of the Bible.

In Theosophy, much is written on the topic of the Divine and the most exalted Beings. However, there seems to be a rejection of any notion of a personal God, particularly the God of Western traditions. As H. P. Blavatsky states in *The Secret Doctrine*, "Esoteric philosophy has never rejected God in Nature, nor Deity as the absolute and abstract *Ens* [an entity or being in the most general sense]. It only refuses to accept any of the gods of the so-called monotheistic religions, gods created by man in his own image and likeness, a blasphemous and sorry caricature of the Ever-Unknowable."[1]

In *The Key to Theosophy*, HPB is asked directly by "Enquirer" whether she believes in God. She notes that this depends on the definition applied to that term; she is then asked whether she believes in the biblical God, a concept she does not endorse. She states, "We reject the idea of a personal, or an extra-cosmic and anthropomorphic God, who is but the gigantic shadow of *man*, and not of man at his best, either. The God of theology, we say—and prove it—is a bundle of contradictions and a logical impossibility. Therefore, we will have nothing to do with him."[2]

She also rejects the application of the terms *atheist* and *pantheist*, going on to say:

"We believe in a Universal Divine Principle, the root of ALL, from which all proceeds, and within which all shall be absorbed at the end of the great cycle of Being."[3]

The Masters appear to reject the concept of a unique God as well. The Master KH writes quite clearly in his notes in Mahatma letter 88:

> Therefore, we deny God both as philosophers and as Buddhists. We know there are planetary and other spiritual lives, and we know there is in our system no such thing as God, either personal or impersonal. . . . The word "God" was invented to designate the unknown cause of those effects which man has either admired or dreaded without understanding them.[4]

These statements have challenged students since they were first published. Why are the Masters so abrupt and dismissive on the matter of the "personal God," an apparent reference to the monotheistic concepts of Judeo-Christian-Islamic religions? Is it due to the precept that human beings are made "in his image" and that therefore God has been anthropomorphized? Perhaps it is the abstract attributes of omniscience, omnipotence, and omnipresence as applied to a particular being that are rejected. No being in HPB's concept of the hierarchy of the universe (see p. 146 above), to which it seems Master KH alludes in the above quotation, is said to have these qualities. Also, in *The Key* she appears to reject the existence of an omniscient God when she says, "And it is they again, who virtually blaspheme, in teaching that an Omniscient and Omnipotent God needs uttered prayers to know what he has to do!"[5] How is the modern student to react? Can we accept a universe without God? What are the characteristics of God? The very term has great historical and political implications. Each of us has his or her own concept of what God is. We speak of *God*, but although we use a common term, do we communicate a common image? God must be an abstract idea, as it cannot be measured, described, or examined. Any effort to name or qualify God in any sense must of necessity fall short. Is it God that the Masters deny, or is it our concepts of God—personal and doctrinal—that are rejected? Is there a "God equivalent" in Theosophy, and, if so, what is its nature?

S. S. Varma examines this struggle in *Teachings on Discipleship*, noting that Master Serapis uses the term *God* in his blessing, "God's blessing upon thee, Brother mine." Varma writes that while the Masters "accept the idea of One Life," they "do not wish to call it God, probably because the word is heavily loaded." Later, he notes that Master Serapis "might have meant by God the One Life, and it does not seem justified to think that he meant by it the popular conception regarding God."[6]

Master KH writes in letter 88: "The God of the Theologians is simply an imaginary power . . . a power which has never yet manifested itself. Our chief aim is to deliver humanity of this nightmare."[7] The implication appears to be that the human interpretation of God is what has led to the circumstances Master KH describes as "a nightmare." It is the human misunderstanding, misuse, and consequent abuse of one another that leads to this criticism. Much could be written on the misuse of religion and would run parallel to the history of civilization up to the present day. Yet this reality does not resolve the quandary of whether a God or God-like being (or nonbeing) exists.

Further in letter 88, the Master KH writes,

> (1) We deny the existence of a thinking conscious God, on the grounds that such a God must either be conditioned, limited and subject to change, therefore *not* infinite, or (2) if he is represented to us as an eternal, unchangeable and independent being, with not a particle of matter in him, then we answer that it is no being but an immutable blind principle, a law.[8]

It could be that the concept of God as a Being is what that Master KH rejects. Later in the same letter, when summing up the Masters' position, he writes,

> As to God—since no one has ever or at any time seen him or it—*unless he or it is the very essence and nature of this boundless eternal*

> *matter, its energy and motion*, we cannot regard him as either eternal or infinite or yet self existing. We refuse to admit a being or an existence of which we know absolutely nothing.[9]

Then Master KH goes on to expound on the reasons for this position.

We are reminded of the Theosophical Society's motto, "There is no religion higher than truth." To have knowledge of the spiritual world, we must rely on our own experience or the teachings of others who may be in a position to know. Those teachers who offer commentary and instruction are seen as wise and elevated, further along the path of our humanity or ascended from it entirely. As we explore possible interpretations of the Divine, whether through Theosophy or the greater world of metaphysical writings, we must be mindful of two caveats inherent in this motto: The first is not to pursue only what we know. The personal God, the traditional father figure, may be reassuring to many, but the desire for the Divine to be similar to earthly life is anthropomorphizing and therefore prone to engendering error. Equally important is the second caveat, which is not to be biased in favor of what we want. The truth depends not at all on what we may wish it to be. However attractive a particular alternative might appear, our specific vantage point may well delude us into accepting as truth something that is merely illusion.

Must truth be only absolute, or can it be relative at times and in certain circumstances? Can something be true for an individual yet *not* for the greater Unity? By definition, truth must be consistent, yet our own version of it, necessarily incomplete, may be a distortion. We look for guideposts for the Divine and understand, to lesser or greater degrees, the truth. We must consider logic in our search but not depend too heavily on it, for rational explanations may lead us far afield. Intuition is often valuable when practiced, but it can be just as misleading. A healthy skepticism is warranted, but the mind shows great limitations.

The Universal may be described indirectly only, using terms such as the "Rootless Root," the "Unknowable," the "Tao," the "One Life," the "Causeless Cause," the "Parentless Logos." *Parabrahman* is the word for the Absolute in Sanskrit—the "Supreme Infinite Brahman" or "Beyond Brahman"—referring to the impersonal and nameless universal principle. In *The Secret Doctrine*, Blavatsky cites three fundamental propositions taken from *The Stanzas of Dzyan*. The first of these is as follows: "An Omnipresent, Eternal, Boundless, and Immutable PRINCIPLE on which all speculation is impossible, since it transcends the power of human conception and could only be dwarfed by any human expression or similitude. It is beyond the range and reach of thought—in the words of *Māndūkya Upanishad*, 'unthinkable and unspeakable.'"[10]

The "Immutable Principle" of which HPB speaks is impossible to conceive of at all (see ch. 10). If it is impersonal, can it equate to a deity or God? HPB writes that "it is of course devoid of all attributes and is essentially without any relation to manifested, finite Being. It is 'Be-ness' rather than Being, (in Sanskrit, *Sat*), and is beyond all thought or speculation."[11] Further, Blavatsky notes,

> Parabrahman (the One Reality, the Absolute) is the field of Absolute Consciousness, *i.e.*, that Essence which is out of all relation to conditioned existence, and of which conscious existence is a conditioned symbol. But once that we pass in thought from this (to us) Absolute Negation, duality supervenes in the contrast of Spirit (or consciousness) and Matter, Subject and Object.[12]

Master KH, again in letter 88, states, "If people are willing to accept and to regard as God our ONE LIFE, immutable and unconscious in its eternity, they may do so and thus keep to one more gigantic misnomer."[13]

The Master says here that the "misnomer" is the classic monotheistic image of a personal God, especially of the nineteenth century. However, there may be room for a broader definition of God or at least for a divine Presence if not specifically a Being. What qualities do we attribute to God? Perhaps these are divine order, compassion, understanding, justice, teachings, and eternal presence. Can these qualities be present without a specific Being to encapsulate them? If so, what is that Presence, and can we experience and know it in any way?

In the summing-up section of *The Secret Doctrine*, Madame Blavatsky writes, "The Secret Doctrine teaches no *Atheism*, except in the Hindu sense of the word nāstika, or the rejection of *idols*, including every anthropomorphic god. In this sense every Occultist is a nāstika."[14]

This statement appears clearly to acknowledge that *The Secret Doctrine* does not teach atheism (and so, presumably, nor do Blavatsky and the Masters). The absence of a personal God, as noted by the previous discussion and quotations, does not equate to a godless universe in the broader sense and does not imply the lack of individual divine beings or the universal Divine. HPB notes that any atheism is only the rejection of idols or an anthropomorphic god. She goes on to say that the Secret Doctrine

> admits a Logos or a collective "Creator" of the Universe; a *Demiourgos* [Gk. *Demiurge*]—in the sense implied when one speaks of an "Architect" as the "Creator" of an edifice, whereas that Architect has never touched one stone of it, but, while furnishing the plan, left all the manual labor to the masons; in our case the plan was furnished by the Ideation of the Universe, and the constructive labor was left to the hosts of intelligent Powers and Forces. But that *Demiourgos* is

> no *personal* deity—*i.e.*, an imperfect, *extra-cosmic god*—but only the aggregate of the Dhyāni-Chohans and the other forces.[15]

HPB's *Theosophical Glossary* defines *Demiurgos* as the "Supernal Power which built the universe."[16] It is the third manifested Logos. Coming from the Platonic and Neo-Platonic schools of philosophy, *Demiourgos* is a concept for a figure or force responsible for the creation of the physical universe. It is derived from Plato's *Timaeus* (360 BC), wherein the demiurge is the organizer of the universe rather than the creator of the matter. Here again is an analogy to the architect who conceives and designs but does not implement the actual creation or construction.

Can any of these Collective Hosts, Dhyan Chohans, or Intelligent Powers be considered God or God-like, individually or in aggregate? Even if we could answer yes, defining these entities as God does not answer the question regarding God's nature. They are divine Forces that helped design and create the universe and direct the life force within it. Although limited human conception cannot fathom the deepest secrets of the beginnings of this world, are the descriptions of these elevated entities clues to the "creators," and do they have any relevance to an inquiry to God and the Divine?

Returning to Mahatma letter 88, the Master KH says, "Pantheistic we may be called—agnostic NEVER."[17] He may be indicating that there is not an individual, personal God or even an overarching, monotheistic God but rather many gods operating within an ordered, created, planned system with purpose and progression, even if their existence is beyond our understanding and awareness. We do see order in nature's physical laws, which science continues to unravel. Is it therefore possible that there are higher laws to which we are subject? Theosophy teaches that this is true and inherent in the greater creation of the universe.

In the *Stanzas of Dzyan*, passage 11 of stanza 3 reads: "The lord of the lords (demiurge) came. From her body he separated the waters (those below from those above), and that was heaven above, the first heaven (atmosphere, air, firmament)."[18] And here is passage 12:

> The great lords called the lords of the moon (lunar ancestors, progenitors, fathers, who give men three of the lower principles—desire, life, double) of the airy bodies: "Bring forth men, men of your nature. Give them their forms within. She will build coverings without (the earth gives the lowest principle, the physical body). Males-females will they be. Lords of the flame also (who give men the fifth principle, mind)."[19]

These words certainly convey a sense of creation, purpose, and intelligent manifestation of previously latent form and life. They describe exactly who or what the causative agent is only as the "great lords" and the "lords of the moon." These beings, if beings they are, appear to be divine and even "God-like," although cosmogenesis and anthropogenesis can often be described only in symbolic language. Is there anything we can know about them that is helpful in our search? Or is the mere purported fact that they exist (or existed), at least in this context, able to provide a clearer understanding? Some may search for reassurance and comfort, but that endeavor is inherently prejudicial to the question.

Theosophists study the septenary nature of humans, addressed in much of their literature including Annie Besant's *The Seven Principles of Man*. In describing the Atma, or the higher Self, she says (quoting HPB) that it is the "inseparable ray of the Universal and ONE SELF. It is the God *above*, more than within us. Happy the man who succeeds in saturating his *inner Ego* with it."[20]

Each vehicle (or body) has increasingly dense matter and a more restricted spiritual sense, until the physical body is reached as the densest manifestation of the universal matter. The highest, most refined matter is the Atma, which is far above (spiritually) the conscious level for most of humanity. This divine spark, although latent in our awareness, is uniform in its presence and our own personal connection to Divinity. Perhaps this aspect of ourselves, although not God in the traditional sense, may serve as a "God-equivalent" or "God-substitute," partially or possibly even totally. Blavatsky notes that *The Secret Doctrine* teaches, as the third fundamental proposition, "the fundamental identity of all Souls with the Universal Over-Soul, the latter being itself an aspect of the Unknown Root; and the obligatory pilgrimage for every Soul—a spark of the former—through the Cycle of Incarnation (or 'Necessity') in accordance with Cyclic and Karmic law, during the whole term."[21] Here she indicates not only a connection between the Atma and the universal over-soul but an identity in which each is contained in the other.

Each human contains the divine spark, not in metaphor, but in actuality. Unknown to most of us, each is contiguous with the cosmic fire that is the basis for all Reality, manifested and unmanifested. Is it possible to be lost in such a cosmos, once the illusion is shed and true sight is restored?

Jiddu Krishnamurti (Alcyone) uses the term *God* frequently in his classic work, *At the Feet of the Master*. One might point out that it is the writings of a young boy; he may have used the familiar term as one of convenience to summarize divine principles. The author, however, states in the preface, "These are not my words; they are the words of the Master who taught me";[22] and, in the foreword, Annie Besant writes of the book and its author, "The teachings contained in it were given to him by his Master in preparing him for initiation."[23] In the first chapter, Krishnamurti writes,

> What religion we hold, to what race we belong—these things are not important; the really important thing is this knowledge—the knowledge of God's plan for us. For God has a plan and that plan is evolution. . . . If you are on God's side, you are one of us, and it does not matter in the least whether you call yourself a Hindu, or a Buddhist, a Christian or a Muslim, whether you are from India or England, China or Russia.[24]

Later, Krishnamurti uses the term *God* in a slightly different context: "For *you* are God, and you will only what God wills; but you must dig deep down into yourself to find the God within you, and listen to his voice, which is *your* voice."[25]

What does Krishnamurti mean here by *voice*? HPB writes about this in *The Voice of the Silence*. Are we to think of a literal voice, or is the word a metaphor? People may experience the phenomenon differently and to different degrees. Perhaps to some it is a literal sound from within (or even from without) with specific information or directions. For others it might be a sensation, a feeling, an inspiration, or a motivation. It matters little. The experience may manifest in a suitable way for that particular time, place, and individual. It may be open to misinterpretation in its subtler forms, but for those that experience true contact with the Divine, certainty is usually inherent in the occurrence.

We must also ask ourselves from where the voice comes. Is it from "God," from an essential part of one's inner being, or from some other contact with the unseen worlds? Every impression made on our astral and mental bodies does not necessarily originate from a purely divine source. We must learn to exercise *viveka* (Skt. discrimination) when we attempt to interpret these experiences (see ch. 15). In Hinduism, there are three traditional occult paths to seek this union: the path of knowledge (*jnana marga*), the path of devotion (*bhakti marga*), and the path of action (*karma marga*).

In *Talks on the Path of Occultism*, commenting on rules nine through twelve that Mabel Collins articulates in *Light on the Path*, C. W. Leadbeater writes, "God hides Himself in matter, but He is not dead because He hides Himself there; all the time His activities, His Forces, are playing upon all His creatures."[26]

Annie Besant, in her article "Brotherhood and War" in *The Theosophist*, states:

> God, Ishvara, Allah—call Him by what name you will—is a Fact; Nature is His Self-Expression; Evolution is His Plan; the laws of Nature are the laws of such part of Him, as is manifested in our universe; life and death are His methods; joys and sorrows, pleasures and pains are His tools—the tools of the Supreme Artist—in fashioning the crude material into the perfect masterpiece embodying His idea; the worlds are His studio, crowded with unfinished models, with hints of exquisite future beauty here and there. For us, who believe in Universal Brotherhood, God is a FACT, ever-present, ever-immanent.[27]

In this passage, Mrs. Besant is quite clear in her description of a divine, orchestrating Presence. She notes that the specific name is not important. Even the nature and image are not relevant, but the existence of a divine Power and Order is not to be missed. She wrote this article at the time of World War I, when the manifested civilization was in great turmoil and suffering was widespread. The future was dark and the reestablishment of order uncertain. Many questioned the purpose of their lives and whether there was an underlying Divinity. Her expression of the unseen forces and intentions in the universe is reassuring.

Dr. George S. Arundale, third international president of the Theosophical Society, writing in *The Theosophist* had the following observations:

> If Theosophy is concerned at all with God, it is concerned with the God within each individual rather than with any extraneous God—anthropomorphic in appearance as every such God must necessarily be. Yet Theosophy knows God as an inner Reality, formless and indescribable to humanity. By no means is Theosophy Godless, for the God–Principle is one of the most wonderful and universal facts of Life.[28]

Although it is not clear that Dr. Arundale had clairvoyant knowledge or any special access to the spiritual planes, he did represent theosophical thought at the time of his presidency (1934–1945), which was based on the work of the Founders and the Masters. Further, he had long studied with and was the assistant of Dr. Annie Besant.

Dr. Arundale uses the terms *God*, *God-principle*, and *Godless*. If the term *God* is indefinable, then the others must be so as well. But he does describe the God-principle, at least in the context of Theosophy, as an inner Reality, formless and "indescribable." This God-principle may have the advantage of not being as historically preconceived as the concept of God per se has been.

Succeeding Dr. Arundale, C. Jinarajadasa (known as Brother Raja) was a prominent theosophical writer and the fourth international president of the Society. In his inaugural speech, he states:

> This work is to be done by us by resuscitating in the religions a divine Truth as to man and God that has been so overlaid by the dust of ages as to be completely forgotten as a living factor in daily religious thought and conduct. We know that divine Truth well here in India in the proclamation of the sages that God and man are one, not two. *Tat tvam asi*, "THAT art thou," is still found written in the scriptures; but it is trampled underfoot by the human institutions which Hindu religion has created and sustained. What more ghastly

> denial of "THAT art thou" could there be than the treatment meted out throughout the ages to the outcaste Depressed Classes, now termed Harijans, the "children of God"? Changing the label has not changed the desecration of a divine Truth.[29]

Jinarajadasa's comment about "resuscitating a divine Truth" that has "been so overlaid by the dust of ages" is essential. Whatever is divine in us is not a distant historical study but a living, pulsing Presence, infusing all life and all forms, animate and inanimate, manifest and unmanifest. It is a constant and all-pervading Energy, whether we are aware of it or not, similar to the rays of the sun, always emanating, but falling on us disproportionately. As the poet Tennyson expressed it:

> Speak to Him, thou, for He hears, and Spirit with Spirit can
> meet—
> Closer is He than breathing, nearer than hands and feet.
> ("The Higher Pantheism," stanza 6)

The fifth international president, N. Sri Ram, wrote of the Divine often in his extensive body of work. He was aware of the apparent paradox of the Masters' denial of God and their support for the Liberal Catholic Church. In *The Theosophist*, he describes this Unity as the divine Wisdom, present in all things:

> Theosophy has been translated as the Divine Wisdom. If so, it must be a Wisdom which is both immanent, that is to say, present in all things, and transcendent. We use such words as immanent and transcendent very freely, but then we have to try to discover their deep meaning. Since the Wisdom is in all things, in the smallest as well as the biggest, in the totality as well as in the unit, if we can understand the unit, which is the single life, we shall be able to perceive there as in a drop the same Wisdom which is in the ocean.[30]

The nature of the Divine is that it is not confined to time or space. It supersedes the three-dimensional universe and cannot be attributed to any location. It can be contained in a drop of water as easily as in the ocean. Our search need not lead to any geographical place. We can touch the omnipresent Spirit as soon as the blindfold is removed from our eyes. It can be the work of many lifetimes or of a moment, timeless. We need but to recognize and embrace It.

We can see from these comments that the concept of God is central in the pursuit of spirituality within much of the Theosophical Society, past and present. The terms we may choose to describe this concept will vary, but the sense of a divine energy in the universe and in all beings is intrinsic to the process of seeking, whether we accept its existence or not. There are many ways to experience this energy, consciously and unconsciously. Perhaps the spiritual sense of it is a memory of the Divine of which we are a part, and experiencing it is the impetus to reconnect and find meaning and understanding in the courses of our lives.

Events challenge us, and we question immoral purpose, injustice, greed, suffering, and inhumanity. We attempt to cope with loss, separation, rejection, humiliation, defeat, and shame. How do we weave these difficult realities into meaning for ourselves and our world? To see the strife, devastation, and poverty of our neighbors at home and in the least developed countries and regions of the globe gives pause. How are we to integrate the pain and ignorance (some would say *evil*) we see around us every day? Is this evidence of a godless universe? Or are we merely blind to a Divinity we cannot fully integrate?

In a world of opposites, both are necessary. Each can be a teacher, and there are many lessons to learn. As Sankaracharya says in the *Vivekacudamani*: "As the most muddy water appears pure water on the removal of the mud, even so the *atman* shines clearly when it is removed from unreality. Therefore, the *atman* should be separated from all that pertains to the false self."[31]

How can we find the Reality within the maya of unreality? We must strive for realization. We must use our faculties, as limited as they are. We must train the mind and body to find the inner self that knows the way, the way of the heart.

Technical arguments are largely fruitless. Does God exist? What, precisely, is God? Where does God begin and end? Is God "out there somewhere," or is God internal in each of us? We must open ourselves to the Divinity of the Universe. We want to know the Logos reflected in each being—not intellectually, but experientially. We must knock at the door, with humility and earnestness, but with confidence that we are immortal pilgrims that will one day reach that spiritual Sun. The path to such knowledge can be long and arduous, but a true heart is our talisman. We proceed with the comfort that we are not alone.

How are we to understand the Divine, especially as it is expressed through Theosophy? What is the true nature of our Reality, and can we know it? The task is daunting, as the human mind seems to lack the capacity to encompass such a vast and nuanced world. Additionally, many doctrines and commentaries, seen as divine by many, appear to directly contradict one another. Does God exist as a Being, as a Presence, or in some other way? Is *God* simply a term we use as a conventional expression for that of which we cannot speak and cannot know?

Beings further along the path of evolution such as the Masters—and, through them, Madame Blavatsky—are among those in a position to know more. Fortunately, they have written on the subject and given us direct information as well as clues to the divine nature of the Universe and the great evolutionary schemes. They seem clearly to reject the existence of any personal God but not of Divinity. There may not be a place for God, as an infallible omnipotent Being, but Godliness is ever present, from the greatest galaxy to the minutest molecule. Far from being a dead and soulless universe, it is teeming with Life, mostly unseen and unknown.

Not knowing our place in the Universe, we suffer in ignorance and pain. We tremble before the magnitude and mysteries of the Unknown. We are blind to the purpose and progress of the development of ourselves and of our race. But we are secure in the embrace of the Universal, held with Infinite Compassion and Intelligence, however distant it may seem at present. Once the Light is known, none can remove it, none can subdue it, none can erase it. We are as at home as fish in the water or birds in the air.

What is our divine purpose? How can we find our way? Are we as alone and lost as we seem? Or are we part of a grand, divine plan, as Theosophy teaches? Can we take comfort and find peace in the wholeness of something larger than ourselves? Can we know in our hearts that our love is but the tiniest and feeblest reflection of divine Love, infinite and endless and accessible to all? We seek connection. We seek community. Yet we are part of the indivisible unity of life. We are already whole. We are already loved. We are already divine. We are already One.

As Mabel Collins writes in *The Idyll of the White Lotus*: "The soul of man is immortal, and its future is the future of a thing whose growth and splendor have no limit."[32]

PART THREE

PRACTICAL, LIVING THEOSOPHY

13

The Golden Stairs

It is worth remembering that the time of greatest gain in terms of wisdom and inner strength is often that of greatest difficulty.

—HIS HOLINESS, THE FOURTEENTH DALAI LAMA

Many who come into contact with theosophical ideas—especially those concerning esoteric descriptions of planes and subplanes, disincarnated beings of various descriptions, and vast dimensions of space and time begin to wonder about the application of such knowledge. It is natural to wonder how this information affects our lives. How can we utilize the tenets of this knowledge to enrich and improve ourselves on a daily basis? There is a need to make Theosophy practical for all who become curious and to investigate its principles either casually or in deeper inquiry.

Although there are many teachers and treatises on spiritual development, both within and outside Theosophy, perhaps none is more comprehensive and yet succinct as the advice given by H.P. Blavatsky in what has come to be known as the "Golden Stairs":

> Behold the truth before you: A clean life, an open mind, a pure heart, an eager intellect, an unveiled spiritual perception, a brotherliness for one's co-disciple, a readiness to give and receive advice and instruction, a loyal sense of duty to the Teacher, a willing obedience to the behests of TRUTH, once we have placed our confidence in, and believe that Teacher to be in possession of it; a courageous endurance of personal injustice, a brave declaration of principles, a valiant defense of those who are unjustly attacked, and a constant eye to the ideal of human progression and perfection which the Secret Science (*Gupta-Vidyā*) depicts—these are the Golden Stairs up the steps of which the learner may climb to the Temple of Divine Wisdom.[1]

The writing was originally taken "from the letter of a Master" and provided by Mme. Blavatsky in 1888 to an inner circle of students who were eager for specific recommendations on how best to live a spiritual life. In 1890 the text was made public for all who might be interested in such teachings.

In a talk on the significance of the Golden Stairs, Joy Mills notes that "each of these steps deserves very careful examination and detailed study, as well as long practice. They all point to ethical and moral attributes which are essential for the individual ultimately to lead the kind of life [i.e., a spiritually meaningful existence] of which I am speaking."[2]

We can list these thirteen "steps" in different ways, and authors disagree about exactly how they should be studied. Sidney Cook, president of the Theosophical Society in America from 1931 to 1945 and later international vice president, writes:

> In the Golden Stairs, H. P. Blavatsky gives us thirteen points, or thirteen steps up the stairs to be mounted. And it should not surprise us if we find that HPB has given us much more than a random list of steps or stages. Does not the fact that she names them a stairway suggest that there must be order and sequence to the steps on the stairs; that the stairway has structure and form and that every step must therefore be trodden in its proper turn? Is there not a suggestion in this idea that no step can be omitted if we would climb to the top, that none can be taken out of order, that it is indeed a stairway, not in symbolic language only, but in actual living fact?[3]

This is a fairly regimented approach. This author believes that the order of the required developments of character is not arbitrary; rather, each step builds on the earlier steps, a foundation without which the more advanced attributes would not be possible. However, mastery of each specific recommendation is likely not possible during one human lifetime. Further, several of the suggested qualities are interdependent. Like strands of a rope, each string must be strengthened and intertwined, in order for the rope as a whole to become more durable.

A later president of the TSA, John Algeo, expressed a different perspective:

> All metaphors have their limits; and if we think of this set of ethical principles that we call "The Golden Stairs" too literally as steps that we climb, one at a time, to reach some pinnacle of moral perfection, we will have trespassed the limits of the metaphor. We do not climb the Golden Stairs once only, but many times, repeatedly; every action of ours is a step in some direction on these stairs. And so the first step is not taken once only, but over and over again. When we at last take the step of a clean life perfectly, we will have passed over all the other steps and arrived at the temple to which they lead.[4]

A word is warranted about HPB's initial sentence quoted above, "Behold the truth before you." Introductory statements to gain the attention of the listener or reader are common prior to spiritual teachings. In this instance, Blavatsky uses the word *behold*, meaning not simply to look or recognize, to listen or read, but to awaken and to understand deeply the wisdom that is about to be conveyed. We should not be distracted or read in a superficial manner but try to ascertain the full dimensions of the message. *Behold* is then followed by the word *truth* in the deepest spiritual sense, indicating that it comes from an unerring source. The statement concludes with the second-person pronoun *you* as the potential recipient of this teaching, placing the responsibility on us as readers to intuit the more profound aspects inherent in the passage.

These steps are often organized into groups that appear naturally to be related, and here I will largely follow Sidney Cook's grouping. He refers to the initial steps one through four as "preparation." Step one is to lead "a clean life." What exactly is meant by that phrase? Certainly, it can be interpreted at multiple levels, including physical, emotional, mental, and moral. In its apparent meaning of living and completing a perfect life, it seems unattainable for any incarnated human being. Such an accomplishment would, by definition, also include any other attempts at purification, since by nature it would have to include all other thoughts, feelings, and actions.

Should we not be able to claim such lofty status, of what use would it be to proceed with the consideration of other attributes, since, as Cook recommends, taking the next step would always depend on the accomplishment of the previous one? However, if we take the stance that we can work on each of these steps in combination and in different orders, then it does make sense logically to proceed with attention to each and conscious effort to improve behavior in an effort to strengthen our character and purify our motives.

The next three steps may be seen as focusing on specific aspects of a clean life, namely, an open mind, a pure heart, and an eager intellect. These are developmental stages that reflect in part the Eightfold Path in Buddhism.

The second step, having an open mind, suggests the qualities of *viveka* (Skt. discrimination) and *vairagya* (Skt. desirelessness). Chapter 15 in this book, discussing Krishnamurti's *At the Feet of the Master*, further elaborates on these qualities. An open mind cannot be achieved in the setting of bias or prejudice. Although we may see ourselves as having an open mind, to be truly free of all unreal influences is not easily obtained. N. Sri Ram, the fifth international president of the Theosophical Society, writes, "It is only in freedom from reactions arising from the past that there can be the perception of the truth which arises freshly in the present."[5]

The third step, having a "pure heart," refers to the passion and compassion of the individual. We may see ourselves as compassionate, but does selflessness extend deep within our nature? Selfishness may be hidden, or we may delude ourselves into thinking that we have conquered it. One of the Masters, K.H., writes, "Selfishness and the want of self-sacrifice are the greatest impediments on the path of adeptship."[6] The heart is often seen as the seat of the emotions that appear to have independent reign in our bodies. We often have varying degrees of control, given the idiosyncrasies of our personalities and characteristics that have emerged through nature and nurture. The Sanskrit terms *raga* (attachments) and *dvesa* (aversions) are two of the five *kleshas* (impediments, afflictions, or poisons) described as causes of suffering in the Hindu text, *The Yoga Sutras of Patanjali*.[7] These are powerful influencers of emotions and obstructive to the purification of the heart. It is only with concentrated and persistent effort that these can be mitigated and ultimately broken to be servants of the Higher Self.

The fourth step is having "an eager intellect." Note that Blavatsky does not say a comprehensive intellect, a refined intellect, or a superior intellect, but rather an *eager* intellect. This reflects a curiosity for knowledge and understanding that may lead to the quality of wisdom. We have been given intellectual abilities to investigate, process, and organize information to assist us in evaluation and education regarding persons and events. Although we wish to maximize clarity and objectivity, intellect can serve us in a myriad of ways. As Krishnamurti notes in *At the Feet of the Master*, "However much you wish to help, if you are ignorant you may do more harm than good."[8] Information is more accessible than ever before, and trying to assimilate even basic developments across the world can easily be overwhelming. With news reaching us 24/7 through the Internet, radio, television, and a variety of other sources, finding a filter, or even a barrier, is essential.

An "eager intellect" also refers to spiritual exploration. We are encouraged to explore and determine for ourselves the truth of any proposed verities and not accept another's testimony, no matter how revered the author or text. Ultimately, it is only we, as individuals, who can tread the slopes of spiritual inquiry. Perhaps a trusted guide can help, but it is only through our own individual effort that even a single step on the pathway may be tread. In order to navigate the peaks and valleys in this and other worlds, we must rely on our essential being and use the tools (qualities) that we are given or able to develop.

The fifth step, "an unveiled spiritual perception," is perhaps a bridging step from lower self-development to relationship. Sidney Cook categorizes step five as the "unveiling and the vision."[9] As we are able to lift the veil, even minimally, we can begin to see our true nature and that of our universe. This can be accomplished through the Higher Self, the *atma-buddhi*, the purest intuition, and the grandest vision. This panorama of the larger purpose of life and the nature of our surroundings is afforded very few on a regular basis, but it comes to each of us at specific times in the cycle of reincarnation. Blavatsky uses the term *unveiled* to indicate the full removal of illusion (maya)—meaning not partial illumination or occasional insights but a full, unobstructed perception of spirituality. Such an ideal may seem unknowable, much less achievable, and yet the concept can burn as brightly as a beacon. With the smallest step, we draw closer to the ideal and can shed illusions, if only a bit. We don't know where breakthroughs may come, or why, but constant selflessness may bring the day closer. Works of art, music, oration, and other human expressions are often seen to be divinely inspired. This is a form of spiritual perception that can be transmitted through the human vehicle, whether the source be recognized or not. We can all benefit from such insights and performances.

The next set of four instructions can be taken together as they relate to interactions with others, and three specifically mention a teacher or instruction. The sixth step is a "brotherliness" for all. The historic term *brotherliness* is intended to be gender neutral and apply to men and women equally. This is advice for disciples especially, and because discipleship spans many lives that occur in bodies of any gender, we would expect one's higher nature to be genderless. *The Golden Stairs* was first published in the late 1880s, clearly a time of male dominance socially, but it was written by a woman who uses the term without hesitation due to its universal implication. We are encouraged to have a brotherliness for all, implying compassion and respect, even for (perhaps especially for) those with whom we disagree socially or intellectually. We are challenged to offer aid and assistance to each of our brothers and sisters, regardless of certain judgments. We honor the Divinity of each pilgrim, even if that divine nature is not readily apparent. No one individual or group has a monopoly on Truth, no matter how faithful its adherents. Andrew Rooke in his commentary on *The Golden Stairs* writes:

> All religions emanate from one source of Being where truth is one. There, various perspectives on reality coexist happily as facets of the single diamond of truth. Through the ages great teachers have brought facets of this gem to various cultures, and people have clasped tightly their little facet of the truth and said: "See, here I have the whole diamond!" If truth shines like the sun from a single source, how much sense does it make to condemn any brother on the spiritual path?[10]

We must realize that every human being has a long stretch of incarnations in the lower kingdoms behind him or her and likely many human incarnations as well. No matter how selfish or corrupt the behavior, we know that in the long duration of human and planetary development, each must realize his own true inner nature and be elevated to his inherent divinity. Although the process may be difficult to visualize, this passage is a reminder to foster compassionate feelings toward all. We must look past the superficial, when necessary, and see the potential disciple within.

Next follows the related step seven, "a readiness to give and receive advice and instruction," which is a natural extension of brotherliness. Once we can recognize the Divinity in each of our fellows, we realize that we can benefit each other, as each has different experience and knowledge. We must be willing to learn both from those who are sometimes a little further along the path and from those who are often just more adept in a certain domain in which we need some assistance. They may not even have expertise but simply experience in a similar situation. We need not follow any advice or instruction for it to be beneficial. We might evaluate it and realize that it does not apply to our particular circumstance or character, and yet it would still be to our benefit to hear it. In this sense, everyone can be our teacher.

We must be cautious, however, not to be just on the receiving end of this teaching. Blavatsky clearly states to "give and receive."

We may be humble, feeling we have little or nothing to give as far as advice goes, but this is far from true. Through life experience, virtues, love, and compassion, we have much to offer to others struggling to find their way in the world. We need not necessarily recommend a specific decision, such as choosing a partner or a vocation; rather, we can help with the internal process toward reaching an independent choice. We can always serve as a model, for actions speak much louder than words and create more vibrant impressions. As Ram Dass has insightfully observed, "We are all just walking each other home."[11]

The eighth step, giving the direction of holding "a loyal sense of duty to the Teacher," may seem implicitly understood and therefore unnecessary. However, the sense of duty is central to the relationship and a critical ingredient if any learning is to take place. The capitalization of *Teacher* in the step indicates that a spiritual teacher, while not infallible, has intrinsic credibility that might be lacking in the world of human affairs. Our loyalty is not misplaced in that any teacher of spiritual lessons makes a sacrifice on our behalf. Therefore, this loyal sense of duty is a recognition and appreciation of the teacher and the message being imparted to us.

The ninth step appears a bit more complicated. We are encouraged to have "a willing obedience to the behests of Truth, once we have placed our confidence in, and believe that Teacher to be in possession of it." We are told to have a willing obedience but only under specific conditions. Many are uncomfortable with the concept of obedience and feel a reluctance to "obey" any given authority. This may be appropriate from a social perspective, but obedience to a spiritual truism implies not weakness but strength. It entails not subservience to a secular authority but rather a surrender of our lower nature to our higher. This may be difficult to appreciate if we see that higher nature as "other."

What, specifically, are these "behests of Truth"? A behest is usually defined as an authoritative order or command. Therefore, a behest of Truth would be an order based on some universal or divine truth, particularly since *truth* is capitalized in this passage. Therefore, the author is urging us to be obedient to spiritual and authoritative truisms as they are expressed in this passage and other writings. Further, they should be accepted only once we have placed our confidence in that Teacher (again capitalized to indicate divine knowledge) and believe that teacher to be in possession of the Truth. *Truth* is a term we hear much of in religious pursuits as well as in society at large. Truth by its definition cannot be false, but humanity's truth can be partial or even flawed. Divine Truth, however, cannot be compromised and cannot fail if we adhere to its teachings. We must decide for ourselves which of these teachings are purest in the sense of spiritual Truth and how best to apply them to our lives.

Moving on to the next group of steps, we will take a closer look at numbers ten through twelve, all relating to justice. Justice is a concept that ideally is objective, but it is often fraught with subjective interpretation. Like beauty, it contains elements of both. It can depend on your perspective, at least in part, in the manifested world. Justice is usually defined as "fair treatment and due reward." But substituting the concept of fairness for justice does not significantly advance clarity. In any specific instance, we may disagree on the most just outcome of a particular circumstance because our perspective as humans is limited. Ideal justice, on the other hand, would leave no room for dispute; administered from a divine source that knows all circumstances, it would universally be seen not only as fair but also as true and proportional. Additionally, for our purposes here, we need not to determine justice in every particular circumstance but merely to recognize that it does exist; and we should work toward it whenever and wherever we are able.

The first of these steps—number ten—is written as "a courageous endurance of personal injustice." Why should we be told that we should suffer and even "endure" personal injustice? All can agree that the world we live in is frequently unjust, and we may frequently feel that we have personally not been treated fairly in a particular instance. Should we complain to all those we see? Should we begrudge our suffering? As is common in our current society, should we retain legal counsel and determine who to sue? The author of *The Golden Stairs* answers no. We should be willing to accept the imagined injustice and endure its consequences. In time, we may even realize that the apparent injustice is not unjust spiritually, due to karmic circumstances. If we are truly able to operate from a selfless perspective, then our own personal circumstances should be less of a concern.

This step is immediately followed by the eleventh step, which encourages "a brave declaration of principles." We must be willing to stand up for our beliefs, particularly in the face of opposition. We need to be willing to "declare" those beliefs publicly and privately. This concept is enshrined in the US Constitution as free speech, but the moral obligation goes far beyond this freedom, to the point of stating those beliefs with the goal of influencing and persuading others. We must be tolerant of others' perspectives without yielding to domination of thought or control of choice. Those who live in modern democratic societies may take this ability for granted, but even in parts of the world today the very act of declaring principles and beliefs is grounds for incarceration or worse—just as it has been for long centuries. For generations, even studying sacred texts while living in authoritarian countries placed one's life at risk. Consequences could be invoked not only by the state but also by the church.

The last in this group of steps—number twelve—is the "valiant defense of those that are unjustly attacked." This again relates to the defense of justice, but this time as it applies to others. Even if the attack on justice does not affect us personally, it is critical that we speak in defense and act in righting the injustice whenever possible. This should be done altruistically, without any expectation to benefit personally. Martin Luther King Jr. reminded us that "Injustice anywhere is a threat to justice everywhere."[12]

We need not wait until we ourselves are at risk but rather must fight on behalf of our brothers and sisters for social justice for all global citizens. We must be careful not to ascribe the injustice and ills of others to a manifestation of their personal karma, despite the above-mentioned role karma might play regarding our own personal injustice, which might influence our own feelings of fairness. It may be easy to attribute suffering to "cosmic causes," but whatever they may be is unknown to us and in no way limits the burden of responsibility to assist in any way possible. We know not the other person's karma; even so, it may be our responsibility to intervene.

"Identity politics" is in vogue, wherein each demographic group works politically to advance its own agenda for recognition, compensation, and legal fairness. But the effort should not be left only to the particular group involved. It is the responsibility of everyone to work toward human rights. In truth, there are not "women rights," "minority rights," or "gay rights"; each are human rights that we must all advocate regardless of our personal identity and position. For freedom to be present, we must all be free. The well-known quotation of Pastor Martin Niemoller on display at the United States Holocaust Memorial Museum is relevant here: "First they came for the socialists, and I did not speak out—because I was not a socialist. Then they came for the trade unionists, and I did not speak out—because I was not a trade unionist. Then they came for the Jews, and I did not speak out—because I was not a Jew. Then they came for me—and there was no one left to speak for me."[13] Even if we retain the desire for self-preservation, for personal freedom and for justice, it is in our mutual interest to advocate for those who may not be able to do so for themselves.

The thirteenth and final recommendation is to have "a constant eye to the ideal of human progression and perfection which the secret science depicts" (the Sanskrit term *Gupta Vidya* is sometimes included in parentheses). The purpose is not so much to give a specific direction but rather to encourage a knowledge and awareness of the "secret science." What is the meaning of the secret science, and, more importantly, what was the meaning in the 1880s? The inclusion of the Sanskrit term is helpful in that *Gupta* can be translated as "to preserve," while *Vidya* is translated as "knowledge" or "wisdom." The translation of the combined term indicates preserving "the secret wisdom and the source of all known religions and philosophies."[14] In this way, Mme. Blavatsky urges us to follow the teachings contained in the divine wisdom, which by its very nature cannot be quantified or limited. She does not tell us to acquire divine wisdom, for to do so would require perfection on an individual basis; rather, she tells us merely to keep a constant eye on the ideal that is depicted in this wisdom. This must be our lodestar by which we orient ourselves in both major and minor choices and even apparently trivial decisions, as reflected in the term *constant*. Many may find achieving this goal daunting, and yet by efforts to approach it we will inevitably experience a purification in our daily lives.

The conclusion to the short but monumental offering of *The Golden Stairs* recaps that "these are the Golden Stairs up the steps of which the learner may climb to the Temple of Divine Wisdom." She evokes the metaphor of Golden Stairs made up of steps that the "learner may climb." And what is the goal of this journey? *Divine wisdom*. However this term is interpreted, it corresponds to the search for meaning in our universe and in ourselves. Divine wisdom is elusive in our day, for it is not easily won. But there is a path (in this case stairs) that we may take. Sidney Cook has said, "The entire world, all experience, and all of living, constitute the Golden Stairs."[15] We must learn how to ascend them, and this is welcome, although intuitive, advice. Each step, at its core, reflects selflessness in thought, feeling, and action. While we may try to achieve success in each step simultaneously—and should, as occasions arise—doing so will become natural if we cultivate selflessness.

The Noble Eightfold Path of Buddhism lists eight practices that, if followed, lead to enlightenment, that is, Nirvana. These are listed in simple translation as right understanding, right resolve, right speech, right action, right livelihood, right effort, right mindfulness, and right meditation.[16] These practices are given in a specific order to nurture progress, emphasizing the necessity of placing right view as the initial step. To create a consciousness with the absence of selfishness prepares us for the diversity of challenges we are to face.

How can we bring this "right view" or selflessness into manifestation? One helpful aspect is the recognition of unity. In *The Human Interest*, N. Sri Ram writes, "What the world needs more than ever before is Brotherhood, first in the heart of man and as its reflection in the outer world an integration, a synthesis of its scattered parts and functions . . . This synthesis has to be brought about through an increasing realization of unities, through the dedication to those unities of the differences which lie about us on every side."[17] We must make efforts to recognize the inherent unity of all life, despite its apparent differences and contradictions. We must strive to see our connectedness with our fellow human beings, and in fact, all life. Theosophy instructs that all matter, manifest and unmanifest, is alive and contained in one, integrated Whole.

As we search for meaning in our lives, we wish for more than comfort, knowledge, sensation, and success. We wish to find ways to contribute in some small way, ultimately leading to the lifting of the burden of humanity, be it physical, mental, or spiritual. Joy Mills, while speaking on this passage, describes it as leading to becoming a "participant in life itself, a participant in the world about us, a real participant in universal process, a participant in the life in the world with our fellow man, with all creatures in the world."[18] It is this desire—the desire to awaken to the illusion of maya, to open our eyes and hearts to the Reality of the universe—that the golden-stairs sequence addresses. We are participating in our own evolution as well as the evolution of the planet, whether we are aware of it or not. We can work for the forces of harmony or for its opposite. This is not to say that we should adopt an attitude of passivity or avoid conflict at all times. When we realize that we are truly a coworker with the universal forces for the future, a cocreator of the new world that must unfold, then we aspire to have some influence on how it develops. We wish to recognize our role and how we can play a part. The Golden Stairs shows us that direction. It teaches how we cannot only progress but elevate. Opportunity will come to us in our ordinary lives. Of this we may be sure. It may not be labeled as a critical occurrence and may even slip by, barely noticed. But each choice we make leads to another. And it is through these choices, large and small, that behaviors follow, defining who we are.

14

The Worker for Theosophy

As beautiful flowers are found in barren places,
so is the most beautiful service that is rendered
in the times and places of the greatest need.

—G. S. ARUNDALE

Through the study of Theosophy, we realize that we are individuals in appearance only. Our true nature is inherently intertwined with all others; in fact, all life is part of the one universal and indivisible whole. How, then, can we express our beliefs in a coherent and harmonious way that may benefit all those with whom we are inseparable? How can we find a life's purpose that is compatible with our values? How can we find practical implementation of our ideals in our daily lives? How can we work through community to elevate humankind? These are questions that have been expressed through the generations of seekers of light.

As we experience the world, both directly and indirectly, we wish our lives in some way to benefit parts of humanity. This wish is at times expressed somewhat wryly of an idealist as wanting to "save the world." However, to live to benefit humanity is a noble pursuit.

In his talk on the subject, Edward Abdill notes that many philanthropists, artists, musicians, engineers, medical researchers, educators, industrialists, and others have contributed toward elevating the experience and comfort of our daily lives.[1] But is this sort of creative activity really the same thing? Those who truly follow the course in life of selflessness and service are often unrecognized and unnoted. In *Light on the Path*, Mabel Collins writes, "And that power which the disciples shall covet is that which shall make them appear as nothing in the eyes of others."[2]

H. P. Blavatsky has quoted words by a Master in her article, "Some Words on Daily Life":

> Theosophy should not represent merely a collection of moral verities, a bundle of metaphysical ethics, epitomized in theoretical dissertations. Theosophy *must be made practical*; and it has, therefore, to be disencumbered of useless digressions, in the sense of desultory orations and fine talk. Let every Theosophist only do his duty, that which he can and ought to do, and very soon the sum of human misery, within and around the areas of every Branch of your Society, will be found visibly diminished.[3]

Certainly, we can focus on our own development. We can attempt to follow the Ten Commandments of Judeo-Christianity, the Paramitas of Buddhism, the Yoga Sutras of Hinduism, the Golden Stairs of Theosophy (see ch. 13), albeit imperfectly. However, individual progress is not generally sufficient in the course of service, and so we also seek ways in which to contribute to the betterment of humankind. If we are alive, we must act, for even inaction is a form of action. Karma is the path of action and ultimately has the ability to lift the burden of humanity.

Each of us will strive for meaningful work. This will generally be in service to our brothers and sisters in some fashion. While our lives unfold, we hope to find ways to purify and expand our consciousness so that we may become better agents of divine intention. We struggle in our daily lives for basic physical necessities, substantive personal relationships, relevant vocations, and methods to contribute to our community and society at large. A plethora of choices faces us every day. Each choice will lead to a different outcome.

As Annie Besant, in *The Spiritual Life*, states,

> Only by service is fullness of life made possible; the whole of the universe is yoked to the service of humankind. Every individual should be pledged to the service of humanity, past, present, and future, humanity evolving up to the divine personage, eternal, immortal, indestructible. That should be the object of life, the goal of evolution.[4]

How then can we contribute to the service of humanity? Of course, there are many ways to serve the human species. The provision for physical, emotional, and mental needs are critical. However, the addressing of spiritual needs is even more essential. The Theosophical Society was created by the Masters of Wisdom as an experiment. It was unknown if the world was yet ready for such concepts and sacrifice. The fact that the Society is still extant nearly 150 years later is testimony that it continues to have relevance. However, its public profile and membership in a relative sense have diminished. Its work is not finished, nor has it even reached its vital potential. How can we work within the Society and more broadly to bring about the goals of compassion and brotherhood? Its mission, as chapter 1 states, has recently been reformulated as "to serve humanity by cultivating an ever-deepening understanding and realization of the Ageless Wisdom, spiritual self-transformation, and the unity of all life." How can we realize the full meaning of that mission?

Modern theosophical writer Dorothy Bell, in an article entitled "True Theosophical Service," begins:

> By definition, Theosophical service is Action Theosophy—the application of fundamental Theosophical principles to inner and outer action. Both HPB and Annie Besant identified it as altruism. Thus Theosophy's central principle is altruism. As a principle, altruism expresses the true root meaning of the words *theos* and *Brahma*—the motion of expansion from within outwardly, which is also associated with the outbreathing of the Great Breath. It means giving unconditionally to the whole from within outwardly. It realizes the wholeness and unity of all. And every movement of that realization of wholeness is open and generous and all-embracing. It is compassion, love, gentleness, kindness, and the full expression of who we truly are.[5]

Therefore, service, however we may define it, must include altruism as its basis. Energy moves from our inward nature to our outer world. Consequently, it is not simply our actions that matter but the motivation behind them. We wish to bring some essential aspect of ourselves, our true being in its most purified form, to the outer experiences in which we are involved. If our motives are selfish, no matter how beneficial the activity, we do not grow spiritually. Yet if we are selfless, nearly any activity will likely be rooted in divine intention. Internal purification is therefore necessarily entwined with external performance. It is helpful to reflect intuitively on intention and choice. The appearance of service only is a hollow shadow of true service. If our motivation is pure, results are not essential. We need to work intelligently and be willing to learn from our mistakes. Success is not always measured by outcome in a spiritual sense.

George Arundale, the third international president of the Theosophical Society, wrote a small, inspirational manual entitled *The Way of Service*. He opens with three principles of service in the theosophical view:

> IF you desire to be of service to others with advantage to them and without danger to yourself, see that these three principles guide you in your service:
>
> (i) That your greatest joy is to tread the path of service;
>
> (ii) That you know yourself to be but the agent of some force greater than your own which sends the power of service through you;
>
> (iii) That you see in others the same divine nature you yourself possess.[6]

As mentioned, central to this idea of service is the theosophical premise of unity of all life and all objects. Realizing that we are on a path of service can be the greatest joy. You need not act entirely on your own account but realize that you are a conduit of empathy and assistance brought about through divine forces. We must assist each other, for all of us have needs in different arenas and at different times that can be served by our brothers and sisters. It is this unconditional service, without want of reward or recognition, that is the practical application of altruism, respect, and compassion. Over time, we may refine our wishes regarding service and look for opportunities where we can be useful. If we set aside any self interest, there is no end to the instances in which we can help. We must be cautious not to interfere with others' work or overextend ourselves to the point that we are ineffective, or worse, harmful, but within these parameters, we can lift our fellow humans.

B. P. Wadia was a member of the Theosophical Society in India in the early twentieth century and worked with Annie Besant and

C. W. Leadbeater at Adyar. Among Wadia's nearly two hundred articles is one entitled "Growth through Service." This article is divided into two sections: Individual Progress and World Service. An excerpt from the section on World Service reads:

> Many kinds of activity, many forms of service, are rendered by many types of people in the world of today. Our task in the T. S. is to render a peculiar kind of service, to give a particular type of assistance to the world. As H.P.B. said, "We believe in relieving the starvation of the Soul, as much, if not more, than the emptiness of the stomach." Our aim for the individual members of the Society is, or should be, to enable them to make an all-round *spiritual* progress, so that our task of rendering that specific service may be achieved. Our aim should not be to help the world in spheres where our members are not competent to hold their own as helpers and assistants. If we undertake a task which is not our own, we fall into the double error of trying to do something which is not our work, while that which is our work remains undone. Our members should find their own sphere of spiritual service.[7]

The reason for this basic idea—that the TS should serve the world spiritually and perhaps less in other ways—is to be found in the root idea to which HPB gives expression:

> Right thought is a good thing, but thought alone does not count for much unless it is translated into action. There is not a single member in the Society who is not able to do *something* to aid the cause of truth and universal brotherhood; it only depends on his own will, to make that *something* an accomplished fact.[8]

In his book *Principles of Theosophical Work*, Dr. I. K. Taimni begins, "The work of the Theosophical Society can be organized efficiently only when the large majority of its members scattered throughout the world understand clearly the aims of the Society and the general principles which should guide them in planning and carrying out this work."[9]

Although much laudable work is being done every day throughout the world by individuals and organizations through caring and compassion, humility and honesty, generosity and genuineness, the Theosophical Society affords a special opportunity for working with like-minded individuals. Members and friends can join together to promote these teachings to a world in dire need of understanding in terms of our deeper nature and development. How might this manifest, and how can we as individuals contribute to the movement known as Theosophy?

Firstly, as Dr. Taimni suggests, we can contribute to the movement by becoming familiar with the language of Theosophy and the divine plan behind it. There is a purpose to the universe that becomes evident, no matter how obscure and inscrutable it appears to most of us. Theosophy describes the septenary (sevenfold) nature of existence, both human and cosmic, and how these planes interrelate. It may be helpful to use the analogy of a seven-story building, the first floor being the physical. Science has been enormously successful in describing that first floor, from the macrocosmic to the microcosmic, from the near to the far, from the ancient to the present. It focuses primarily on the physical (that which can be measured) and to a large extent is atheistic or agnostic regarding higher planes (floors) in our metaphorical building. Science and the academic arts have much to offer us, but their description is, by necessity, incomplete. Science and religion have had their differences over the years (witness Galileo), but this need not be so. Each is addressing a different domain that is understood to coexist, once we are able to comprehend the broader perspective of the multidimensional, multifaceted, multi-vibrational strata in which we exist. Theosophical texts (especially *The Secret Doctrine* by Mme. Blavatsky) describe in various perspectives more detail, not only about this occult structure but also about the purpose of its unfoldment. Dr. Taimni writes:

> As this Divine Plan which we see working in the evolution of life and form everywhere is not a mere pious belief or a philosophical speculation but as matter of fact as the working of a modern factory, it naturally requires the services of a vast army of agents who are responsible for the working of its different parts and their successful completion. These agents are the hierarchies of Angels and Adepts who from the subtler planes guide the forces of Nature and bring about those changes and adjustments in human institutions which are needed for the harmonious and efficient working of the Plan.[10]

Paramount among many, the Theosophical Society is one organization that has been created and directed to assist the higher beings with implementation of this endeavor. Understanding and purity of purpose, achieved by awakening and becoming a coworker through the harmony of intention with the divine powers of our planet, fosters effective contributions. No matter how lofty its aims, such an organization needs careful planning, clear goals, inspired adherents, efficient coordination, boundless energy, and a widespread dedication and commitment to the goals of the movement. Each effort, no matter how limited, may further this divine plan in its outer as well as inner manifestation.

The second way we as individuals might contribute to the theosophical movement could be stated as training. This applies both to the head (knowledge) and the heart (compassion). After we have a basic familiarity with theosophical principles and the divine purpose behind them, we may wish to commit to deeper study. This is the path of *jnana* (Skt.), or knowledge. This path appeals to some seekers more than others. We can train ourselves to be effective advocates for spiritual awareness and dispersion of the Ageless Wisdom in whatever relevant form may apply. The deeper our understanding, the more effective we may be in teaching and persuasion. We may be able to speak from that inner peace that is intrinsic to divine understanding. This is a never-ending process. As Mabel Collins says, "You will enter the light, but you will never touch the Flame."[11]

This training need not be only for our own development and unfoldment. As we become increasingly aware of unseen energies and entities, we can be of service in ways that may be less obvious. As we become a center for peace and harmony, not only can we influence those with whom we come into daily contact, but, through openness and meditation, we can send healing thoughts and messages. We all constantly create thoughts, some under more control than others. However, thoughts and desires can actually be manifested as forms, seen to the clairvoyant eye, consisting of colors and shapes. In Annie Besant's book *Thought Forms*, she describes two effects of thought:

> Each definite thought produces a double effect—a radiating vibration and a floating form. The thought itself appears first to clairvoyant sight as a vibration in the mental body, and this may be either simple or complex. If the thought itself is absolutely simple, there is only the one rate of vibration, and only one type of mental matter will be strongly affected. The mental body is composed of matter of several degrees of density, which we commonly arrange in classes according to the sub planes.[12]

She goes on to describe how these thought-forms can affect others in our environment or even at a distance. Unbeknownst to most of us, we are constantly intersecting with nonvisible forms of thought and emotion that influence us in complicated ways.

Beyond individual blessings, we can access higher powers that, when channeled, can have even more dramatic effects. We can send benevolent wishes to large groups of people with wishes of healing and elevation. This is a dynamic and limitless resource.

Geoffrey Hodson wrote an article for *The Theosophist* in 1933 entitled "Nature and the Gods," in which he states, "There came also an Angel visitor who 'said'. . . ."[13] The rest of the article is in quotation marks, presumably relaying the angel's statements, part of which as is follows:

> Those who serve by thought-power and the evocation of superphysical energies, seeking to heal, to inspire, to uplift, to bless, to influence the mind of their fellows in the direction of brotherhood and peace, may greatly increase their effectiveness through cooperation with the gods. They bring to such work knowledge of the operation of natural forces; capacity to direct their flow, and freedom from the limitations of time and matter and are therefore valuable allies in all altruistic work.[14]

Lastly, we turn to group work. This is useful in a variety of ways. As we recognize the unity of humanity, we realize how critical it is to be inclusive of others, co-pilgrims on this adventure of life. Most of us have various "networks" in which we operate on a day-to-day basis. We have family, friends of various origins, professional relationships, social groups, avocational clusters, political affiliations, geographical connections, and other collections of acquaintances across the spectrum. Some of the relationships are purpose driven, while others are simply for comradeship, leisure, and enjoyment. It is through interacting with other people that we can learn about and improve ourselves. We may learn the "social graces"; share mutual respect and support as well as time and ideas; and gain skill in how to advance and when to retreat and generally in how to engage in human discourse. If the group is purpose driven, it is helpful to learn organization and efficiency, task sharing, distribution of expertise, the effectiveness of personality and behavior types, and ability for real-time and retrospective evaluation. These characteristics are not easily accomplished, and many projects and businesses fail due to the want of them.

The Theosophical Society provides many opportunities to engage with other workers for common purpose. The Society is built on a hierarchical structure of local lodges and study groups. These coalesce into federations, districts, and sections, often corresponding to the national headquarters and then with the international headquarters at Adyar, India. Ideally, communication can occur among all levels of the organization and through appropriate channels in applicable situations. While the skeletal structure may consist of the international and sectional leadership, the flesh and blood of the society is the local membership affiliated through lodges and study centers. Although these groups exist in most major metropolitan areas, there are many areas without representation.

How, then, can we use our work in local groups to advance the vision of the Theosophical Society? The many answers to this question may vary by the specific location and makeup of each lodge and study center. The work may be done by supplying education through teaching, by deep reflection through meditation and similar practices, by providing altruistic community services, and by opening opportunities for those who might not be aware of the TS by sharing its concepts and tenets. Public lectures, given by local members as well as by national speakers, can be instrumental in generating interest. Study groups may be appealing to those who want to delve deeper into specific books and classes.

In addition, and beyond study centers and lodges, Dr. Taimni suggests the creation of Theosophical training centers for the specific purpose of training members for Theosophical work. The aims of these centers will be threefold: Firstly, "to provide systematic and graded teaching of Theosophy for workers and other members of the society who may wish to avail themselves of the facilities." Secondly, "to provide systematic and graded training of different kinds for workers who want to do public work in accordance with Theosophical ideals." And thirdly, "to provide instruction and practical guidance on scientific lines, for those who want to build a strong and pure character and to unfold their spiritual faculties with a view to becoming more efficient instruments in the working of the Great Plan."[15]

Of course, some of this activity could be accomplished in our existing study groups, but this threefold plan of Taimni's would formalize the specific purpose of training individual members to impact the world favorably in terms of both inner and outer aspects. It is through the mutual and harmonious efforts of theosophical workers worldwide that such an effort can have tangible and long-lasting results. It is a call to action for all dedicated workers to become effective conduits for the Masters' work at this stage in our evolutionary cycle.

Imagine, for a moment, the potential of having tens of thousands of theosophical workers in the field, striving for the highest levels of service and ethics for the benefit of humankind. Extend this vision to the potential of hundreds of thousands or even millions of workers all interconnected and holding the beliefs of unity, compassion, and fairness. The impact on the affairs of peoples around the world could be enormous socially, politically, economically, and spiritually. In addition, consider the impact that could be made with harmonization of large numbers of members connected to the higher planes. Geoffrey Hodson did this with a small number of groups in New Zealand in the 1940s. The effect, of course, cannot be exactly known. He writes about this effort in an article entitled "Cooperation between Angels and Men":

> The power of individuals mentally to influence the thought, character, and conduct of others increases by geometrical progression, we are taught, when they think together in groups. The enormous potentiality for good of groups of dedicated and trained servants of the race who deliberately use their thought power for beneficent purposes at once becomes obvious. Organized efforts for these purposes could lead to the establishment of numerous extremely potent mind "radio stations" or groups of trained thinkers. Mental work of incalculable value could be performed by such groups.[16]

In summary, theosophical work can exhibit numerous facets. We can work individually as advocates for some human need. We can develop ourselves internally in order to purify our efforts to be compassionate and selfless in our attentions. We can connect with the deeper aspects of our being and access hidden powers that can be a source of nourishment spiritually for ourselves and for those who struggle. We can work through our theosophical organizations to promote unity in all aspects of human endeavor. We can educate ourselves and others through examining comparative religion and theosophical principles. We can work in harmony with divine principles (and beings?). And we can understand unexplained laws of nature and use latent powers to implement beneficent interventions in the global community. With this knowledge, we realize that any efforts to assist in bringing forth the divine plan are not wasted but instead a true step forward in the pursuit of evolutionary progress that ultimately will manifest as significant elevation in health, relationships, and consciousness.

Mr. Arundale writes, "As even a little flame shines brightly in surrounding darkness, so does a little act of service shine out clearly amidst surrounding selfishness."[17]

15

At the Feet of the Master

Considerations

You have the making of your own future in your own hands . . . and every day you may be weaving its woof.

—MASTER KH

At the Feet of the Master, by Alcyone (J. Krishnamurti), is one of the short classics of theosophical literature. It is among what are often called the three jewels, along with *Light on the Path* and *The Voice of the Silence* (see the following chapters). Although much has been written and spoken about this little volume, I wish to add some reflections.

This slim exposition can be easily overlooked as a key to profound spiritual teaching. The language is straightforward. The concepts are multidimensional. They reflect spiritual teachings going back to antiquity, including those of the Bhagavad Gita, the Vedas, Aristotle's philosophy, and the Christian church. Spiritual writings are purported to be able to be understood on several different levels, so no matter how many times we have read, studied, and discussed the principles, they remain a fountain of teaching that is ever fresh and inspiring. To follow the precepts put forth in *At the Feet of the Master* in our practical lives is not something we can achieve in a few months or even a few years; it could generally stretch over many lifetimes and still be imperfect. However, this is not a reason to avoid gleaning the benefits of the instruction as we currently may. It is a guidebook, a manual for living, a template for those that wish to understand and aspire to higher service.

The inscription reads "To Those Who Knock." It was added by Annie Besant, who wrote the foreword to this work and was the international president of the Theosophical Society at the time of its publication. This inscription should be deeply considered before delving into the text itself. The implication is that the book was written for those in search of higher learning in the spiritual dimensions. It is clearly not intended for the general reader or the masses of humanity as yet indifferent to the golden treasures that it contains. It requires great devotion and selflessness to proceed and to gain the fruits of its wisdom. As the author states in the preface about the words therein written, "It is not enough to say that they are true and beautiful; anyone who wishes to succeed must do exactly what is said."[1] The words can be read superficially and some points observed and even thoughtfully considered, but to derive the deepest meaning, they must be truly lived. For those who knock (request entry into the secrets of the universe) there is always a price or commitment that will be asked of us. Once we are given inner knowledge, we cannot unlearn it. After seeing deeper meaning, we cannot unsee it. So, we must ask ourselves whether we are seekers of the perennial wisdom and, once we have a taste of it, what we will do with what we are given. Are we prepared to follow the teachings, however imperfectly? Will we take responsibility for our actions and our choices? We must be cautious with our intentions, devotional in our desires, and reverent in our requests.

Dr. Besant, in her foreword to this work, writes that the "greater part is a reproduction of the Master's own words; that which is not such a verbal reproduction is the Master's thought clothed in his pupil's words."[2] Charles Leadbeater, a clergyman and mentor to the young Krishnamurti, explains further in *Talks on the Path of Occultism*,

> Every night I had to take this boy in his astral body to the house of the Master, that instruction might be given to him. The Master devoted perhaps fifteen minutes each night to talking to him, but at the end of each talk, He always gathered up the main points of what He had said into a single sentence, or a few sentences, thus making an easy little summary which was repeated to the boy, so that he learnt it by heart. He remembered that summary in the morning and wrote it down.[3]

Whether the words in *At the Feet of the Master* came literally from the Master's mind to that of his pupil is intriguing but not essential to understanding the weight of the words. The message is extraordinarily simple on the surface, so that even this boy of fourteen could understand and transmit it, however complex the essential meaning and implementation.

Preceding the preface of the book is the English translation from an ancient prayer, translated from the Sanskrit:

> From the unreal lead me to the Real.
> From darkness lead me to Light.
> From death lead me to Immortality.

For what reason is this prayer included? Is it not the prayer of all seekers? How do we learn of our divine nature and realize our potential, if not through deep inquiry into ourselves and the universe? Clearly, a central theme of this treatise is to be able to distinguish between the unreal and the Real and move from the darkness into the Light. The terms *unreal* and *Real*, commonly used in Theosophy and other traditions, can be misleading, as they are used somewhat differently than in the greater society. Perhaps more accurately, the Hindu translation compares the impermanent with the Permanent. The word *Permanent* here indicates "Eternal," "Universal," "Divine," "Oneness." It applies to the immortal aspects of ourselves and of the universe. All living forms, even stars and galaxies, experience birth and death. But, as some certainly attest and believe, there are aspects that survive and cannot be destroyed. Leadbeater further explains,

> So far as we know all manifestation is impermanent; only the Unmanifested is absolutely and always the same. All manifestation, even that of the highest planes, will one day pass again into the changeless, so the difference between what we commonly call the impermanent and those higher planes is only a matter of time, which in comparison to eternity can be as nothing.[4]

So, how can we find that which is Real? How do we find the Light? Can we become Immortal, even as we are still incarnate? These are the ageless questions that Krishnamurti's small work undertakes to answer. Therefore, it is critical to listen in the deepest sense to the lessons it has to give. To consider the teachings with an open mind—and perhaps with a much more holistic part of our being than what we would classify as mind only—is vital. We must listen with our soul and spirit.

In his book, *Thoughts on "At the Feet of the Master,"* published in 1911, George Arundale, who was to become the third international president of the Theosophical Society, commented on these opening lines:

> The Sanskrit verse which precedes Alcyone's own Foreword or Introduction sums up, as it were, the whole of the teaching that any Master can give His pupil. "From the unreal lead me to the real" is the cry of all who are in earnest. More than anything else we desire to distinguish between the true and the false, between that which gives pain and that which brings joy; and in every life the lessons we learn from pain are teaching us to recognize more unerringly, and, therefore, to cast aside, those thoughts, feelings and actions which belong to the unreal, to that which separates us from the knowledge of God.[5]

Arundale goes on to say that "it is not enough to know with the mind, you must know with the heart" in order to distinguish the unreal from the Real.[6]

Discrimination (Skt. *viveka*) is the first qualification, for it is necessary to choose what might have value in our lives and purpose in our pursuits. Do we aspire to see meaning beyond our superficial world? Are the common goals of fame, wealth, and power admirable and enduring values for our sense of self, or do we seek a more moral and unifying worldview?

Discrimination, by its very nature, requires us to assign value to a particular object or activity. We often do so mentally, in a process we would term *judgment*. After evaluating a particular situation and weighing various factors, usually colored by our own knowledge and experience, we assign a relative value to a course of action and weigh it against other possibilities. This exercise, of course, is imperfect, as we can never obtain all the relevant information or know the absolute outcome of a particular choice.

Another way of evaluating choices is to use the intuitive process. This largely (or entirely) bypasses the intellectual aspect of our assessment. We must be cautious to differentiate between what is called *lower intuition* (inclination or "gut feeling") and the *higher intuition* process. In the first paragraph of *At the Feet of the Master*, Krishnamurti notes that discrimination must determine whether the inquirer will enter these teachings at all, referred to in this work and many spiritual writings as "the path."[7] He uses the somewhat simplistic concept of being "on God's side."[8] This can be seen metaphorically as working toward virtues in our lives (and in the universe) such as generosity, honesty, and justice. Annie Besant would describe it as being in harmony with the evolutionary forces of development. Krishnamurti notes that the basic determination between right and wrong is inherent in this choice, but these black-and-white decisions are rarely what we struggle over, and we need to be more nuanced in our discrimination. He writes about distinguishing the important from the unimportant, the useful from the useless, the true from the false, and the selfless from the selfish. But more than that, we need to distinguish between the more important and the less important, the more useful and the less useful, the more true and the less true, and the more selfless and the less selfless. We frequently face competing wants and needs, and to see clearly that which is more aligned with the "Real" is not always easy, at least for the novice.

Krishnamurti also refers to our constitutional makeup of many bodies, which can often be in conflict. We can identify at times primarily with our physical needs, our emotional needs, or our mental needs. Each sense of self is fighting for superiority. He writes that we are none of these aspects, but we need to care for each of them meticulously, direct them, and realize that our sense of self is separate from them. Our lower bodies must be reined in so that they can properly serve us when needed for a given task. These bodies can be wild and impulsive and need to be "broken," as a horse is, into obedience. However, just as a horse cannot be optimally responsive if it has been mistreated, we must treat the lower bodies with care, respect, and nourishment.

Krishnamurti addresses each of these bodies in turn. He advises that we should study that which is most useful to help others: "Work patiently at your studies, not that others may think you wise, not even that you may have the happiness of being wise, but because only the wise person can be wisely helpful."[9] Good intentions are not enough. We must find a way to be useful to our fellow beings, and that often begins with knowledge. But even knowledge is not adequate. It must be combined with compassion and love in order to generate wisdom. These qualities are in much need in the world today.

Regarding knowledge, Krishnamurti notes that "you must distinguish between truth and falsehood; you must learn to be true all through, in thought and word and deed."[10] He elaborates on of each of these aspects, particularly thought, as it is the basis of speech and action. If thoughts can be true to our deeper nature, then it is more likely that true speech and true action will follow. Further, in instructing us to discriminate between the selfish and the unselfish, he admonishes us that selfishness has many forms and can often arise in a subtle manner. One method to avoid selfishness is always to make the thought of helping others central in ourselves. We need also to learn to see the best in each person and thing, for the divine Life is there, too.

Krishnamurti says, "Learn how to arouse that in them, learn how to appeal to that in them, and so shall you save your brothers and sisters from wrong."[11] Geoffrey Hodson writes that the ability to see Divinity in others and help them along their spiritual path is the greatest of *siddhis* (Skt. powers) for the evolving human:

> Simply put, the true guide, philosopher and friend endeavours to put people's feet on the right road, and when they stray, steers them

> back again to their true course. This, from the point of view of value to humanity, is the greatest of the occult powers or *Siddhis,* one to be most highly sought for and prized, *wisely to guide when guidance is sought.* Whilst all ministrations and charities are valuable, it is necessary and it is best to set people on the right road at all levels at which they are capable of living—spiritual, intellectual, personal and physical.[12]

Desirelessness (Skt. *vairagya*) is a word that is often chosen for the second qualification, but this can be misleading to those who may not be familiar with this terminology. A literal meaning would be lack of all desire, suggesting passivity or ennui, in which state all preference and commitment have evaporated. But this meaning is clearly not the intention of the translation. The implication instead is of a freedom from desire in the lower nature that would bias one in a particular direction. It has to do with an impartiality, perhaps akin to the Lady Justice symbol of Roman mythology.

Another translation for this qualification is the "uncolored mind." This is more suggestive of the quality of neutrality and the ability to look at our world without personal filters that would distort the images in a prejudicial way. This part on desirelessness is the shortest section in this book and yet one of its most challenging. We often define ourselves by our desires, values, and judgments. Who are we, indeed, without desires? Krishnamurti writes that for those who meet the Master, all desires die except "the desire to be like him."[13] We must obtain the ability to forget ourselves, or selfish desire will bind us. Annie Besant notes that this assertion of Krishnamurti's recalls the verse in the Bhagavad Gita: "The objects of sense, but not the taste for them, turn away from the abstemious dweller in the body; and even taste turneth away from him after the Supreme is seen."[14]

The author writes of the desire to see the fruits of our action. We want to see results, and we want others to see them, too, but this desire colors our mind and actions. Krishnamurti writes that "you must give yourself to the service of the world because you love it and cannot help giving yourself to it."[15] It is the joy of service that we must find instead of being attached to specific outcomes, for we know them not, and they might come much later or in ways that we cannot imagine. He emphasizes, as well, that we should not desire and pursue psychic powers, for they will come in due course when most needed, when we are mature enough and can utilize them in unselfish ways. We must never wish to shine or appear clever in daily life. He reminds us that the four qualifications often given are "to know, to dare, to will, and to be silent; and the last of the four is the hardest of them all."[16] Any effort to seek self-importance is to be observed carefully, assessed, and modified to omit selfishness. There should be caution when interfering with the affairs of others, unless we have direct responsibility to do so, for it is likely we have an incomplete understanding of that person's needs as it applies to their own spiritual path. Certainly, we can give compassionate and constructive advice when we are asked. We have a responsibility to intervene when we witness cruelty or injustice, even if we are at risk of harm ourselves.

We easily become conditioned to our culture, our experience, and our aptitudes. This conditioning creates filters to our worldview that we must overcome. Later in his life, Krishnamurti published a book entitled *Freedom from the Known*, which addresses similar concepts.[17] We may be aware of how our individual history creates certain modifications of our thinking, but many of us are not. For this reason, it can be very useful to bypass the filters of our physical, astral, and mental bodies and relate directly to the outer world from the highest aspects of our inner selves.

John Algeo, in his talk on *At the Feet of the Master*,[18] makes the interesting observation that there is an inherent paradox, or "catch 22," regarding the first two qualities described in this work: In order to have true discrimination, one would need true desirelessness, and in order to have true desirelessness, one would need to have true discrimination. Can we develop these qualities separately, or are they forever intertwined? Can we have one absent the other? He shows that the solution to this quandary is contained in the book's last two parts, entitled "Good Conduct" and "Love."

In part 3, concerning the qualification of "Good Conduct," Krishnamurti lists six points requiring attention: self-control regarding the mind, self-control in action, tolerance, cheerfulness, one-pointedness, and confidence. These qualities are translations from the Sanskrit again, and, as is true in all translations, do not necessarily capture the entire meaning of the original. For instance, Annie Besant feels that for the Sanskrit word *uparati*, "cessation" may be a better translation than "tolerance," but she also notes that cessation of criticism and discontent do lead to tolerance.[19] The fourth quality—*titiksha*—she had understood as indicating endurance, but she adds that clearly "a person who has endurance will necessarily be cheerful."[20] Further, she suggests that *samadhana*, translated as "one-pointedness," can also be translated as "balance."[21] Lastly, while the quality of *shraddha* is translated as "confidence," an alternative could be "faith."[22] As Krishnamurti states in the text, the translations he provides were given to him through his teacher (often ascribed to the Master Koot Hoomi), but it is likely that no one English word can capture the depth and breadth of the original Sanskrit. This narrative, however, describes the essential qualities.

The first—self-control of the mind—may be the most difficult to achieve. The mind is mercurial and often seems to have a will of its own. In the Bhagavad Gita, Arjuna states that "the mind is restless, Krishna, impetuous, self-willed, hard to train: to master the mind seems as difficult as to master the mighty winds" (BG 6:34). Krishna answers,

> The mind is indeed restless, Arjuna: it is indeed hard to train. But by constant practice and by freedom from passions the mind in truth can be trained. When the mind is not in harmony, this divine communion is hard to attain; but the man whose mind is in harmony attains it, if he knows and if he strives. (BG 6:35–36)

And Bishop Charles Leadbeater, in *Talks on the Path*, states, "Control of temper is precisely one of the things which are difficult for us. . . . Our victory is so much the greater because of these difficulties, the overcoming of which shows that we have progressed further in strength of will than has the monk or the hermit."[23]

Many authors, both classic and modern, spiritual and popular, have addressed the control of the mind. Examples include J. Allen in *As a Man Thinketh*, Annie Besant in *Thought Power*, and *The Cloud of Unknowing* by an unknown Christian monk. Various spiritual disciplines and mental exercises might be helpful to an individual at a specific time and place. Krishnamurti suggests that we strive for a calm mind, becoming unperturbed by bodily sensations, environmental irritations, mental obsessions, and other distractions that keep us from our center. He states that "the calm mind means also courage, so that you may face without fear the trials and difficulties of the path; it means also steadiness, so that you may make light of the troubles which come into everyone's life, and avoid the incessant worry over little things in which many people spend most of their time."[24] He notes that we should shun suffering over losses, pride, sadness, and depression as well as idle wandering. By constantly focusing on good purposes and emphasizing selflessness, the mind can become disciplined.

Krishnamurti goes on to describe well and with examples the other qualities relevant to good conduct. Their daily application, though, is more challenging. Can any of us say that we are tolerant and cheerful every day and in all situations? Do we demonstrate one-pointedness in all our efforts? Do we have confidence and trust in ourselves and in the divine angels (or in the Masters) that help show us our way? Have we expunged all our doubts and hesitations? Is our faith unshakable? Do we know that we will make the right decisions now and in the future? These qualities and their descriptions are useful reminders and contain practical suggestions that we can incorporate into our daily living and the human interactions we all experience. It is an ideal to which we can aspire. At times we will fail to meet it, but we can rise again with determination that we can improve ourselves and our world by our continued awareness of and integration toward that which is perfect.

In part 4 of *At the Feet of the Master*, Krishnamurti notes that, of all the qualifications discussed, "love is the most important, for if it is strong enough in us, it forces us to acquire all the rest, and all the rest without it would never be sufficient."[25] Intuitively, it seems evident that love (or compassion), the highest expression of devotion, is necessary to incorporate into our attitude and behavior as a necessary component for spiritual progress.

The chosen term *love* can be easily misunderstood, however. Krishnamurti writes that often this qualification "is translated as an intense desire for liberation from the round of births and deaths and for union with God. But to put it in that way sounds selfish and gives only part of the meaning."[26] As these concepts come from ancient Hindu texts and are translated from Sanskrit words, the full meaning is often difficult to transmit. Leadbeater, in his commentary, notes that the translations Krishnamurti gives are departures from ordinary ones and that "of all those departures this one is the most daring—the presentation of *mumukshatva* as Love."[27] Leadbeater explores the Sanskrit root, explaining that the more literal translation might be "the state of desire for release," which has the same root that forms the word *moksha*, often translated as "deliverance" as well as "liberation."[28] Krishnamurti's next passage transmitted from the Master reads:

> It is not so much desire as *will*, resolve, determination. To produce its result, this resolve must fill your whole nature, so as to leave no room for any other feeling. It is indeed the will to be one with God, not in order that you may escape from weariness and suffering, but in order that because of your deep love you may act with God and as God does. Because God is Love, you, if you would become one with God, must be filled with perfect unselfishness and love also.[29]

This expansion of the interpretation of love as the desire to "act with God" and to "become one with God" has a different nuance to it. The choice of the word *God* appears to be a likely intentional oversimplification, as each tradition, and in fact each human being, has a slightly different understanding of the word and the concept it is meant to convey. Many other words could be substituted, depending on the reader's preference, such as the *Universal*, the *Divine*, *Logos*, *Oneness*, and *Light*. In this understanding, the intense desire for liberation can sound selfish as it indicates personal achievement, which cannot be consistent with divine love. Geoffrey Hodson, in a short passage entitled "Purity of Heart," states that

> Only he who is free of even the slightest thought of reward, material or spiritual, in return for his labours can ever tread to its end the steep and narrow way which leadeth to eternal life.

> Blessed indeed are the pure of heart, for not only shall they see and know that God which is their highest self, but they shall bestow their powers of vision upon their fellow men.[30]

In order for us to love unselfishly, Krishnamurti instructs us "first, to do no hurt" and then lists three practices that are very damaging to love: they are "sins which work more harm than all else in the world—gossip, cruelty, and superstition—because they are sins against love."[31] While these characteristics are not necessarily illegal, Krishnamurti likely chose them because they are detrimental, painful, and common. He addresses each of them in turn, categorically and with illustrations. Each such negative practice must be carefully guarded against in the effort of purification as we attempt to expand and elevate the love we hold. If we strive to maintain a deep respect for all life and recognize the unity of manifestation, then it may be easier to avert impulses to participate in these behaviors.

After describing "these three great crimes," Krishnamurti goes on to say:

> But not only must you thus refrain from evil, but you must also be active in doing good. You must be so filled with the intense desire of service that you are ever on the watch to render it to all around you—not to human beings alone, but even to animals and plants. You must render it in small things every day, that the habit may be formed, so that you may not miss the rare opportunity when the great thing offers itself to be done. For if you yearn to be one with God, it is not for your own sake; it is that you may be a channel through which God's love may flow to reach your fellow human beings.[32]

In his commentary on this passage, George Arundale amplifies the phrase "intense desire of service" and states that it

> is to be found the most powerful qualification for admission to the Master's training school. The keener the intensity, the surer the admission, and one who, as it were, palpitates with an intensity of desire of service and who is, on that account, ready to go anywhere and do anything, is on the threshold of admission.[33]

Arundale interprets the Master's message as conveying that love and service of humanity are indistinguishable. Love of the Universal is therefore love of all manifestation, for each living being contains and reflects the divine nature of the Oneness of life.

It now becomes clear that all of these qualifications—discrimination, desirelessness, good conduct, and love—although listed and described separately, are intertwined, mutually enhancing, and inseparable for those who wish to develop and purify themselves on the path of spiritual evolution. Each one of us is a bud waiting to blossom. What ingredients are necessary to allow this natural unfolding to occur? Krishnamurti's small signpost, easily overlooked perhaps, contains profound teachings, reflecting those that have been transmitted throughout the ages, and brings to us this Ageless Wisdom. Each rereading and reflective understanding can stimulate inspiration in our daily lives.

Krishnamurti ends his instruction by stating that "the wisdom which enables you to help, the will which directs the wisdom, the love which inspires the will—these are your qualifications. Will, wisdom, and love are the three aspects of the Logos; and you, who wish to enroll yourselves to serve God, must show forth these aspects in the world."[34]

Summary of Concepts

Sanskrit	*Viveka*	*Vairagya*	*Shatsampatti*	*Mumukshutva*
Qualification in *At the Feet of the Master*	Discrimination	Desirelessness	Good conduct	Love
Alternative	Discernment	Uncolored mind	Correct living	Desire for liberation
Method	Wise choice	Uncondi-tioned state	Constant practice	Self-Knowledge
Aristotelian quality	Prudence	Temperance	Fortitude	Justice
Hindu texts (added by author)	Adi Shankara's *Vivekachu-damani* by Shankara-charya	Patanjali's *Yoga Sutras*	Amritabindu Upanishad	Vedas, Sri Karapatra Swami's *Advaita Bodha Deepika*

Figure 3. Summary of Concepts. Source: John Algeo, "Guideposts for Living: At the Feet of the Master," video found on YouTube.

16

LIGHT ON THE PATH

CONSIDERATIONS

So now, you my chela, choose and grasp your own destiny.

—MASTER MORYA

Light on the Path is a short work by Mabel Collins, a member of the Theosophical Society in England when she wrote it in 1885, only ten years after the founding of the Theosophical Society in New York City. The ideas and some of the language in the work are said to be quite ancient, its purpose being to reintroduce these precepts to the world and particularly the West.

The book is divided into two parts (followed by a short section on karma not addressed here). Each part presents enumerated rules for leading a spiritual life, the principal ones rendered in bold type, the others considered commentaries. Interspersed among the rules are longer notes of further explanation.

Annie Besant states that the text

> was given to the Western world by Master Hilarion, one of the great Teachers belonging to the White [not meaning ethnicity] Lodge—a Master who played a great part in the Gnostic and Neoplatonic movements, one of the great persons who made attempts to keep Christianity alive. . . . He obtained the book as we have it, without the notes, from the Venetian Master, one of the great Teachers whom H.P.B. spoke of as Chohans.[1]

She further writes that all the rules it sets forth, "except the thirty short aphorisms, were written by the Chohan [an elevated Master], who gave it to the Master Hilarion."[2] So, it is clear at the outset that this short guidebook has at least three authors and likely many more, as it is a manifestation of timeless instruction to aspirants through the ages. The more ancient version of this book consists of only thirty short sentences. In Mabel Collins's later version, a portion of the "rules" are ancient; the Chohan (sometimes spoken of as the "Venetian Master") added some clarifying rules and comments, and some further notes were added by Master Hilarion.

Collins's subtitle for the book is "a treatise written for the personal use of those who are ignorant of the Eastern Wisdom, and who desire to enter within its influence."[3] She also wrote many commentaries on the subject, including *Through the Gates of Gold*, published in 1887, where she delves much more deeply into the inner meaning of the original publication.

Part 1 opens, as is true of many spiritual texts, with words that are not casual or incidental. It is critical to read, reflect on, consider, and understand them before proceeding, for they give context to the entire communication. Here we read, "These rules are written for all disciples: Attend you to them."[4] While this statement may appear to be simple and introductory, we must examine it more closely.

The author uses the term *rules*. Why would we pay attention to new rules to follow? A definition of a rule is a "prescribed guide for conduct or action." Rules are stricter than suggestions and often seen as requirements, the infraction of which, if observed, results in consequences, potentially punitive. Reading further, we are told that these rules are "for all disciples." A disciple is a follower or learner in any school, especially a spiritual one, and an accepted pupil in many spiritual traditions. Hence, Collins is saying, these rules are not for all, but only for those who seek deeper spiritual wisdom and instruction for self-purification. The related word, *discipline*, implies obedience to rules in a code of behavior inherent to the activity that the participant chooses.

The second sentence amplifies the first. "Attend you to them" emphasizes the importance of understanding and following the rules that are to be presented. They are not given lightly and are of a critical nature, requiring attention of the deepest intuition and adherence. It is proper to pause, as one might at a precipice, before taking the next step.

The reader might be anxious to see what these rules contain and anticipate gleaning the instruction that they provide. Before they begin, however, there are four apparently simple declarations, each beginning with the word *before*:

> Before the eyes can see, they must be incapable of tears. Before the ear can hear, it must have lost its sensitiveness. Before the voice can speak in the presence of the Masters, it must have lost the power to wound. Before the soul can stand in the presence of the Masters, its feet must be washed in the blood of the heart.[5]

Suddenly, we are at a full stop. This small paragraph contains requirements that the reader must fulfill in preparation for the proper instruction. The study of these requirements could fill multiple chapters, and accomplishing them would likely require multiple lifetimes. They cannot be passed by easily, and the understanding of them cannot be superficial. Mabel Collins herself, in commenting on her book, states that "the first four aphorisms of *Light on the Path* refer entirely to astral development. This development must be accomplished to a certain extent—that is to say must be fully entered upon—before the remainder of the book is really intelligible, except to the intellect; in fact, before it can be read as a practical, not a metaphysical treatise."[6] Additionally, she writes that the "four truths written on the first page . . . refer to the trial initiation of the would-be occultist. Until he has passed it, he cannot even reach to the latch of the gate which admits to knowledge."[7] Therefore, we should consider the import of this message, one sentence at a time:

"*Before the eyes can see they must be incapable of tears.*" This declaration can be mystifying if taken literally. Should we conform ourselves to be incapable of compassion, empathy, and love and impervious to pain? Sight is receptive (as, we will discover, is hearing) and indicates perception, knowledge, judgment, and discrimination. If we are to think clearly, we must have discernment and dispassion, uncolored by bias and prejudice in our world and in ourselves. Here, tears can represent the emotional self (astral), the lower body that can contain undue sentimentality. It can also represent impurities in our vision, for when we are tearful it is much more difficult to see clearly, both literally and figuratively. The plural of the term, *eyes*, can be interpreted as having one represent the Higher Self and one the lower mind (manas). For optimal vision and depth perception, persons benefit from having two eyes at slightly different locations brought into conjugate gaze. The metaphor can be extended in that when our mental vision from our lower and higher selves is brought into focus through alignment, our knowledge is enhanced.

Annie Besant states that

> this and the following three statements are intended for two classes of disciples. In the first class are those who are on the probationary path, and therefore being taught to get rid of all that we speak of as the personality; these preliminary instructions are intended to show them that they must begin by eliminating the lower self. In the second class are those who are already initiated. Something more is demanded from them.[8]

"*Before the ear can hear, it must have lost its sensitiveness.*" Again, we recoil. Do we not want to gain sensitivity? Do we not wish to be aware of others' needs and wishes? Do we not wish to understand more precisely our environment and ourselves?

We must think in spiritual terms. Hearing is often invoked as a symbol when discussing deeper intuition. How can we "hear" our deepest nature? How can we "listen" to the voice of the silence? Mrs. Besant writes that "the disciple must become entirely indifferent to the opinions of others about himself, as far as his own feelings are concerned. . . . Yet at the same time he must not be indifferent to the opinions of others as they affect the people who hold them."[9] This statement can be more broadly thought of as gaining the capacity to stay focused on our higher purpose and intuition without being distracted by the lower sensations. Minor sounds (as well as sights, smells, and even thoughts) can be distracting and divert our attention from our higher purpose and intuition. Here, the singular is used to emphasize the need of our entire being to be focused on the divine aspect of our nature and the wisdom of our intuition.

"*Before the voice can speak in the presence of the Masters, it must have lost its power to wound.*" This third declaration is expressive. Speech represents creativity, thought, feeling, and action, and it can be used for healing or for injury. We can in many ways define ourselves by our speech and how it is used. It is how we express our greatest wishes and our darkest fears. It connects us to the past and future as well as to others. In order to speak "in the presence of the Masters," which can also be thought of as in a pure form or in the presence of our higher selves, our speech must no longer be able to cause pain. We can achieve this goal initially through efforts at self-regulation, avoiding unkind, needless, and hurtful speech. As we progress with purification of our lower feelings and thoughts, we will no longer have the inclination to speak negatively about others, for those thoughts will have been expunged.

Charles Leadbeater comments,

> Anyone who wishes to approach the Master must already have given up the *desire* to wound others by his speech. But there is still the possibility of wounding unintentionally and unconsciously, on account of want of sensitiveness. As we go further and raise our consciousness to a higher level, we shall more and more understand how things strike others.[10]

"*Before the soul can stand in the presence of the Masters, its feet must be washed in the blood of the heart.*" What is the meaning here? Again, the action required is expressive: to stand. The presence of the Masters again refers to purification and being in an elevated state. But what of "its feet must be washed in the blood of the heart"? Mrs. Besant comments that it "has to do with the teaching of sacrifice, which still appears in different religions in various forms, though they have generally lost its true meaning."[11] The blood of the heart in spirituality often represents suffering, pain, and experience. Through the consequences (karma) of many experiences of numerous lives, one gains maturity and knowledge, developed through the difficulties of incarnation. The novice cannot expect to be able to stand firmly in this situation due to inexperience and naïveté. It is only through learning life's lessons, generally through pain and remorse, that one can ascend beyond lower passions and be worthy of attention from divine elements.

Joy Mills, in her book *Entering on the Sacred Way*, discusses *Light on the Path* in considerable depth. She compares the four statements we have just reviewed this way:

> These four functions, expounded in the Jungian school of depth psychology, are thinking and feeling (as rational functions) and intuition and sensation (as nonrational functions). . . . They concern a need to "perfect" the manner in which consciousness functions in relation to the world about us (including objects, situations, and people) so as to ensure our wholeness (or, to use a Jungian term, to help us achieve full "individuation").[12]

A passage early in part 2 of the work gives an additional clue to the four opening aphorisms: "To be able to stand is to have confidence; to be able to hear is to have opened the doors of the soul; to be able to see is to have attained perception; to be able to speak is to have attained the power of helping others."[13] More insights can likely be found, but we will move on to the body of this teaching.

As we look at the rules in the first section, it is usually beneficial to examine them as groups rather than individual directives. Of these rules, six of the first seven—with the exception of the fourth, being a commentary that I will address below—begin with the words "Kill out":

1. Kill out ambition.
2. Kill out desire of life.
3. Kill out desire of comfort.
5. Kill out all sense of separateness.
6. Kill out desire for sensation.
7. Kill out the hunger for growth.[14]

This directive may seem quite abrupt to those reading the work for the first time. As we enter the spiritual path, we seek to purify and expand ourselves, and learning that we must "kill out" is disharmonious at best, regardless of the object of this potential violent act. However, killing and overcoming obstacles is common in mythology and spiritual writings. Metaphorically, we must wrestle with demons, slay dragons, and vanquish monsters of every description. We must destroy the limits of our lower nature in order to reach the higher. Joy Mills expresses it this way:

> The first adventures encountered by the mythic hero usually involve either an actual or ritual killing of enemies who embody qualities that would prevent the achievement of the goal. These enemies may be vices that would deflect or distract the hero-soul from its purpose. In some mythologies the hero is called on to perform sacrifices in which the victims are either animals or other human beings, but in some manner they are symbolic and represent a projection of qualities or tendencies within the aspirant (the candidate for initiation) which must be slain. All such mythologies portray the psychological necessity of removing from the personal nature those elements that prevent the light of the Self from breaking through into full consciousness.[15]

The first eight rules are about the sense of self and self-preservation. They are essential to the development and maintenance of individuality. Human beings are strongly motivated to establish themselves in the world, and historically they quest for the objects of ambition, status, and comfort as driven individuals in their own evolution and that of society.

In his book of commentary, *Seek Out the Way,* Rohit Mehta equates the first three rules—kill out ambition, desire for life, and desire of comfort—with our desire for success, continuity, and security, respectively. Rules 5, 6, and 7—kill out all sense of separateness, desire for sensation, and the hunger for growth—are a higher spiral of the first three, this time in the reverse order. Therefore, ambition equates with a hunger for growth, desire for life equates with a desire for sensation, and the desire for comfort equates with a sense of separateness. Mehta states that "this is obviously to show to the neophyte that success, continuity and security lead to frustration at all levels, that there are limitations beyond which conscious effort cannot go."[16]

Three of the first seven rules admonish us to "kill out" desire of or for something. Yet our desires are integral to our sense of self and define who we are, so why are we being told to eliminate desire? Is it only certain types of desire that we should avoid? It is not the action that the author counsels us to reject. The commentary labeled number 4 helps to clarify the meaning: "Work as those work who are ambitious. Respect life as do those who desire it. Be happy as those who live for happiness."[17] So, it appears that it is not the activity that is prohibited but the motivation. We can work as those do who are ambitious and yet not be ambitious ourselves. We can work arduously without being attached to the result. We can work to lift humanity but not for our own recognition or benefit. As Krishna says to Arjuna in the Bhagavad Gita (3:26), "Let not the wise disturb the mind of the unwise in their selfish work. Let him, working with devotion, show them the joy of good work."

The passage for the commentary labeled 4 in *Light on the Path* goes on to explain that the source of evil (here, selfishness) lives in the heart and can only be killed out by the strong and by great suffering. It cannot be removed by indulgence or suppression. In the end, we are told, however, how to escape this burden of pain and misery. It is by living "neither in the present nor the future, but in the Eternal. This giant weed cannot flower there; this blot upon existence is wiped out by the very atmosphere of eternal thought."[18]

How do we find this Eternal? These lessons attempt to show us the way. We must see ourselves as part of all humanity, in fact, of all existence. We cannot separate ourselves from others and protect ourselves from the world. We cannot judge that some are unworthy of our attention or our sympathy. All men and women are brothers and sisters and should be regarded with respect and compassion. We cannot expect to surpass or "outrun" them. We may be quick to judge another, but we may share that state sooner than we know. Self-righteousness is shortsighted and should be avoided. It is only with humility that we can begin to expand our consciousness.

It is important to note that rules 2, 3, and 6 instruct us to kill out *desire* of life, *desire* for comfort, and *desire* for sensation, respectively. These rules do not, however, recommend killing out life, comfort, and sensation themselves. Pablo Sender elaborates on this point in part 2 of his talks on the subject.[19] We need to learn from life, sensation, and, to some degree, comfort. Experiences in life are critical to our learning and evolution. It is the *desire* in the form of attachment that can become problematic. Once we are attached to life, comfort, and sensation, this attachment distorts our vision, thoughts, and activities. To what ends will we go to seek out these three values? What compromises might we make? What ethical boundaries might we breach? We may sacrifice our neutrality or dispassion (Skt. *vairayga*) to gratify these needs. Sensation is unavoidable in life, but our desire for it can be controlled.

The next set of six rules—from the ninth to the fifteenth, with the exception of the twelfth—appear paradoxical, not only to the first six but within themselves:

9. Desire only that which is within you.
10. Desire only that which is beyond you.

11. Desire only that which is unattainable.
13. Desire power ardently.
14. Desire peace fervently.
15. Desire possessions above all.[20]

After claiming we should kill out ambition and desire for several aspects of life comes a hard turn telling us what we *should* desire. The first set of three here—rules 9 through 11—note that our desires should be only for that which is within us, that which is beyond us, and that which is unattainable. These statements are confusing on their surface. Why should we desire only what is already within us? And to desire what is beyond us appears vague and generally unhelpful. Finally, to desire that which is unattainable would appear to be fruitless and frustrating. How can we reconcile these directives with the previous ones to enhance our understanding? Many spiritual texts use paradox to hint at esoteric truths. We must examine the deeper meaning of these words.

The second set of three directives in this section indicate specifically what we should desire and how intensely. Ostensibly, they advocate for power, peace, and possessions, which in a literal sense supports materialism. As Rohit Mehta points out, "These rules seem absolutely contrary to the instructions given in the earlier part of the book. By themselves [they] seem to point to the path of black magic. . . . These rules seem to be bringing back success, continuity and security after rejecting them in the earlier part of the book."[21]

But when we read the explanatory passages that comprise rules 12 and 16, each of which elaborates on the prior three rules, the messages become tempered. The twelfth entry (a commentary) begins, "For within you is the light of the world—the only light that can be shed upon the path. If you are unable to perceive it within you, it is useless to look for it elsewhere."[22] Thus, it becomes clear that the author is not being contradictory but rather speaking to the indefinable quality of which we are part. Joy Mills, in her commentary, notes that

> these six rules point to the unfoldment of the higher triad of our nature and to the qualities that characterize the higher triad. The elimination of the elements in our personality (the lower quaternity as it has been called) that bind us to sensate experience releases energy (desire) which may now be directed toward the attainment of faculties that are inherent in the individuality.[23]

It is therefore useful to understand that the first set of six rules pertain to the lower nature—physical body, personality, emotions and lower mind—while the second set of six direct us to help find our higher nature, which is more difficult to locate and describe. It is deep within ourselves (metaphorically speaking) while simultaneously being far beyond us. We wish to reach it, but it is "unattainable," at least by the lower aspects of self. The well-known conclusion to the twelfth entry states that "you will enter the light, but you will never touch the Flame."[24] This is explained by some authors as the heart of universal consciousness. Leadbeater notes that "to whatever height we raise our consciousness, into whatever ineffable glories we can rise, we always see something more glorious still beyond. The Flame ever recedes."[25] He then quotes the Lord Buddha, "Veil after veil will lift, but there must be veil after veil behind."[26]

Rule 17 warrants special mention: "Seek out the way."[27] It appears astoundingly simple and yet has untold layers of complexity. Fortunately, the explanatory note adds a great deal of depth and also indicates a link with rule 17 in part 2. The note states, in part, "When the final secret of this great lesson is told, in it is opened the mystery of the new way—a path which leads out of all human experience and which is utterly beyond human perception or imagination."[28] This is an indication of the power of our potential and the sacredness of this teaching.

Rule 17 is also in a set of three (with a fourth as commentary). We are then told to seek the way by "retreating within" (rule 18) and by "advancing boldly without" (rule 19).[29] This again apparent contradiction can be interpreted in different ways. It may suggest the difference between meditation and activity (Joy Mills), between living a reclusive life or a life in the world (Pablo Sender), or between a subjective existence and one of pure objectivity (Rohit Metha). Both the contemplative life (retreating within) and the active life in the world (advancing boldly without) are necessary in different ways and at different times for spiritual progress and ultimately connecting to the Divine.

This Divinity has no physical location, and allusions to it are not literal. The language here is meant to stimulate and inspire, giving us a sense of the Eternal. We will have to nurture our connection to our higher consciousness, often dormant and unrecognized but inherent nonetheless.

Part 1 concludes with rule 21: "Look for the flower to bloom in the silence that follows the storm: not till then."[30] The explanatory note is helpful here but still mystical and metaphorical. The deep peace and silence can come only after the battle has been waged; only after the storm has raged can the lessons have been learned. The secret must be fought for, and, when hard won, the peace of wisdom is obtained; the deep silence of Unity is felt. The strength of immortality is known. The yearning of aspiration is satisfied. This pause is a temporary one, however, of undetermined length, for further battles await. There are more lessons to be learned.

Part 2 of the book is often not emphasized as much; some note that it is reserved for disciples. However, wherever we are on the path, these lessons can be useful, as a spiritual journey is not linear but has many twists and turns, cycles and spirals. The second paragraph opens with, "You who are now a disciple—able to stand, able to hear, able to see, able to speak . . ."[31] But whether the use of the term *disciple* is literal is not known and perhaps not necessary to know now. The author states, "Go to the Hall of Learning and read what is written there for you."[32] This directive is described in the note as entering "the state in which learning becomes possible. Then will many words be written there for you, and written in fiery letters for you to read easily."[33]

The first three rules of the second section are then given:

1. Stand aside in the coming battle, and though thou fightest be not thou the warrior.
2. Look for the Warrior and let him fight in thee.
3. Take his orders for battle and obey them.[34]

In "battle," we are to recuse ourselves and look for the Warrior (the Higher Self), letting it fight and taking its orders. This military metaphor appears belligerent initially, but it describes the battle of life and the struggle between the attachments of the lower self and the illumined equipoise of the higher.

Entry 4 then states that when we surrender our physical and psychological wishes to the "Warrior," then "it will be impossible for you to strike one blow amiss."[35] Yet it is up to each one of us to find our warrior during the battle we are all living, for it will not find us. Once found, it is forever available, forever willing to advocate for our cause, if it is pure and genuine. "He is yourself, yet you are but finite and liable to error. He is eternal and is sure. He is eternal truth."[36]

The text in part 2 makes another turn in rule 5: "Listen to the song of life."[37] The note advises us to look deeply for it, not once or twice, but three times. So obscurely it might be hidden that our greatest efforts in seeking it may seem to fail.

What is the song for which we must listen? It has many names, including the Divine Seed and the Voice of the Silence. Joy Mills notes, "That primordial sound or primordial vibration has been called *Nada*, a term used by Blavatsky in *The Voice of the Silence* to signify the 'Soundless Sound' of the essential Self."[38] Dr. Taimni writes, "There is according to Occultism a mysterious integrated state of vibration from which all possible kinds of vibrations can be derived by a process of differentiation. This is called *Nada* in Sanskrit."[39] And, as the Chohan has written, "Life itself has speech and is never silent. And its utterance is not, as you that are deaf may suppose, a cry; it is a song."[40]

The next set of rules in the second part, numbers 9 through 12, are gentle and encouraging:

9. Regard earnestly all the life that surrounds you.
10. Learn to look intelligently into the hearts of men.
11. Regard most earnestly your own heart.[41]

Notice that the order of direction—to look at "all the life that surrounds you," "into the hearts of men," and into "your own heart"—begins at the outer and progresses to the inner. In her commentary, Joy Mills suggests the reverse may be more apt: "The distortion comes from our own prejudices, our own cultural and social conditioning, and all the veils that we have made and thrown about ourselves to obscure right perception. For that reason, we might reverse the order of the rules and begin with who and what we are in our present state."[42]

Following rule 11, the Chohan's commentary in number 12 reads, "For through your own heart comes the one light which can illuminate life and make it clear to your eyes."[43] About this statement Charles Leadbeater writes, "Unless you recognize God within yourself you can never find Him outside. . . . Your Master himself cannot give you that light, though he can help you to awaken it within yourself; it must come from within, and it *is* within, whether you know it or not."[44]

After the pause following the note for rule 13, Mabel Collins writes that the remaining notes are for "those who can read what I have written with the inner as well as the outer sense."[45] Next are three entries advising that we inquire regarding secrets:

15. Inquire of the earth, the air, and the water of the secrets they hold for you.
16. Inquire of the Holy Ones of the earth of the secrets they hold for you.
17. Inquire of the inmost, the One, of its final secret, which it holds for you through the ages.[46]

What secrets are held for us we can only imagine. What wonders of the universe will one day be revealed in the far future when we can truly comprehend? What mysteries lie before us, and what adventures await us along the way? We cannot begin to guess, but simply knowing the majesty of what is in store for us is inspiring.

The book concludes with three short instructions without commentary:

19. Hold fast to that which has neither substance nor existence.
20. Listen only to the voice which is soundless.
21. Look only on that which is invisible alike to the inner and outer sense.[47]

These instructions may seem contradictory, but in essence they are a summary of all that has gone before. We must listen with our inner mind, and even beyond that, with our intuition. This is a call to open to our true nature, our immortal being, our deepest vision. There are worlds to discover, both inner and outer.

17

The Voice of the Silence

Considerations

Purity of earthly love purifies and prepares for the realization of the Divine Love.

—MASTER SERAPIS

Commenting on H. P. Blavatsky's small classic—*The Voice of the Silence*—is intimidating for two reasons: The first is the depth and complexity of the work itself, revered since its publication more than 130 years ago as a window into the great mysteries of the universe and a set of instructions for the serious esoteric student. Secondly, because of the reasons just given, it has been studied and commented on by a variety of esteemed authors who have contemplated these pages and the occult concepts they contain for decades. Thus, it is with humility that I offer a few thoughts, especially to the student who may be less familiar with the work.

HPB wrote this book in the summer of 1889, completing the bulk of it in Fontainebleau, France, where she had gone for a period of respite due to failing health. She writes in a letter while there: "I am here to rest for a month or so. . . . Mrs. Garrison Candler . . . has almost forced me to come to rest a little with her in this (now) lovely forest and country. I am here incognito . . ."[1] Dr. Annie Besant, who visited Fontainebleau during that time, writes about HPB's process in creating the book:

> Now there is another point about another book of hers which is to me of special interest, a book you may know, *The Voice of the Silence*: that book happened to be written while I was with her in Fontainebleau. It is a small book and in what I am going to say I speak only of the book itself. . . . I know that she did not write it referring to any books, but she wrote it down steadily, hour after hour, exactly as though she were writing either from memory or from reading it where no book was. She produced, in the evening, that manuscript that I saw her write as I sat with her, and asked myself and others to correct it for English, for she said that she had written it so quickly that it was sure to be bad. We did not alter in that more than a few words, and it remains as a specimen of marvelously beautiful literary work. . . . The book is, as I said, prose poem, full of spiritual inspiration, full of food for the heart, stimulating the loftiest virtue and containing the noblest ideals. It is not a hotch-potch drawn from various sources, but a coherent, ethical whole.[2]

The origins of the book prior to Mme. Blavatsky's writing are not entirely clear. She notes in its preface that the work is made of three fragments derived from ancient writings known as *The Book of the Golden Precepts*, an esoteric work whose origins are even more distant in time. In this reference, she says,

> *The Book of the Golden Precepts*—some of which are pre-Buddhistic while others belong to a later date—contains about ninety distinct little treatises. Of these I learned thirty-nine by heart, years ago. To translate the rest, I should have to resort to notes scattered among a too large number of papers and memoranda collected for the last twenty years and never put in order, to make of it by any means an easy task.[3]

C. W. Leadbeater, in *Talks on the Path of Occultism*, goes into quite a bit of detail regarding the obscure origins of this work and in turn *The Book of the Golden Precepts*. He notes that one of the authors of the *Golden Precepts* was Aryasanga, the "great preacher and reformer of Buddhism," who founded a monastery in Tibet "in the early centuries of the Christian era."[4] It is known that HPB spent up to three years in Tibet during a period of travel and study and may have come across some of these manuscripts then. However, she may have also accessed this material clairvoyantly, as she did for much of her other writing. Regardless of her sources, the origins appear to be spiritual and remote.

The inscription to this book is "Dedicated to the Few." Mme. Blavatsky does not elaborate on who those few might be. Joy Mills suggests that "it may well have been—and this is conjecture only—that this inner group, which became known as the Esoteric School of Theosophy or E.S.T., in entreating H.P.B. for more instruction led her to set down in writing the small book which we now have."[5] Certainly, it is directed toward spiritual seekers and aspirants who may wish to know more of Eastern mysticism.

The book is arranged in three "fragments," entitled "The Voice of the Silence," "The Two Paths," and "The Seven Portals." According to Pablo Sender, these sections correspond to the topics of meditation, the bodhisattva path, and initiations, respectively.[6] Because HPB put these teachings in writing, she must have felt them to be essential for her students to learn; however, they comprise only a small sample of the much larger work containing thirty times the number of treatises that she conveyed. We are left to wonder what additional secrets are left untold.

Fragment 1, entitled identically to the larger book, begins with the statement that "these instructions are for those ignorant of the dangers of the lower *iddhi*."[7] Notice that HPB indicates here that, in fact, the contents are "instructions." The corresponding note indicates that "the Pali word *iddhi* is a synonym of the Sanskrit *siddhis*, or psychic faculties, the abnormal powers in man."[8] She goes on to explain that there are two types of iddhis, one associated with the lower psychic and the other with the higher spiritual. This is a warning, common in spiritual literature, to avoid the seduction of the phenomena of lower powers. While one is being introduced to occult teachings such phenomena can be enticing; they are often at best distracting and at worst devastating if one does not have the purity of purpose to move past them unflinchingly until their natural unfoldment becomes part of one's own evolution.

Leadbeater comments on the concept of iddhis that

> there is a vast amount of misunderstanding on this subject of psychic powers, and it will save the student a great deal of trouble if he will try to get a reasonable conception of it to begin with. First, let him not attach a wrong interpretation to the word "abnormal." These powers are abnormal only in the sense that they are at present uncommon—not in the least in the sense that they are in any way unnatural. They are perfectly natural to every man—indeed they are latent in every man here and now; a few people have developed them from latency into activity, but the majority have as yet made no effort in that direction, and so the powers still remain dormant.[9]

There will come a time when manifestation of these powers will be appropriate for the individual and even common in evolution, but we have not reached that point. The potential for misuse is enormous until we have dissolved (or at least strictly controlled) our lower impulses and desires. The appropriate timing will be made clear when these abilities are useful in achieving our role in society and do not need to be sought or artificially developed.

There are one hundred instructions listed in this first section (and more than three hundred in the full work), so they cannot all be discussed individually. The next several, however, appear to be particularly critical. The second one reads, "He who would hear the voice of *nada*, 'the Soundless Sound,' and comprehend it, he has to learn the nature of *Dharana*."[10] Here, *nada* is another term indicating "spiritual sound," equivalent both to the "Soundless Voice" and to the "Voice of this Silence." *Dharana*, we are told, is the "intense and perfect concentration of the mind upon some one interior object, accompanied by complete abstraction from everything pertaining to the external universe, or the world of the senses."[11] HPB seems to suggest that only by exclusion of all external awareness and sensation are we able to gain access to the Voice, metaphorically representing spiritual intuition or divine essence. In the cacophony of our everyday world, it is lost. We obtain awareness of its existence only through the effort of perfect concentration. By becoming "indifferent to objects of perception" we must identify this "*raga* of the senses" that can see beyond illusion.[12]

Numbers 4 and 5 are two of the best known in Theosophy: "The mind is the great slayer of the Real" and "Let the disciple slay the slayer."[13] What is the essence of the instruction here? As Pablo Sender notes, It is not an instruction to destroy the mind. It is simply an instruction to destroy the illusion of the mind known as maya.[14] The mental faculties are necessary for many of our activities and relationships; however, they distort the true nature of things. We develop illusions and biases based on sensation, preconceptions, distortions, and naïveté. In this sense, the mind deforms (slays) the Real (Eternal). We must surmount this distortion in order to know the essential nature of ourselves and our environment. We must be able to parse the inaccuracies of our sensations from the true vibrations of the world, both inner and outer. This is the process of intense concentration, meditation, and contemplation.

HPB follows these instructions shortly with the seventh: "When he has ceased to hear the many, he may discern the ONE—the inner sound which kills the outer."[15] As N. Sri Ram interprets these words,

> And then the soul hears a Voice—not an actual voice, for it is heard in realms that are beyond the range of sound. Although it can be likened to sound, it is a Voice that is born out of the silence, and it is only when there is silence that you will be able to listen to it. This is the silence of the mind which comes about by itself when the mind ceases from those pursuits which agitate the consciousness.[16]

The next several entries amplify this theme:

> 9. Before the soul can see, the harmony within must be attained. . . .
> 10. Before the soul can hear, the image (man) has to become as deaf to roarings as to whispers. . . .
> 11. Before the soul can comprehend and may remember, she must unto the Silent Speaker be united. . . .
> 13. And then to the inner ear will speak THE VOICE OF THE SILENCE.[17]

Instruction 20 reads, "Bestride the Bird of Life, if thou wouldst know."[18] In her notes, HPB writes that "a Yogi who bestrides the Hamsa (thus contemplates on Aum) is not affected by karmic influences or crores of sins."[19] Joy Mills comments that

> The "bird of life" has many meanings, just as has the sacred word, the Aum or Om. In the Mandukya Upanishad, the Aum represents the four stages of consciousness, and therefore to sound the word is to move from our present state of consciousness, the waking state, through the dream state to the deep-sleep state to that transformed fourth state "Turiya," which means simply four, which is a transformed state of awareness. . . . So the Hamsa [is] a mythological bird which is supposed to have had the capacity to separate milk from water, indicating the quality of discrimination, symbolizing wisdom.[20]

HPB then uses the metaphor of the three Halls: the Hall of Ignorance, the Hall of Learning, and the Hall of Wisdom. She notes that the earth is the Hall of Sorrow, where delusions entrap the seeker and probationary student. Only through traversing the three Halls can we shed the sorrow, which is due to a lack of understanding. Instruction 26 tells us that we are enticed in the Hall of Learning by finding "the blossoms of life, but under every flower a serpent coiled,"[21] meaning that for each appealing activity there is a shadow side, an illusion of pleasure, but with hidden pain. This is further explained in instruction 29: "If thou wouldst cross the second safely, stop not the fragrance of its stupefying blossoms to inhale. If freed thou wouldst be from the karmic chains, seek not for thy guru in those mayavic regions."[22] Here we see that these attractions can be from "karmic chains," so that much of our attachment may be karma that we've brought into this lifetime or developed earlier. Such attachments are barriers to spiritual progress and must be identified and broken if we are to proceed.

In instructions 41–50, she describes the seven sounds of Divinity to which one must be attuned before being able to access the Voice. Instruction 41 reads, "Before thou settest thy foot upon the ladder's upper rung, the ladder of the mystic sounds, thou hast to hear the voice of thy *inner* God [the Higher Self] in seven manners."[23] She goes on to list these manners specifically and poetically.

Service is an essential part of the path. One must be willing to sacrifice any and all comfort in order to assist another, particularly those in need. As instruction 60 states, "Let not the fierce sun dry one tear of pain before thyself hast wiped it from the sufferer's eye."[24]

We are told to look forward and not to dwell in the past, for the past is gone and cannot be changed. Those who dwell in the past indulge in past attachments and desires. We must free ourselves from these burdens, clean the slate, and move forward, unencumbered by karmic chains. HPB writes in instruction 74, "Long and weary is the way before thee, O disciple. One single thought about the past that thou has left behind, will drag thee down and thou wilt have to start the climb anew."[25]

Many other instructions are given regarding steps toward purification. These are in mystical metaphor, at times inscrutable but worthy of consideration and deep reflection. Near the end of the first fragment, in instruction 99, she states, "Behold! Thou hast become the light, thou hast become the sound, thou art thy Master and thy God. Thou art Thyself the object of thy search: the VOICE unbroken, that resounds throughout eternities, exempt from change, from sin exempt, the seven sounds in one, THE VOICE OF THE SILENCE."[26]

N. Sri Ram notes that "the illumination of the culminating state makes all things intelligible and clear. 'The Sound' is a certain definite utterance; it takes form, it creates forms in the worlds of form, whereas the light is always formless. The disciple has become one with the Master within; he becomes that for which he had been searching."[27]

Unity has been achieved.

"The Two Paths" is the title of the second fragment. The preceding fragment has instructed us on how to achieve unity with the Divine or the Universal. Now, immediately, we are presented with a choice of *two* paths—signifying divergence, or *non*unity. What can this apparent contradiction mean? Granted, these first two fragments were sourced separately, but Mme. Blavatsky juxtaposes them in a particular sequence. The inference is that the spiritual path divides. This sense is expressed more explicitly later.

The candidate implores the Master in instruction 102, "Shall not thou, Master of thine own mercy, reveal the Doctrine of the Heart? Shalt thou refuse to lead thy servants unto the Path of Liberation?"[28] We can easily be confused as HPB quotes the Teacher's answer in instruction 103: "The Paths are two; the great Perfections three; six are the Virtues that transform the body into the Tree of Knowledge."[29]

What is this "Doctrine of the Heart"? Blavatsky explains in the notes and elsewhere that the "Heart Doctrine" is the esoteric path named due to emanation from the Buddha's heart, whereas the Eye Doctrine is the exoteric path and was derived from "the work of his head or brain."[30] In the text, the candidate asks again for "the truth unveiled about the Secret Heart."[31] The Teacher's response is in instruction 108:

> Behold how like the moon, reflected in the tranquil waves, Alaya [the Real Self] is reflected by the small and by the great, is mirrored in the tiniest atoms, yet fails to reach the heart of all. Alas, that so few men should profit by the gift, the priceless boon of learning truth, the right perception of existing things, the knowledge of the nonexistent![32]

The author appears to be suggesting that the higher energies are ever present—here analogous to the moon, shining on all, whether we are cognizant of it or not—but those energies go unrecognized in the heart, the true nature, of the individual. So few can benefit because we are asleep (some would say blind) to the inner life and all its potential. It is analogous to cursing the absence of the sun on a cloudy day or in the darkness of night. It is the *connection* that is absent, not the message.

Fragment 2 goes on to compare the Doctrine of the Eye and the Doctrine of the Heart. HPB writes in instruction 111, "Learn above all to separate head learning from soul wisdom, the "Eye" from the "Heart" doctrine."[33] Both these doctrines are essential to provide valuable skills in treading a spiritual path. C. W. Leadbeater writes that

> no occult progress at all is possible for a man while he is extremely ignorant, however much he may be developed in other ways. Without some knowledge of the Truth, and of the Path, he will not move in a definite direction. Most people have very little knowledge of what it means to be really a man, what are the qualities and actions which make for progress and what for retrogression, and they have no conception of the great destiny to which all are slowly moving.[34]

As we examine the two "paths," we must realize that the term is often used in spiritual literature metaphorically. The path is not literal, of course, but a journey in consciousness. As Joy Mills has pointed out, on a material path we are generally little changed—except for some experiences we may encounter—when we reach the end. However, on a spiritual path, our very nature is transformed:

> On the path of transformation, on the other hand, on the path we are undertaking, everything in us must be changed. That is not easy. For that kind of transformation, the starting point and goal are also equally important but another factor has entered into the picture. That factor is pointed up rather early in our text: "Thou canst not travel on the Path before thou hast become that Path itself"

[fragment 1, verse 58]. A paradoxical and mystical statement. In other words, we are not separate from the path, from the process.[35]

So, how are we to travel this path? If all action results in karma, will absence of action protect us from the karmic consequences of actions—good and bad—in the world? Pablo Sender notes that some seekers in Eastern traditions follow this belief by detaching from society (and apparent action) in order to free themselves from karma and ultimately rebirth.[36] This rationale, however, is flawed in the context of our present work. Action is contained in inaction as inaction is in action. Refusal to act is still a form of action. Even if we physically refrain from significant activities, in esoteric traditions, emotions and thoughts are also actions. In instruction 130, HPB writes: "Both action and inaction may find room in thee; thy body agitated, thy mind tranquil, thy soul as limpid as a mountain lake."[37] And in the well-known instruction 136: "Shalt thou abstain from action? Not so shall gain thy soul her freedom. To reach Nirvana one must reach self-knowledge, and self-knowledge is of loving deeds the child."[38] Therefore, abstaining from action is not a strategy for spiritual progress in general, although there may be times when it is appropriate.

Much of the rest of the section contains advice on what to embrace and what to avoid as we "follow the wheel of life; follow the wheel of duty to race and kin, to friend and foe," as we close our minds "to pleasures as to pain"[39] until we are brought back to the topic of the two paths. In instruction 180, HPB writes, "The one becomes the two, the Open and the Secret. The first one leadeth to the goal, the second, to self-immolation."[40] We are told that the choice is ours: both the "first Path" of liberation that leads to the glorious state of Nirvana and the "Path of Woe"—the sacrifice of Nirvana in order to assist the "men of karmic sorrow"—are equally of merit. However, the author appears to criticize the former by stating, "The Open Way, no sooner has thou reached its goal, will lead thee to reject the Bodhisattvic body and make thee enter the thrice glorious state of Dharmakaya, which is oblivion of the world and men forever."[41] But the second path—that of forsaking Nirvana when on the cusp of eternal bliss—is greater, about which instructions 191 and 192 are explicit: "The Bodhisattva who has won the battle, who holds the prize within his palm, yet says in his divine compassion: 'For others' sake this great reward I yield'—accomplishes the greater renunciation."[42]

The third fragment, "The Seven Portals," describes a path of initiation. The seven portals are gates through which each aspirant must pass. And each gate has a key, which in this case correspond to the *paramitas*. These are virtues or character qualities, sometimes translated from the Buddhist tradition as "perfections." They vary, usually listed as six or ten in number, but here Mme. Blavatsky lists them as seven. Each paramita corresponds to a key, which can unlock the portal gate, or barrier to passage. Although these qualities are listed sequentially, their development is not necessarily so separate. Joy Mills comments on the origin of the word:

> The very term, *paramita*, is an interesting one, for it is a compound word in Sanskrit which can be divided in two different ways, giving us two complementary meanings. We can divide it as *para*, meaning beyond, superior, and *mita*, which means to proceed by measured steps. Or the word may be divided into *param*, having the connotation of the other shore, and *ita*, to go, indicating that by means of these ideals we move toward the other shore from which a new view of the world is gained.[43]

In instructions 196 and 197, the pupil petitions the teacher for instruction: "Thy servant here is ready for thy guidance," and the teacher answers, "'Tis well, Shravaka [Skt. a listener, or student who attends religious instruction]. Prepare thyself, for thou wilt have to travel on alone. The Teacher can but point the way."[44] With this caveat, the journey begins. The teacher writes in verse 206: "Thou seest well, lanoo [Skt. spiritual student]. These Portals lead the aspirant across the waters on to the other shore. Each Portal hath a golden key that openeth its gate; and these keys are. . . ."[45]

HPB then gives the seven keys in a list of Sanskrit words. The first is "Dana, the key of charity and love immortal."[46] The true meaning of *dana* is broader than the modern concept of charity alone. According to Clara Codd, an English Theosophist, lecturer, and writer, "the first Paramita is *Dana*, generally translated by the word *charity* or *love*, but the root *da* means 'giving' so it may also be thought of as the spirit of eternal giving instead of taking, this being the central sign of spirit."[47]

The other keys are similarly translated, but with broad and layered meaning. Each applies to the development of an aspect of ourselves, to a depth of which we may be unaware in our waking, conscious mind. Pablo Sender notes that there's a correlation between the first key, *dana* (charity), and the physical body; the second key, *shila* (harmony), and the emotional body; and the third key, *kshanti* (patience), and the mental body or lower mind.[48] This patience goes beyond the ability to postpone desire but addresses equanimity, which HPB states as "patience sweet, that naught can ruffle."[49] It is the patience that comes with wisdom.

I have mentioned that *vairagya*, the fourth key, is the quality of desirelessness, of an uncolored mind, as Krishnamurti discusses at some length in *At the Feet of the Master*. The fifth key, *virya*, is a quality of spiritual energy and perseverance. Leadbeater notes that this quality can be disruptive if not combined with the quality of patience:

> A person who has this energy and hears about the path wants immediately to tread it to the very end—but without patience he will cause such a disturbance all along the way, and create such a quantity of troublesome karma that he will delay himself considerably. On the other hand the man who has the patience and not the energy will perhaps be content to go along very slowly—and his progress will then be slow indeed.[50]

Dhyana, the sixth key, is often translated as "profound meditation" and "contemplation," but, even more fully, as "spiritual awareness." And the seventh key is "prajna, the key to which makes of a man a god."[51] This is divine wisdom and higher consciousness, eternal without distortion or disturbance.

The subject of verse 306 is the three higher states in Buddhism described as vestures (or robes): "The stream is crossed. 'Tis true thou hast a right to Dharmakaya vesture, but Sambhogakaya is greater than a Nirvani, and greater still is a Nirmanakaya—the Buddha of Compassion."[52] HPB's endnote 117 goes more deeply into the Buddhist doctrine of higher states. These may not be relevant to the student attempting early portions of the long spiritual path, but conceptually they can be intriguing regarding ultimate steps. John Algeo, in reflecting on the writings of Leadbeater, notes that the state of Nirmanakaya connects to the personality, of Sambhogakaya to the individuality (higher mind), and of Dharmakaya to the monad, or Buddha nature. He notes that these three states comprise a choice of how we are to continue to function in the higher planes.[53]

In Geoffrey Hodson's essay about His Holiness, the Fourteenth Dalai Lama, Hodson references *The Voice of the Silence* in discussing the principles of reincarnation of Adepts:

> The first of these, the *Nirmanakaya*, is that form which an Adept assumes when leaving His physical body, then appearing in His Astral

> Body and possessing in addition all the knowledge of an Adept. . . . *Sambhogakaya* is the same, but with additional lustre of three perfections, one of which is entire obliteration of all earthly concerns. The *Dharmakaya* body is that of a complete Buddha, actually no true body at all, but "an ideal breath."[54]

While all spiritual writing can be opaque, in part due to the multiple levels of communication, *The Voice of the Silence* can be particularly challenging. It is instructional and yet poetic and mystical at the same time. It contains truths that are ancient and yet relevant today. B. P. Wadia comments,

> Esoteric Philosophy has always taught the art of all-round development—a healthy mind in a healthy body; but also, it has always taught that the course of unfoldment is from within without, and that therefore mind and not body should be the starting point, and that motive and not method should receive primary consideration. Not that body and method were neglected, but ever and always mind and motive were made the starting point.[55]

The enormity of the spiritual path can be overwhelming when we compare ourselves to the ideal. However, it can be a joyful journey—not easy, of course, but with the knowledge of our final destiny in the heights of the mountains of illumination of consciousness, the beauty of compassion and the bliss of selflessness. Each of us can find our way, despite the apparent darkness, if we listen to our inner nature. Everyone can lift another and thereby ensure that none are left behind. Where we may be on such a path is less important than the direction in which we are oriented. If we forget ourselves and open our hearts, our unfoldment will follow nature's laws.

Perhaps it is best to close with words from Clara Codd regarding the path of initiation:

A newly made Initiate gives the blessing of the Brotherhood to the world. Mrs. Besant said that this blessing is felt by everybody. A little child playing in the sun would feel a thrill of joy, a sufferer in the hospital would feel his pain lessened for a second. Everybody would feel it, though they would not know what it was. That is what *The Voice of the Silence* says. Once that Sowani hath crossed the seventh path, all Nature thrills with joyous awe and feels subdued. The silver star now twinkles out the news to the night blossoms, the streamlet to the pebbles replies out the tale; dark ocean waves will roar it to the rocks surf-bound, scent laden breezes sing it to the vales, and stately pines mysteriously whisper: A Master has arisen, a Master of the Day.[56]

AFTERWORD

Our world is full of cycles, but, as in a spiral, there is progress, too. To use a common metaphor, we are circling up the mountain path. There are periods of ebb and flow, times to expand and times to consolidate our experiences. Each day is an opportunity to learn more about ourselves and our journey. Each day comes with circumstances that are relevant to our lives. Each day we have occasion to sense the wonder of our world. Each day we can explore the mystery of what it is to be human. Each day we can live the connection with our fellow travelers. Each day we can sense the beauty of our universe. Each day we can explore a little further and excavate a little more. Each day we can open the blinders a bit wider and absorb the radiant Now.

Theosophy, and spiritual Reality more generally, is not confined to books, to history, to some dusty, bygone era. It is vibrant in every interaction, every new activity, every breath we take, and every thought we create. It is the totality of who we are and yet much more. Our potential is unending and our existence eternal. There is a thrill in the universe that can be sensed. There is a joy that is unending. There is a bliss unbounded.

We must remember, in our hearts as well as our minds, that there is a reverence in the routine, a perfection in the (seemingly) ordinary, a delight in the everyday. Each of us is on a divine pilgrimage, although at times it is obscure. Additionally, most of us are unaware of the forces acting within us and around us. We can think of it as sleepwalking through our days. And yet, like a dream, once we realize where we are, we can awaken, we can see new vistas, we can elevate our consciousness. All things are possible. As Master Koot Hoomi has written,

> There are innumerable pages of your life-record still to be written up; fair and blank they are as yet. Child of your race and of your age, seize the diamond-pen and inscribe them with the history of noble deeds, days well-spent, years of holy striving. So will you win your way ever upward to the higher planes of spiritual consciousness.[1]

NOTES

Chapter 1

1. Annie Besant, *The Ancient Wisdom*, (Adyar, India: Theosophical Publishing House, 1939), 1.
2. H. P. Blavatsky, *The Key to Theosophy* (London: Theosophical Publishing Company, 1889; Pasadena, CA: Theosophical University Press, 1995), 1. Citations refer to the 1995 edition.
3. Ibid., 1–2.
4. Ibid., 57.
5. C. W. Leadbeater, *A Textbook of Theosophy* (Adyar, India: Theosophical Publishing House, 1912), 1.
6. Reed Carlson, "Foreknowledge of the Wave/Particle Duality of Light," *Theosophy World Resource Centre*, December 1, 1997, https://www.theosophy.world/resource/foreknowledge-waveparticle-duality-light.
7. Leadbeater, *Textbook of Theosophy*, 2.
8. H. P. Blavatsky, *Collected Writings*, ed. Boris de Zirkoff, vol. 10, *1888–1889*, 2nd ed. (Wheaton, IL: Theosophical Publishing House, 1974), 167.
9. H. P. Blavatsky, *The Secret Doctrine*, vol. 1, *Cosmogenesis*, ed. Boris de Zirkoff. First Quest ed. (Wheaton, IL: Theosophical Publishing House, 1993), 631.
10. Leadbeater, *Textbook of Theosophy*, 3.
11. Annie Besant, *Esoteric Christianity*, 2nd ed. (Wheaton, IL: Quest Books, 2006), 165.

12. Leadbeater, *Textbook of Theosophy*, 121–22.
13. Ibid., 124.
14. Blavatsky, *Secret Doctrine*, 1:16–17.
15. Annie Besant, *The Masters*, 8th repr. (Adyar, India: Theosophical Publishing House, 2007), 1.
16. Blavatsky, *Collected Writings*, ed. Boris de Zirkoff, vol 6, *1883–1884–1885*, 2nd ed. (Wheaton, IL: Theosophical Publishing House, 1975), 239.
17. N. Sri Ram, *Seeking Wisdom* (Adyar, India: Theosophical Publishing House, 1969), 5.
18. Katherine. A. Beechey, comp., *Daily Meditations: Extracts from Letters of the Masters of Wisdom*, 2nd ed. (Adyar, India: Theosophical Publishing House, 1984), 109–10.
19. Annie Besant, *An Introduction to Yoga* (Adyar, India: Theosophical Publishing House, 1908), 134.
20. Leadbeater, *Textbook of Theosophy*, 108–9.
21. Blavatsky, *Collected Writings*, vol. 13, *1890–1891*. (Wheaton, IL: Theosophical Publishing House, 1982), 219.

Chapter 2

1. Blavatsky, *Secret Doctrine*, 1:17 (see ch. 1, n. 9).
2. Ibid., 57–58.
3. Blavatsky, *Key to Theosophy*, 351 (see ch. 1, n. 2).
4. I. K. Taimni, *Man, God, and the Universe* (Wheaton, IL: Quest Books, 1974), Kindle ed., 97.
5. Leadbeater, *Textbook of Theosophy*, 41–42 (see ch. 1, n. 5).
6. Pablo Sender, *Evolution of the Higher Consciousness: An In-Depth Study into H. P. Blavatsky's Teachings* (Ojai, CA: Fohat, 2018), 86–88.
7. Annie Besant, *The Spiritual Life*, rev. ed. (Wheaton, IL: Quest Books, 1991), 91.

8. Mabel Collins, *Light on the Path* in *Inspirations from Ancient Wisdom: At the Feet of the Master; Light on the Path; The Voice of the Silence* (Wheaton, IL: Quest Books, 1999), 53.
9. Blavatsky, *Secret Doctrine*, 1:14 (see ch. 1, n. 9).
10. H. P. Blavatsky, *The Voice of the Silence* in *Inspirations from Ancient Wisdom* (Wheaton, IL: Quest Books, 1999), 106.
11. Pablo Sender, "A Universe of Purpose," lecture at the Summer National Convention, Theosophical Society in America, Wheaton, IL, 2019.
12. Beechey, *Daily Meditations*, 145 (see ch. 1, n. 18).
13. Mabel Collins, *Light on the Path* and *Through the Gates of Gold* (Pasadena, CA: Theosophical University Press, 1997), 75–76.
14. Annie Besant, *London Lectures of 1907* (London: Theosophical Publishing Society, 1909), 43.
15. Besant, *Spiritual Life*, 78.
16. Blavatsky, *Key to Theosophy*, 59.

Chapter 3

1. David Hume, "Of the Standard of Taste," in *Essays Moral and Political* (London: George Routledge and Sons, 1894). See *Stanford Encyclopedia of Philosophy*, https://plato.stanford.edu/entries/beauty.
2. Heinrich Wölfflin, *Principles of Art History* (London: Bell, 1932), 9–10, 15. See *Stanford Encyclopedia of Philosophy*, https://plato.stanford.edu/entries/beauty.
3. Christopher Marlowe, *Doctor Faustus*, Chorus 4–Epilogue.
4. John Denver and Mike Taylor, "Rocky Mountain High," on *Rocky Mountain High*, RCA Records, 1972.
5. "Thailand: Jewel of the Orient," *PBS*, n.d., accessed August 21, 2021, www.pbs.org/edens/thailand/buddhism.htm.
6. Kurt Spellmeyer, "Awakened by Beauty," *Tricycle*, Fall 2019, https://tricycle.org/magazine-issue/fall-2019/.

7. "The Mirror of Insight," *Dhammatalks.org: Talks, Writings, and Translations of Thānissaro Bhikku*, n.d., accessed July 13, 2022, https:// www.dhammatalks.org/books/Mirror_ofInsight/Section0008.html.
8. Spellmeyer, "Awakened by Beauty."
9. Buddha, "The Just," Poem 19, *Pearls of Wisdom*, copyright 2002–2021, http://www.sapphyr.net/buddhist/buddhist-dhammapada.
10. Blavatsky, *Voice of the Silence* in *Inspirations,* 74 (see ch. 2, n. 10).
11. Besant, *Introduction to Yoga*, 43 (see ch. 1, n. 19).
12. David Tame, *Beethoven and the Spiritual Path* (Wheaton, IL: Quest Books, 1994), 65.
13. Taimni, *Man, God, and the Universe*, xxxv (see ch. 2, n. 4).
14. Ibid., xxxv–xxxvi.
15. Ravi Ravindra, *The Bhagavad Gita: A Guide to Navigating the Battle of Life* (Boulder, CO: Shambhala, 2017), 149.
16. Ibid.
17. Blavatsky, *Key to Theosophy*, 155 (see ch. 1, n. 2).

Chapter 4

1. C. W. Leadbeater, *The Masters and the Path*, 3rd ed. (Adyar, India: Theosophical Publishing House, 1992), 58.
2. Besant, *Spiritual Life*, 7 (see ch. 2, n. 7).
3. Vicente Hao Chin, ed. *The Mahatma Letters to A. P. Sinnett from the Mahatmas M. and K.H.: In Chronological Sequence* (Adyar, India: Theosophical Publishing House, 1998), 295.

Chapter 5

1. Mette Ebbesen, Svend Andersen, and Birthe D. Pedersen, "Further Development of Beauchamp and Childress's Theory Based on Empirical Ethics," *Journal of Clinical Research and Bioethics*, 2012, accessed September 7, 2021, https://www.longdom.org/open-access/further-development-of-beauchamp-and-childress-theory-based-on-empirical-ethics-2155-9627.S6-e001.pdf.

2. "Ethics: The Five Precepts," *The Buddhist Centre*, n.d., accessed August 20, 2021, https://thebuddhistcentre.com/text/ethics.
3. Himanshu Bhatt, "Ethics of Hinduism," *Hindupedia*, n.d., accessed August 20, 2021, http://www.hindupedia.com/en/Ethics_of_Hinduism.
4. Ibid.
5. "Ahimsa," *Wikipedia*, July 18, 2022, https://en.wikipedia.org/wiki/Ahimsa.
6. Ravi Ravindra, *The Wisdom of Patanjali's Yoga Sutras* (Nova Scotia: Shaila Press, 2015), 85.
7. "Yoga's Ethical Guide to Living: The Yamas and Niyamas," *Kripalu,* ©2022, https://kripalu.org/resources/yoga-s-ethical-guide-living-yamas-and-niyamas.
8. Ravindra, *Wisdom of Patanjali*, 91.
9. Blavatsky, *Key to Theosophy*, 14 (see ch. 1, n. 2).
10. Sender, *Evolution*, 80 (see ch. 2, n. 6).
11. Ibid., 86.
12. Blavatsky, *Key to Theosophy*, 229.
13. Collins, *Light on the Path* in *Inspirations*, 55 (see ch. 2, n. 8).
14. Blavatsky, *Key to Theosophy*, 229–30.
15. Ravindra, *Wisdom of Patanjali*, 132.

Chapter 6

1. Ron Chernow, *Alexander Hamilton* (New York: Penguin, 2004), Kindle ed., 75.
2. Nelson Mandela, *Long Walk to Freedom: The Autobiography of Nelson Mandela* (New York: Little, Brown and Company, 2008), Kindle ed., 364.
3. Lawrence O'Donnell, *Playing with Fire* (New York: Penguin, 2017), Kindle ed., 241.
4. "Gautama Buddha," *Goodreads*, n.d., accessed September 9, 2021, https://www.goodreads.com/quotes/57004-hatred-does-not-cease-by-hatred-but-only-by-love.

5. Matt. 5:39, Holy Bible, New King James Version (Nashville: Thomas Nelson, 1982).
6. Ravindra, *Bhagavad Gita*, 161 (see ch. 3, n. 15).
7. Ibid.
8. "Three Objects," *Theosophical Society in* America, ©2022, https://www.theosophical.org/about/about-the-society.
9. Ravindra, *Bhagavad Gita*, 161.
10. Chin, *Mahatma Letters*, 295 (see ch. 4, n. 3).

Chapter 7

1. Kris Kristofferson, "Me and Bobby McGee," sung by Janis Joplin, on *Pearl*, Columbia Records, 1971.
2. "Four Freedoms," *Wikipedia*, last updated April 25, 2022, https://en.wikipedia.org/wiki/Four_Freedoms.
3. Buddha, from MagiQuotes, n.d., accessed August 21, 2021, https://www.magiquotes.com/en/author/buddha.html.
4. The sentence has been attributed to Eleanor Roosevelt since it appeared in the *Reader's Digest* 37 (September 1940) 84, but there is no evidence that she wrote it.
5. "Mumukshutva," *Yogapedia*, n.d., accessed August 21, 2021, https://www.yogapedia.com/definition/8496/mumukshutva.
6. Ibid.
7. Ravindra, *Bhagavad Gita*, 3 (see ch. 3, n. 15).
8. "Free will," *Oxford Languages*, ©2022, http://languages.oup.com.
9. "Determinism vs. Free Will: Crash Course Philosophy #24," *PBS Digital Studios*, 2016, https//www.voicetube.com/v3/videos/42029.
10. "Karma," *Oxford Languages*, ©2022, http://languages.oup.com.
11. See Annie Besant, *A Study in Karma*, 3rd ed. (Adyar, India: Theosophical Publishing House, 2019) and Collins, *Light on the Path* in *Inspirations* (see ch. 2, n. 8).
12. Besant, *Karma*, 3rd ed. (Adyar, India: Theosophical Publishing House, 1905), 2–3.

13. Geoffrey Hodson, quoted in John Sell and Elizabeth Sell, comp., *Sharing the Light: The Collected Articles of Geoffrey Hodson*, vol. 1 (Quezon City, Philippines: Theosophical Publishing House, 2008), 195.
14. Ibid., 197.
15. Taimni, *Man, God, and the Universe*, 40–41 (see ch. 2, n. 4).
16. Ibid., xxxvi.
17. Blavatsky, *Voice of the Silence*, in *Inspirations,* 98 (see ch. 2, n. 10).
18. Blavatsky, *Secret Doctrine* 1:17 (see ch. 1, n. 9).
19. Blavatsky, *Voice of the Silence* in *Inspirations*, 97.
20. Collins, *Light on the Path* in *Inspirations*, 42.
21. Hodson, in *Sharing the Light*, 198.
22. Ibid., 198.
23. Beechey, *Daily Meditations*, 4 (see ch. 1, n. 18).

Chapter 8

1. Annie Besant, *The Seven Principles of Man*, 12th repr. (Adyar, India: Theosophical Publishing House, 2015), 2.
2. "What Are Possible Causes of Stillbirth?" *National Institute of Child Health and Human Development* (*NIH*), last updated December 1, 2016, https://www.nichd.nih.gov/health/topics/stillbirth/topicinfo/causes.
3. "Infant Mortality," *World Health Organization*, n.d., accessed June 6, 2022, https://www.who.int/data/gho/data/themes/topics/indicator-groups/indicator-group-details/GHO/infant-mortality.
4. Annie Besant, *Mahabharata: The Story of the Great War* (Adyar, India: Theosophical Publishing House, 1927), 25–26.
5. Socrates, from Plato's *Apology*, *Goodreads*, n.d., accessed August 21, 2021; https://www.goodreads.com.
6. "Disability Impacts All of Us," *Center for Disease Control and Prevention* (CDC), last updated September 16, 2020, www.cdc.gov/ncbddd/disabilityandhealth/infographic-disability-impacts-all.html.
7. Richard W. Johnson, "What Is the Lifetime Risk of Needing and Receiving Long-Term Services and Supports?" *US Department of Health and Human*

Services (DHHS), April 3, 2019, https://www.aspe.hhs.gov/reports/what-lifetime-risk-needing-receiving-long-term-services-supports-0.

8. Anne Kelly et al., "Length of Stay for Older Adults Residing in Nursing Homes at the End of Life," *NIH: National Library of Medicine*, August 24, 2010, https://www.pubmed.ncbi.nlm.nih.gov/20738438/.
9. Katharina Allers, Falk Hoffmann, and Rieke Schnakenberg, "Hospitalizations of Nursing Home Residents at the End of Life: A Systematic Review," *Sage Journals*, August 1, 2019, https://journals.sagepub.com/doi/pdf/10.1177/0269216319866648
10. Blavatsky, *Key to Theosophy*, 24 (see ch. 1, n. 2).

Chapter 9

1. Martin Luther King, Jr., quoted by Cynthia Haven, *Stanford University*, n.d., accessed August 25, 2021, https://www.bookhaven.stanford.edu/2012/01/martin-luther-king-on-his-day.
2. Blavatsky, *Collected Writings*, 10:351 (see ch. 1, n. 8).
3. Hodson, in *Sharing the Light*, 30 (see ch. 7, n. 13).
4. St. John of the Cross, "Dark Night of the Soul," A. Z. Foreman, trans., *Transformative Writing*, n.d., accessed August 25, 2021, https://transformativewriting.wordpress.com/2011/11/27/the-long-night/.
5. Besant, *Spiritual Life*, 66 (see ch. 2, n. 7).
6. Gopi Krishna, *Kundalini* (Boulder: Shambala, 2017), 16.
7. "Major Depression," *National Institute of Mental Health*, last updated January 2022, https://www.nimh.nih.gov/health/statistics/major-depression.
8. Kevin Culligan, "The Dark Night and Depression," in *Carmelite Prayer: A Tradition for the 21st Century*, Keith J. Egan, ed. (New York: Paulist Press, 2003); quoted by Therese Borchard, "Is It Depression or a Dark Night of the Soul?" *Everyday Health*, April 14, 2015, https://www.everydayhealth.com/columns/therese-borchard-sanity-break/depression-dark-night-soul/.

9. John R. Peteet, "Spiritually Integrated Treatment of Depression: A Conceptual Framework," *Hindawi*, April 19, 2012, https://www.hindawi.com/journals/drt/2012/124370/.
10. William Meader, "The Dark Night of the Soul," *Theosophical Society in America* on *Youtube*, April 24, 2020, https://www.youtube.com/watch?v=-DQsyNDyNGY.
11. Joseph Campbell, quoted by the *Joseph Campbell Foundation*, n.d., accessed August 27, 2021, https://www.jcf.org/works/quote/the-dark-night/.
12. Besant, *Spiritual Life*, 127.
13. Collins, *Light on the Path* in *Inspirations*, 44 (see ch. 2, n. 8).
14. Hodson, in *Sharing the Light*, 30–31.
15. N. Sri Ram, *Thoughts for Aspirants, First Series*, 2nd ed. (Adyar, India: Theosophical Publishing House, 1956), 139.
16. Joseph Campbell, *Goodreads*, n.d., accessed May 21, 2022, https://www.goodreads.com/quotes/505149-you-are-the-hero-of-your-own-story.
17. Master Morya, quoted in Beechey, *Daily Meditations*, 82 (see ch. 1, n. 18).

Chapter 10

1. "Absolute," *New World Encyclopedia*, n.d., accessed August 29, 2021; https://www.newworldencyclopedia.org.Absolute.
2. Blavatsky, *Key to Theosophy*, 212 (see ch. 1, n. 2).
3. Blavatsky, *Secret Doctrine* 1:16 (see ch. 1, n. 9).
4. Ibid., 135.
5. Blavatsky, *Key to Theosophy*, 174.
6. Chin, *Mahatma Letters*, 512 (see ch. 4, n. 3).
7. Ibid., 270.
8. Ibid., 204.
9. Leadbeater, *Textbook of Theosophy*, 9 (see ch. 1, n. 5).
10. Ibid.
11. Besant, *Spiritual Life,* 145 (see ch. 2, n. 7).
12. Ibid., 164.

13. Taimni, *Man, God, and the Universe*, 1 (see ch. 2, n. 4).
14. Ibid.
15. Ibid., 3.
16. Ibid., 7.
17. Ibid., 9–10.
18. Ibid., 15.
19. Mabel Collins, *The Idyll of the White Lotus*, 2nd ed. (Wheaton, IL: Theosophical Publishing House, 1974), 114.

Chapter 11

1. MrMcMillanREvis, "The Problem of Evil, Pt. 1," *Youtube*, April 11, 2014, https://www.youtube.com/watch?v=qilO5AJjkvw.
2. Ibid.
3. Buddha, *AZ Quotes*, n.d., accessed May 21, 2022, https://www.azquotes.com.
4. Ibid.
5. Buddha, *Real Buddha Quotes*, March 11, 2015, https://www.realbuddhaquotes.com/ceasing-to-do-evil.
6. Annie Besant, *The Use of Evil* (Adyar, India: Theosophical Publishing House, 1932), 2–3.
7. Ibid., 5–6.
8. Ibid., 11.
9. Ibid.
10. Ibid., 14–15.
11. Ibid., 20–21.
12. Chin, *Mahatma Letters*, 273–74 (see ch. 4, n. 3).
13. Ibid., 274.
14. H. P. Blavatsky, *The Secret Doctrine*, vol. 2, *Anthropogenesis.* (Wheaton, IL: Theosophical Publishing House, 1993), 475.
15. Joy Mills, *Reflections on an Ageless Wisdom* (Wheaton, IL: Quest Books, 2010), 332–33.
16. Blavatsky, *Secret Doctrine* 2:476.

17. Ibid.
18. Chin, *Mahatma Letters*, 95.
19. Ibid., 96.
20. Robert Ellwood, *Theosophy: A Modern Expression of the Wisdom of the Ages* (Wheaton, IL: Quest Books, 1986), 165–66.
21. Leadbeater, *Masters and the Path*, 118 (see ch. 4, n. 1).
22. Pablo Sender, "The Problem of Evil," *Theosophical Society in America* on *YouTube,* February 28, 2017, https://youtube/5-fQ3RCxTM4.

Chapter 12

1. Blavatsky, *Secret Doctrine*, 1:xx (see ch. 1, n. 9).
2. Blavatsky, *Key to Theosophy*, 61 (see ch. 1, n. 2).
3. Ibid., 63.
4. Chin, *Mahatma Letters*, 270 (see ch. 4, n. 3).
5. Blavatsky, *Key to Theosophy*, 71.
6. S. S. Varma, *Teachings on Discipleship* (Adyar, India: Theosophical Publishing House, 2005), 76–78.
7. Chin, *Mahatma Letters*, 270.
8. bid., 272.
9. Ibid.
10. H. P. Blavatsky, *Secret Doctrine* 1:14.
11. Ibid.
12. Ibid., 15.
13. Chin, *Mahatma Letters*, 270.
14. Blavatsky, *Secret Doctrine*, 1:279.
15. Ibid., 279–80.
16. H. P. Blavatsky, *Theosophical Glossary*, facsimile of the original edition. (London: Theosophical Publishing Society, 1892; London: The Theosophy Company, 1973), 97.
17. Chin, *Mahatma Letters*, 270.
18. H. P. Blavatsky, *Two Books of The Stanzas of Dzyan*, 8th repr. (Adyar, India: Theosophical Publishing House, 2013), 180.

19. Ibid., 180–81.
20. Besant, *Seven Principles of Man*, 80 (see ch. 8, n. 1), quoting from Blavatsky, *Key to Theosophy*, 175 (see ch. 1, n. 2).
21. Blavatsky, *Secret Doctrine*, 1:17.
22. J. Krishnamurti, *At the Feet of the Master* in *Inspirations from Ancient Wisdom* (Wheaton, IL: Quest Books, 1999), 5.
23. Ibid, 3.
24. Ibid., 7–8.
25. Ibid., 9.
26. Annie Besant and C. W. Leadbeater, *Talks on the Path of Occultism*, vol. 3, *Light on the Path*, 6th ed. (Adyar, India: Theosophical Publishing House, 1976), 398.
27. Annie Besant, "Brotherhood and War," *The Theosophist* 36, n. 9 (June 1915): 198.
28. George S. Arundale, "You, Theosophy, and the Society," originally published as an essay in *You* (Adyar, India: Theosophical Publishing House, 1935), https://www.theosophical.org/files/resources/articles/You.pdf.
29. C. Jinarajadasa, "The Work ahead for Theosophists," inaugural address to the International Theosophical Society, Adyar, India, February 17, 1946, pg. 7.
30. N. Sri Ram, ed., "On the Watch Tower," *The Theosophist* 76, no. 6 (February 1955): 290.
31. Sri Sankaracharya, *Viveka-Cudamani*, trans. Mohini M. Chatterji. (Adyar, India: Theosophical Publishing House, 1932), 82.
32. Collins, *Idyll*, 114 (see ch. 10, n. 19).

Chapter 13

1. H. P. Blavatsky, *Collected Writings*, ed. Boris de Zirkott, vol. 12, *1889–1890* (Wheaton, IL: The Theosophical Publishing House, 1980), 503.
2. Joy Mills, "The Golden Stairs: The Ideal of Human Progression and Perfection," audio, accessed December 9, 2021, at "The Golden Stairs,"

Theosophy Wiki, https://www. Theosophy.wiki/en/The_Golden_Stairs and https://ia803100.us.archive.org/30/items/1232_20191205/1232.mp3.

3. Sidney Cook, *The Golden Stairs: A Commentary* (Adyar, India: Theosophical Publishing House, 1957), 3; accessed December 9, 2021, at "The Golden Stairs," *Theosophy Wiki,* https://www. Theosophy.wiki/en/The_Golden_Stairs and https://www.theosophical.org/files/resources/articles/GScom.pdf#.
4. John Algeo, "The Golden Stairs: Ethics in the Ancient Wisdom Tradition," *The American Theosophist* (November 1984), 3; accessed December 9, 2021, at "The Golden Stairs," *Theosophy Wiki,* https://www.Theosophy.wiki/en/The_Golden_Stairs and https://www.theosophical.org/files/resources/articles/GoldenStairsCommentary.pdf#.
5. N. Sri Ram, *Thoughts for Aspirants, Second Series,* 2nd ed. (Adyar, India: Theosophical Publishing House, 1999), 63.
6. Beechey, *Daily Meditations,* 6 (see ch. 1, n. 18).
7. The terms *raga, dvesa,* and *kleshas* are often translated slightly differently. For accuracy, I am using the translations found on the blog *Yoga Matters,* https://www.yogamatters.com. Otherwise, for this discussion I have largely relied on Ravi Ravindra's translation and guide entitled *The Wisdom of Patanjali's Yoga Sutras* (Nova Scotia: Shaila Press, 2015).
8. Krishnamurti, *At the Feet* in *Inspirations,* 11 (see ch. 12, n. 22).
9. Cook, *Golden Stairs,* 5.
10. Andrew Rooke, "Golden Stairs to the Temple of Wisdom," *Sunrise Magazine* (April/May 2005), *Theosophy Wiki,* https://www. Theosophy.wiki/en/The_Golden_Stairs.
11. Ram Dass, *Ram Dass Foundation,* n.d., accessed May 25, 2022, https://www.ramdass.org.
12. Martin Luther King, Jr., Letter from a Birmingham Jail, *US History* Scene, n.d., accessed May 25, 2022, https://www.ushistoryscene.com.

13. Martin Niemoller, “Then They Came for Me,” *Goodreads*, n.d., accessed May 25, 2022, https://www.goodreads.com/search?utf8=✓&query=Martin+Niemoller.
14. “Gupta Vidya,” n.d., accessed July 27, 2022, *Word Finder*, https://findwords.info/term/gupta-vidya#:~:text=Gupta-vidya.
15. Cook, *Golden Stairs*, 12.
16. “Noble Eightfold Path,” *The Buddist Centre*, n.d., accessed February 16, 2022, https://www.thebuddhistcentre.com/text/noble-eightfold-path.
17 N. Sri Ram, *The Human Interest*, 2nd ed. (Adyar, India: Theosophical Publishing House, 1968) 140.
18. Mills, “Golden Stairs.”

Chapter 14

1. Edward Abdill, “To Live to Benefit Mankind,” audio, December 20, 2009, https://archive.org/details/1293norm.
2. Collins, *Light on the Path* in *Inspirations*, 43 (see ch. 2, n. 8).
3. H. P. Blatatsky, “Some Words on Daily Life,” *Lucifer* 1, no. 5 (January 15,1888), 344.
4. Besant, *Spiritual Life*, 94 (see ch. 2, n. 7).
5. Dorothy Bell, “True Theosophical Service,” *Quest Magazine* 96, no. 6 (November–December 2008): 227–29.
6. G. Arundale, *The Way of Service* (Los Angeles: Theosophical Publishing House, 1919), 1; see *Internet Archive*, October 26, 2019, https://archive.org/details/arundalethewayofservice1913.
7. B. P. Wadia, *Growth through Service* (New York: Theosophical Association of New York, 1922), see *Internet Archive*, June 5, 2007, https://archive.org/details/growththroughser00wadiiala.
8. H. P. Blavatsky, *Collected Writings*, 6:336.
9. I. K. Taimni, *Principles of Theosophical Work*, rev. ed. (Adyar, India: Theosophical Publishing House, 1991), v.
10. Ibid., 4.
11. Collins, *Light on the Path* in *Inspirations*, 42.

12. Annie Besant and C. W. Leadbeater, *Thought Forms*, 2nd Quest ed., abridged (Wheaton, IL: Quest Books, 1999), 11.
13. Hodson, in *Sharing the Light*, 485 (see ch. 7, n. 13).
14. Ibid., 488.
15. Taimni, *Principles*, 98–99.
16. Hodson, in *Sharing the Light*, 495.
17. Arundale, *Way of Service*, 19.

Chapter 15

1. Krishnamurti, *At the Feet* in *Inspirations*, 5 (see ch. 12, n. 22).
2. Ibid., 3.
3. Annie Besant and C. W. Leadbeater, *Talks on the Path of Occultism*, vol. 1, *At the Feet of the Master*, 6th ed. (Adyar, India: Theosophical Publishing House, 1971), 24.
4. Ibid., 27.
5. George Arundale, *Thoughts on "At the Feet of the Master"* (Adyar, India: Theosophical Publishing House, 1919); see https://www.theosophy.world/sites/default/files/ebooks/ThoughtsOnAtTheFeetOfTheMaster_GSArundale.pdf, 9.
6. Ibid.
7. Krishnamurti, *At the Feet* in *Inspirations*, 7.
8. Ibid., 8.
9. Ibid., 11.
10. Ibid., 12.
11. Ibid., 14.
12. Hodson, in *Sharing the Light*, 135 (see ch. 7, n. 13).
13. Krishnamurti, *At the Feet* in *Inspirations*, 15.
14. Besant and Leadbeater, *Talks on the Path*, 1:56.
15. Krishnamurti, *At the Feet* in *Inspirations*, 16.
16. Ibid., 17.
17. J. Krishnamurti, *Freedom from the Known* (Brockwood Park, England: Krishnamurti Foundation Trust, 1969).

18. Algeo, "Guideposts for Living: At the Feet of the Master," video lecture; see https://www.youtube.com/watch?v=5Apfb82A53s.
19. Besant and Leadbeater, *Talks on the Path*, 1:218.
20. Ibid., 218.
21. Ibid.
22. Ibid.
23. Besant and Leadbeater, *Talks on the Path*, 1:219.
24. Krishnamurti, *At the Feet* in *Inspirations*, 20.
25. Ibid., 27.
26. Ibid.
27. Besant and Leadbeater, *Talks on the Path*, 1:351.
28. Ibid.
29. Krishnamurti, *At the Feet* in *Inspirations*, 27.
30. Hodson, in *Sharing the Light*, 150 (see ch. 7, n. 13).
31. Krishnamurti, *At the Feet* in *Inspirations*, 28.
32. Ibid., 31.
33. Arundale, *Thoughts*, 191.
34. Krishnamurti, *At the Feet* in *Inspirations*, 32.

Chapter 16

1. Besant and Leadbeater, *Talks on the Path*, 3:4 (see ch. 12, n. 26).
2. Ibid.
3. Collins, *Light on the Path* in *Inspirations*, 37 (see ch. 2, n. 8).
4. Ibid., 39.
5. Ibid.
6. Collins, *Light* and *Through the Gates*, 40 (see ch. 2, n. 13).
7. Ibid., 31–32.
8. Besant and Leadbeater, *Talks on the Path*, 3:17.
9. Ibid., 31.
10. Ibid., 34.
11. Ibid., 35.

12. Joy Mills, *Entering on the Sacred Way* (Wheaton, IL: Quest Books, 2000), 40.
13. Collins, *Light on the Path* in *Inspirations*, 51.
14. Ibid., 39–42.
15. Mills, *Entering on the Sacred Way*, 62–63.
14. Collins, *Light on the Path*, 39–42.
16. Rohit Mehta, *Seek Out the Way: Studies in Light on the Path* (Adyar, India: Theosophical Publishing House, 1955), 34.
17. Collins, *Light on the Path* in *Inspirations*, 40.
18. Ibid., 41.
19. Pablo Sender, “Light on the Path,” part 2, four-part video, *Theosophical Classics,* 2011, https://www.youtube.com/watch?v=6_qG3DGwpCc.
20. Collins, *Light on the Path* in *Inspirations*, 42–43.
21. Mchta, *Seek Out the Way*, 38.
22. Collins, *Light on the Path* in *Inspirations*, 42.
23. Mills, *Entering on the Sacred Way*, 80.
24. Collins, *Light on the Path* in *Inspirations*, 42.
25. Besant and Leadbeater, *Talks on the Path*, 3:159.
26. Ibid.
27. Collins, *Light on the Path* in *Inspirations*, 43.
28. Ibid., 43–44.
29. Ibid., 44.
30. Ibid., 46.
31. Ibid., 51.
32. Ibid.
33. Ibid., 52.
34. Ibid.
35. Ibid.
36. Ibid., 53
37. Ibid.
38. Mills, *Entering on the Sacred Way*, 125.
39. Taimni, *Man, God, and the Universe*, 203 (see ch. 2, n. 4).

40. Collins, *Light on the Path* in *Inspirations*, 54.
41. Ibid., 54–55.
42. Mills, *Entering on the Sacred Way*, 138.
43. Collins, *Light on the Path* in *Inspirations*, 55.
44. Besant and Leadbeater, *Talks on the Path*, 3:415.
45. Collins, *Light on the Path* in *Inspirations*, 56.
46. Ibid., 56–57.
47. Ibid., 58.

Chapter 17

1. Joy Mills quoting H. P. Blavatsky in *From Inner to Outer Transformation: Lectures on "The Voice of the Silence"* (Amsterdam: Uitgeverij der Theosofische Vereniging, 1996), 14–15.
2. Annie Besant, quoted in ibid., 16–17.
3. Blavatsky, *Voice of the Silence* in *Inspirations*, 69–70 (see ch. 2, n. 10).
4. Besant and Leadbeater, *Talks on the Path of Occultism*, vol. 2, *The Voice of the Silence*, 6th ed. (Adyar, India: Theosophical Publishing House, 1973), 7.
5. Mills, *From Inner to Outer Transformation*, 14.
6. Pablo Sender, "The Voice of the Silence," two-part video, *Theosophical Classics,* 2011, https://www.bing.com/videos/search?q=Pablo+Sender%2c+"The+Voice+of+the+Silence"+YouTube&docid=607998757631126975&mid=FF7708F8C7C53C76A34FFF7708F8C7C53C76A34F&view=detail&FORM=VIRE.
7. Blavatsky, *Voice of the Silence* in *Inspirations*, 73.
8. Ibid., 123.
9. Besant and Leadbeater, *Talks on the Path*, 2:25–26.
10. Blavatsky, *Voice of the Silence* in *Inspirations*, 73.
11. Ibid., 123.
12. Ibid., 73.
13. Ibid.
14. Sender, "Voice of the Silence," two-part video.

15. Blavatsky, *Voice of the Silence* in *Inspirations*, 73.
16. N. Sri Ram, *The Way of Wisdom* (Adyar, India: Theosophical Publishing House, 1989), 184.
17. Blavatsky, *Voice of the Silence* in *Inspirations*, 74.
18. Ibid., 76.
19. Ibid., 124.
20. Mills, *From Inner to Outer Transformation*, 32.
21. Blavatsky, *Voice of the Silence*, in *Inspirations*, 76.
22. Ibid.
23. Ibid., 78.
24. Ibid., 80.
25. Ibid., 83.
26. Ibid., 86.
27. Ram, *Way of Wisdom*, 232.
28. Blavatsky, *Voice of the Silence* in *Inspirations*, 87.
29. Ibid.
30. Ibid., 129.
31. Ibid., 87–88.
32. Ibid., 88.
33. Ibid.
34. Besant and Leadbeater, *Talks on the Path*, 2:190.
35. Mills, *From Inner to Outer Transformation*, 36–37.
36. Sender, "Voice of the Silence," two-part video.
37. Blavatsky, *Voice of the Silence* in *Inspirations*, 91.
38. Ibid., 92.
39. Ibid., 95.
40. Ibid., 99.
41. Ibid.
42. Ibid., 100.
43. Mills, *From Inner to Outer Transformation*, 84.
44. Blavatsky, *Voice of the Silence* in *Inspirations*, 103.
45. Ibid., 104.

46. Ibid.
47. Clara Codd, *The Way of the Disciple* (Adyar, India: Theosophical Publishing House, 1964), 125.
48. Sender, "Voice of the Silence," two-part video.
49. Blavatsky, *Voice of the Silence* in *Inspirations*, 105.
50. Besant and Leadbeater, *Talks on the Path*, 2:265–66.
51. Blavatsky, *Voice of the Silence* in *Inspirations*, 105.
52. Ibid., 120.
53. John Algeo, "The Voice of the Silence," lecture series, part 7, *Internet Archive*, 2019, https://archive.org/details/124301/1243_01.flac.
54. Hodson, in *Sharing the Light*, 596–97 (see ch. 7, n. 13).
55. B. P. Wadia, "Studies in *The Voice of the Silence*," *United Lodge of Theosophists, London, UK*, 1–2, accessed May 25, 2022, https://www.theosophy-ult.org.uk/book-review/studies-in-the-voice-of-the-silence/#_Toc101709692.
56. Clara Codd, "Comments on *The Voice of the Silence*," part 5, *Theosophy World Resource Centre*, accessed January 19, 2022; https://www.theosophy.world/resource/comments-voice-silence-clara-codd.

Afterword

1. Beechey, *Daily Meditations*, 118–19 (see ch. 1, n. 18).

Selected Bibliography

Arundale, George. *Thoughts on "At the Feet of the Master."* Adyar, India: Theosophical Publishing House, 1919. www.theosophy.world/sites/default/files/ebooks/ThoughtsOnAtTheFeetOfTheMaster_GSArundale.pdf.

———. *The Way of Service*. Krotona: Theosophical Publishing House, 1919. https:// archive.org/details/arundalethewayofservice1913.

Beechey, Katherine. A., comp. *Daily Meditations: Extracts from Letters of the Masters of Wisdom.* 2nd ed. Adyar, India: Theosophical Publishing House, 1984.

Besant, Annie. *Ancient Wisdom*. Adyar, India: Theosophical Publishing House, 1939.

———. *An Introduction to Yoga.* Adyar, India: Theosophical Publishing House, 1908.

———. *Esoteric Christianity*. 2nd ed. Wheaton, IL: Quest Books, 2006.

———. *Karma*. 3rd ed. Adyar, India: Theosophical Publishing House, 1905.

———. *The London Lectures of 1907*. London: Theosophical Publishing Society, 1909.

———. *Mahabharata: The Story of the Great War*. Adyar, India: Theosophical Publishing House, 1927.

———. *The Masters*. 8th repr. Adyar, India: Theosophical Publishing House, 2007.

———. *The Seven Principles of Man*. 12th repr. Adyar, India: Theosophical Publishing House, 2015.

———. *The Spiritual Life*. Rev. ed. Wheaton, IL: Quest Books, 1991.

———. *A Study in Karma*. 3rd ed. Adyar, India: Theosophical Publishing House, 2019.

———. *The Use of Evil*. Adyar, India: Theosophical Publishing House, 1932.

Besant, Annie, and C. W. Leadbeater. *Talks on the Path of Occultism*. 3 vols. 6th ed. Adyar, India: Theosophical Publishing House, 1971–76.

Besant, Annie, and C. W. Leadbeater. *Thought Forms*. 2nd Quest ed., abridged. Wheaton, IL: Quest Books, 1999.

Blavatsky, H. P. *Collected Writings*. Edited by Boris de Zirkoff. Vol. 6, *1883–1885*; Vol. 10, *1888–1889*; Vol. 12, 1889–1890; Vol. 13, *1890–1891*. Wheaton, IL: Theosophical Publishing House, 1974–1982.

———. *The Key to Theosophy*. Pasadena, CA: Theosophical University Press, 1995. First published by Theosophical Publishing Company, 1889.

———. *The Secret Doctrine: The Synthesis of Science, Religion, and Philosophy.* Edited by Boris de Zirkoff. Vol. 1. Wheaton, IL: Theosophical Publishing House, 1993. First published 1888 by Theosophical Publishing Company.

———. *Theosophical Glossary*. London: Theosophy Company, 1973. Facsimile of the first edition. London: Theosophical Publishing Society, 1892.

———. *Two Books of The Stanzas of Dzyan*. 8th repr. Adyar, India: Theosophical Publishing House, 2013.

———. *The Voice of the Silence*. In *Inspirations from Ancient Wisdom*. Wheaton, IL: Quest Books, 1999.

Chin, Vicente Hao, ed. *The Mahatma Letters to A.P. Sinnett from the Mahatmas M. and K.H.: In Chronological Sequence*. Adyar, India: Theosophical Publishing House, 1998.

Codd, Clara. *The Way of the Disciple*. Adyar, India: Theosophical Publishing House, 1964.

Collins, Mabel. *The Idyll of the White Lotus*. 2nd ed. Wheaton, IL: Theosophical Publishing House, 1974.

———. *Light on the Path*. In *Inspirations from Ancient Wisdom*. Wheaton, IL: Quest Books, 1999.

———. *Light on the Path* and *Through the Gates of Gold*. Pasadena, CA: Theosophical University Press, 1997.

Cook, Sidney. *The Golden Stairs: A Commentary*. Adyar, India: Theosophical Publishing House, 1957.

Ellwood, Robert. *Theosophy: A Modern Expression of the Wisdom of the Ages*. Wheaton, IL: Quest Books, 1986.

Hodson, Geoffrey. *Sharing the Light: The Collected Articles of Geoffrey Hodson*. Compiled by John Sell and Elizabeth Sell. Vol. 1. Quezon City, Philippines: Theosophical Publishing House, 2008.

Krishna, Gopi. *Kundalini*. Boulder: Shambala, 2017.

Krishnamurti, Jiddu. *At the Feet of the Master*. In *Inspirations from Ancient Wisdom*. Wheaton, IL: Quest Books, 1999.

———. *Freedom from the Known*. Brockwood Park, England: Krishnamurti Foundation Trust, 1969.

Leadbeater, C. W. *The Masters and the Path*. 3rd ed. Adyar, India: Theosophical Publishing House, 1992.

———. *A Textbook of Theosophy*. Adyar, India: Theosophical Publishing House, 1912.

Mehta, Rohit. *Seek Out the Way*. Adyar, India: Theosophical Publishing House, 1955.

Mills, Joy. *Entering on the Sacred Way*. Wheaton, IL: Quest Books, 2000.

———. *From Inner to Outer Transformation: Lectures on "The Voice of the Silence."* Amsterdam: Uitgeverij der Theosofische Vereniging, 1996.

———. *Reflections on an Ageless Wisdom*. Wheaton, IL: Quest Books, 2010.

Ravindra, Ravi. *The Bhagavad Gita: A Guide to Navigating the Battle of Life*. Boulder, CO: Shambhala, 2017.

———. *The Wisdom of Patanjali's Yoga Sutras*. Nova Scotia: Shaila Press, 2015.

Sender, Pablo. *Evolution of the Higher Consciousness: An In-Depth Study into H. P. Blavatsky's Teachings*. Ojai, CA: Fohat, 2018.

Sri Ram, N. *The Human Interest.* 2nd ed. Adyar, India: Theosophical Publishing House, 1968.

———. *Seeking Wisdom.* Adyar, India: Theosophical Publishing House, 1969.

———. *Thoughts for Aspirants, First Series.* 2nd ed. Adyar, India: Theosophical Publishing House, 1956.

———. *Thoughts for Aspirants, Second Series.* 2nd ed. Adyar, India: Theosophical Publishing House, 1999.

———. *The Way of Wisdom.* Adyar, India: Theosophical Publishing House, 1989.

Sri Sankaracharya. *Viveka-Cudamani.* Translated by M. M. Chatterji. Adyar, India: Theosophical Publishing House, 1932.

Taimni, I. K. *Man, God, and the Universe.* Wheaton, IL: Quest Books, 1974. Kindle ed.

———. *Principles of Theosophical Work.* Rev. ed. Adyar, India: Theosophical Publishing House, 1991.

Tame, David. *Beethoven and the Spiritual Path.* Wheaton, IL: Quest Books, 1994.

Varma, S. S. *Teachings on Discipleship.* Adyar, India: Theosophical Publishing House, 2005.

Wadia, B. P. *Growth through Service.* New York: Theosophical Association of New York, 1922. https://archive.org/details/growththroughser00wadiiala.

INDEX

Illustrations are indicated by (i).

INDEX

Author Biography

Douglas Keene, MD, MPH, has been a member of the Theosophical Society in America since 1980, first joining in San Antonio, Texas, while in medical school. He was also a member of the inaugural class of the Partners in Theosophy program. He has served for several years on the TSA Board of Directors, initially as Eastern Director then one term as Vice President and currently as President. During this time, Doug has made many visits to the Society's locations in Wheaton, Illinois, Adyar, India, and the Krotona Institute in Ojai, California, for various programs and projects. He has presented at a number of lodges in the eastern United States, at the Ojai Valley TS Lodge, and at the TSA summer national convention in Wheaton. He is a family doctor who has practiced for more than thirty-three years, initially in rural northwest Alaska, above the Arctic Circle. Later in his career, he earned a master's degree in public health with a concentration in global health, following which he worked in Lesotho, Africa, for two years training native doctors. Following this he was a director in an extended care nursing facility for five years before retiring from medicine. When not in Wheaton, Doug and his wife, Risa, live in New Hampshire.

The Universal Spirit is published by
The Theosophical Publishing House, a division of
The Theosophical Society in America.

The Theosophical Society encourages open-minded inquiry into
world religions, philosophy, science, and the arts
in order to understand the wisdom of the ages,
respect the unity of all life, and help people explore
individual spiritual self-transformation.

Its publications are generously supported by
THE KERN FOUNDATION,
a trust committed to Theosophical education.

For information about programs, literature,
online study, membership benefits, and international centers,
see www.theosophical.org
or call 800-669-1571 or (outside the U.S.) 630-668-1571.